Paras in Action

To Derek,

You must be very proud of your son in 'Para Reg'

'Every Man An Emperor'

Best of luck to you both

Jason

Dear ,

You must be very proud of your Son in the Big

Brass Band. the Emperor.

Best of Luck to you all.

Sam

[signature]

# Paras in Action

## Ready for Anything – The Parachute Regiment Through the Eyes of Those who Served

Jason Woods

FRONTLINE BOOKS

First published in Great Britain in 2022 by
Frontline Books
An imprint of
Pen & Sword Books Ltd
Yorkshire – Philadelphia

Copyright © Jason Woods 2022

ISBN 978 1 39904 017 4

The right of Jason Woods to be identified as Author of this work has been asserted by him in accordance with the Copyright, Designs and Patents Act 1988.

A CIP catalogue record for this book is available from the British Library.

All rights reserved. No part of this book may be reproduced or transmitted in any form or by any means, electronic or mechanical including photocopying, recording or by any information storage and retrieval system, without permission from the Publisher in writing.

Typeset by Mac Style
Printed and bound in the UK by CPI Group (UK) Ltd, Croydon, CR0 4YY.

Pen & Sword Books Limited incorporates the imprints of Atlas, Archaeology, Aviation, Discovery, Family History, Fiction, History, Maritime, Military, Military Classics, Politics, Select, Transport, True Crime, Air World, Frontline Publishing, Leo Cooper, Remember When, Seaforth Publishing, The Praetorian Press, Wharncliffe Local History, Wharncliffe Transport, Wharncliffe True Crime and White Owl.

For a complete list of Pen & Sword titles please contact

**PEN & SWORD BOOKS LIMITED**
47 Church Street, Barnsley, South Yorkshire, S70 2AS, England
E-mail: enquiries@pen-and-sword.co.uk
Website: www.pen-and-sword.co.uk

Or

**PEN AND SWORD BOOKS**
1950 Lawrence Rd, Havertown, PA 19083, USA
E-mail: Uspen-and-sword@casematepublishers.com
Website: www.penandswordbooks.com

# Contents

| | | |
|---|---|---|
| *Foreword* | | vii |
| *Introduction* | | viii |
| **Chapter 1** | Inception | 1 |
| **Chapter 2** | Defeating Nazi Germany, 1942 to 1945 | 11 |
| **Chapter 3** | Post-War World | 24 |
| **Chapter 4** | The Squadron | 34 |
| **Chapter 5** | Cyprus Insurgency | 42 |
| **Chapter 6** | Last Drop | 47 |
| **Chapter 7** | Fighting in the Mountains | 53 |
| **Chapter 8** | Secret Wars | 59 |
| **Chapter 9** | The Factory | 66 |
| **Chapter 10** | P Company: Pass or Fail | 76 |
| **Chapter 11** | Jumps | 81 |
| **Chapter 12** | Troubles Closer to Home | 86 |
| **Chapter 13** | Maggie's Boys | 97 |
| **Chapter 14** | The Troubles Continue | 114 |
| **Chapter 15** | Ethnic Cleansing | 122 |
| **Chapter 16** | Operation Certain Death | 133 |
| **Chapter 17** | Liberation of Kabul | 148 |
| **Chapter 18** | Freedom | 154 |

| **Chapter 19** | Helmand | 169 |
| **Chapter 20** | Special Forces Support Group | 193 |
| **Chapter 21** | Return to Kabul | 202 |
| **Chapter 22** | The Circuit | 210 |
| *Afterword* | | 217 |
| *Acknowledgements* | | 219 |
| *Select Bibliography* | | 221 |
| *Glossary* | | 224 |
| *Notes* | | 228 |

# Foreword

This book, *Paras in Action – The history of the Parachute Regiment through the eyes of those who served*, typifies the informal motto of what is rightly seen as being one of the world's most iconic elite fighting forces, the Parachute Regiment: 'Every man an emperor'.

From the very earliest beginnings of the Parachute Regiment, when it was yet to achieve that storied name, or to adopt the distinctive maroon beret, which would earn it the 'Maroon Machine' moniker in due course – Jason Woods, himself a distinguished veteran – traces the enthralling history of a unit, which in the Second World War rapidly earned the fearsome nickname amongst the German enemy, those who had to fight against the Paras in the North African desert – the *rote teufeln*; the Red Devils.

From those exalted early beginnings, Woods chronicles the Parachute Regiment's most daring and iconic missions, many of which have become household names to anyone with even a passing interest in military history. But importantly, Woods seeks to do so by using the words and recollections of those who actually served, lending a very immediate and visceral quality to the accounts and the writing. In doing so, he truly brings these histories alive – from the earliest origins to the present day and covering the key missions in between.

Having written many books myself which tell of the Second World War or later operations of 'the Paras' – either featuring those who served in that elite unit, or the special forces with whom they went on to operate – I can safely say that he has captured what it means to pass the rigorous selection regime and join the exalted ranks of the Parachute Regiment; the quality and essence and unique esprit de corps that really does set the unit apart, distinguishing those who operate within it as being able to go above and beyond.

I commend *Paras In Action* to you. Read it. You will not be disappointed.

Damien Lewis, Dorset, April 2022

# Introduction

The date 1 August 2022 marks the eightieth anniversary of the inauguration of one of the most powerful fighting forces the world has ever seen: the Parachute Regiment. In this book I aim to honour this regiment, in which I was extremely proud to serve, and bring readers right up to date with its impressive achievements. I pay tribute to the illustrious history with examples of the challenges they have faced in the line of duty, and for which many of them have laid down their lives. Specifically aiming to showcase the indomitable spirit of a warrior, I aim to celebrate the courage displayed and the victories achieved in the face of adversity. This book provides an informal snapshot, from the inside looking out, of the integral role that the Paras have played throughout their history in operations all over the world. My intention is to demonstrate not only the courage, strength and fitness of the men who make up this mighty force but also their intelligence, compassion, and wicked sense of humour.

The word warrior immediately conjures up images from ancient history of the Spartans, Roman Centurions, the Samurai or the Vikings amongst others, all of whom had a distinctive, terrifying look about them, and whose reputation on the field of battle struck terror into the hearts of their enemies. There have been several supreme fighting forces who have forged their place in history and with the distinctive maroon beret, and roll of battle honours over recent times, the Parachute Regiment has become one of these elite and illustrious units.

It goes without saying that parachutists would never have come into existence if it hadn't been for significant developments and inventions. It is inherent in Man's nature to strive to accomplish new things, conquer limitations and continually create, develop, and improve. For hundreds if not thousands of years, inventors and experimenters tried to devise methods that would enable them to jump off cliffs without killing themselves. The parachute, named after the French meaning 'against fall', in the late eighteenth century was initially a form of circus entertainment, but following the invention of manned hot-air balloons it was further developed as a safety device. With the development of sustainable flight in a heavier than air machine in the early twentieth century, it was only natural that man began thinking about how conquering the air might be used in warfare. During the First World War aeroplanes were used for reconnaissance, dropping bombs and aerial dogfights, and parachutes provided a means of escape for airmen. However, towards the end of the war a more pro-active use was found for them, and Italy, Germany, Britain and France began to use them to drop spies and saboteurs behind enemy lines.

Improvements that began following the end of the war soon led to the possibility of using parachutes for more expansive offensive roles. The Russians were the first to put this into practice on a large scale and began demonstrating the technique of using parachutes to insert troops behind enemy lines to secure key positions before other forces joined them. When Hermann Goering, Commander in Chief of the Luftwaffe, heard reports of Russia's exhibition of its abilities to use parachutes for this purpose, he immediately ordered the establishment of an airborne corps of paratroopers called the Fallschirmjäger. Their success at the beginning of the Second World War was the inspiration for Britain to develop a Parachute Corps of their own and this proved to be a pivotal decision. The men who volunteered for what was eventually called the Parachute Regiment proved themselves to be indomitable warriors who played a significant role in changing the course of the war.

The Para Regt has been kept extremely busy since its inception in the Second World War and has taken part, one way or another, in just about every deployment, conflict and war in which this country has been involved. From jumping out of rattling, old bombers into flak-filled skies and landing behind enemy lines to engage in ferocious fighting, right up to the heart-breaking but efficient organisation of evacuees from Afghanistan in 2021, they have proved themselves to be warriors in battle as well as capable, well-disciplined peacekeepers in strife-torn regions. Quickly building a fierce reputation for tenacity and valour, the Paras have continuously defied the odds and have cleverly evolved into what you see today as the backbone of 16 Air Assault Brigade and the Special Forces Support Group (SFSG). The Parachute Regiment is also a rich harvesting ground for Special Forces' recruits. Building on strong historical links and a common operating mentality, they have provided more than their fair share of the men who make up the ranks of the Special Air Service (SAS), and I'm sure will continue to do so in the future.

Through historical records, contemporary interviews, and personal experience, I present a fast-moving insight into the underlying nature and abilities of the men who make up the ranks of the Parachute Regiment with their stories of what actually happened on the ground in the chaotic, sometimes gruesome, and certainly extremely dangerous theatres of war in which they operated and upheld the regiment motto, *Utrinque Paratus* (Ready for Anything). I describe the gruelling selection process that the guys must pass before joining their respective battalions, the rigorous ongoing training that follows and explain the often underestimated and misunderstood world of the private security industry, known as the Circuit, that many of them move into and continue to serve within.

I was keen to use as many original quotes from serving and former members of the regiment as possible, and to not regurgitate past stories, unless absolutely pertinent. This was particularly so in the Second World War chapters of this book, where I have tried to carefully weave together old quotes from the original trailblazers who are no longer with us with new unheard perspectives from the current generation of paratroopers.

The scope of this book does not allow for intricate details; entire books have been written on many of the individual operations and I hope that readers will be motivated to read these more in-depth accounts. I am not trying to write a definitive history but aim to portray the engine of this unique machine, the timeline of events, the unbelievable will to win, and where the beat is truly set within the ranks of this regiment. Due to the intricacies of war and different time zones some sources differ on dates and times and those used have been verified by military specialists.

The book should bring a wry smile and a nod of understanding from those who have served within the regiment and hopefully inspire anyone considering joining the Paras to embrace the courage, ethos, and DNA of those who came before, and to work hard to make more glorious history as part of this legendary fighting force in the years ahead. This book is a celebration of the Parachute Regiment, an overview of our history written by a paratrooper from the ranks.

When it comes to times of hostility and adversity, when the nation is on the back foot and needs a flag bearer then there isn't a more powerful and resolute group of warriors to call upon. Field Marshal Bernard Montgomery summed up the whole ethos of the regiment perfectly when he said, 'What manner of men are these that wear the maroon beret? They are firstly all volunteers and are toughened by physical training. As a result, they have infectious optimism and that offensive eagerness which comes from well-being. They have 'jumped' from the air and by doing so have conquered fear. Their duty lies in the van of the battle. They are proud of this honour.

They have the highest standards in all things whether it be skill in battle or smartness in the execution of all peace time duties. They are in fact – men apart – every man an emperor. Of all the factors, which make for success in battle, the spirit of the warrior is the most decisive. That spirit will be found in full measure in the men who wear the maroon beret.'[1]

This is the story of the Paras in action, through the eyes of those who served.

## Chapter 1

# Inception

In May 1940, with Germany invading countries across Europe in the initial stages of the Second World War, Winston Churchill took over from Neville Chamberlain as prime minister. As part of the Allied strategy, he recognised the urgent need for a parachute corps and called for Britain to have its own airborne capability. His actions led to the creation of a military force that soon became known as the Parachute Regiment with a new breed of men who would instil fear and awe in all who confronted them.

Chamberlain's government had underestimated the importance of airborne troops and although the Air Ministry had already set up a parachute training centre, Major John Rock of the Royal Engineers had been put in charge with very little support or information regarding the plan for this new unit. The Germans had been preparing for war for six years and when the Fallschirmjäger (German paratroopers) emerged as a successful fighting force that used parachutes and gliders to drop into enemy territory to overcome opposing forces, the British people lived in fear of being invaded by this enemy from the sky. When Churchill came into power, he immediately galvanised people into action. In his famous letter to Sir General Hastings Ismay, he called for a 'corps of at least 5,000 parachute troops ...' and added, 'Advantage must be taken of the summer to train these men ...'[1] He wasn't allowing much time for the development of this new force and the training centre leapt into action. Once established, the British paratroopers soon made up for lost time and proved themselves to be more than a match for their German counterparts as the war progressed.

The Central Landing School (later changed to 'Establishment') was sited at Ringway Airport, just outside Manchester, and with Churchill's support, Major Rock could now be more proactive in training and building up the new unit of parachutists. Volunteers were called to form the first parachute force, named 2 Commando. They answered adverts put out across the forces network for involvement in hazardous work; there was no mention of the fact that they would be parachutists and barely any of them had experience with flying let alone parachutes. Training got started very quickly with a joint team of RAF and Army physical training instructors, who were literally thrown in at the deep end with no training equipment, no real experience and nothing to guide them. All they had were a few hundred parachutes and six old Armstrong Whitworth Whitley bombers. Nicknamed 'Flying Coffins', these planes were already obsolete due to their lack of speed and vulnerability to anti-aircraft guns.

Over the next two months, instructors worked around the clock improvising with makeshift parachute towers and old aircraft. They developed the training through a process of trial and error and quite a few injuries; sprained and broken ankles or dislocations were commonplace. Exercises were devised to strengthen the muscles required for jumping and landing, and they were taught some basic self-defence skills for close-quarter battle on the ground.

Working out where to jump from was a major issue. At first the rear turret was removed, and the plan for the volunteers in this new role was to stand up in the open turret and wait for their parachute to inflate from above and lift them off the plane in what was called the 'Pull Off' method. This only got as far as the testing phase with the PJIs (Parachute Jump Instructors) demonstrating its use. Unsurprisingly, it proved to be extremely dangerous, so they moved to cutting a hole in the floor of the aircraft. However, this had its own dangers, with men smashing their heads or faces against the edge as they exited the plane through the 3ft-deep ring of metal. The soldiers called it the 'Whitley Kiss' and it was the method of exit for a while before the new Dakotas came into service with side doors installed for jumping, which eventually became known as Para doors. Training was intense as the new para recruits were put through their paces to increase their overall fitness and tactical awareness and learn how to jump from great heights and land with a parachute. It was an innovative method of insertion, but for the guys it was purely a form of transportation; the real work of a paratrooper started once they hit the ground. As they continued, adjustments and improvements were made through trial and error. They changed their initial clothing to be less bulky, with early versions of the Para Smock coming into use. On the 136th descent the first fatality occurred, sadly killing Ralph Evans, who experienced a 'roman candle'. This is a total malfunction of a chute, also known as a 'streamer', where the canopy has failed to open; it is just trailing behind the parachutist, and usually results in death. Unfortunately, it was relatively common during the Second World War for this to occur, and British paratroopers weren't equipped with reserve chutes at this time. Thankfully this situation has been very rare since the addition of anti-inversion skirts to the modern canopies.

A new parachute, the X-type Statichute, was designed, which had the main advantage of opening well after the parachute had cleared the aircraft. Several men died or sustained serious injuries in the early experiments, although one man had a remarkable escape from what was described as a 'hang-up'. The hook from the static line got caught in Frank Garlick's parachute bag and he was left dangling from the plane, unable to get back into the aircraft or be released. The plane came slowly into land with its tail up and he was dragged along the ground on his parachute. Remarkably he survived with only cuts and bruises and went on to serve in North Africa and Arnhem with great distinction.

It is a tribute to these pioneers that, despite the haphazard facilities and men being injured and killed in training, they stuck with it, determined to master the techniques, and get ready for some action. Former RAF Parachute Jump Instructor Rick Wadmore, who served for twenty years up to the early 2000s, gave his view, 'It was literally flying by the seat of your pants stuff in the early days. However, once they realised what was the best way of getting the paratroopers out of the plane and onto the ground as fast as possible, then things settled down. The first parachutes were known as GQ X type, then they moved onto the PX chutes. They were only on to the PX Mark 4 by the mid-nineties when the LLP (Low-Level Parachute) was brought into service, which just goes to show the slow progression of this form of transport.'[2]

There were many who refused to jump or just couldn't meet the requirements but those that made it through demonstrated the characteristics of mixing humour with a 'let's just get on with it' attitude. As one early paratrooper, Tony Hibbert, recalled in an interview with Paradata, 'Everything was about laughter in those days.' On one occasion he jumped out of a balloon at night wearing full mess kit and spurs because he needed to complete another jump for his qualification book and Para pay. 'We had to have a sense of fun, to lighten up and not take life too seriously,' he said.[3]

After six months, 488 men had completed training at Ringway, and they were keen to be given a mission. The war was raging across Europe and North Africa and German bombers had been causing devastation to civilian populations in cities across the land. The guys were pumped up and ready to go but raids kept being cancelled and some began to ask to go back to their original regiments, purely so that they could be involved in the fight again.

By late 1940, things were starting to move fast. The Parachute Training Squadron (previously 'school') was officially named. Most of the modern-day paratroopers remember it as 1 PTS. For those at the time it was merely

PTS, and only became 1 PTS when, later in the war, a second school opened for airborne forces in India. Then they looked for a powerful, unifying symbol to bond this new force together, so 'Pegasus the Slayer of Enemies' was designed by the artist Edward Seago, who at the time was completing his war service in the Royal Engineers.

## Operation Colossus

In response to the feelings of the men and Churchill's own impatience to get his new airborne force into action, a mission was found. It was not a full-blown insertion and volunteers were called to make up the team, which required seven officers and thirty-one from other ranks, for Operation Colossus. Every single man stepped forward and so selections were made before intensive, secret training began. Two men were included to act as interpreters. A civilian, Fortunato Picchi, who was renamed Trooper Pierre Dupont, had emigrated to Britain in the 1920s and worked as head waiter at the Savoy Hotel in London before giving up his job and volunteering. The other was a veteran of the First World War, Flight Lieutenant Ralph Lucky, an RAF Intelligence officer.

The aim of Colossus was to insert the men onto mainland Italy to destroy the Tragino Aqueduct, which provided vital supplies of water to the ports on the Adriatic coast and the Gulf of Taranto from where Italians were embarking on campaigns in North Africa and Albania. A full-scale mock-up of the aqueduct had been constructed and the men, now called X-Troop, trained for the landing and studied maps and aerial photographs in preparation for the mission and subsequent escape back to Britain. Every morning they went on runs and forced marches carrying full equipment, and in the afternoons they rehearsed the task on the mock bridge. In a dress rehearsal some of the men suffered minor injuries, but with an attitude that became the hallmark of the Paras, none of them would give up their place on the team.

Right up until the last minute, no mission details were known to the men of the, now designated, 11 Special Air Service Battalion, not even where the target was located, and when they finally realised that they were going to Italy, they were not so much concerned about completing the task, so much as how they were to be extracted from the country afterwards. The troop was transferred to Malta and from there they flew in six Whitley bombers to the drop zone. Two more planes carried bombs to drop on nearby railway yards as a diversion. On 10 February 1941 the planes took off with the aim of reaching the DZ (drop zone) by 2130 hours. The men had all been issued with supplies including weapons and a commando knife along with various additions sewn into their uniforms including silk maps of Italy, a hacksaw blade, 50,000 Lire and a metallic stud that contained a compass.[4] The Whitleys were small and cramped inside and the men sat on the floor with their backs against the edge of the plane's interior with their kit carefully stored; they were told that if they moved, it would upset the balance of the plane and cause a crash. Before jumping they had to shuffle along the plane on their backsides to the hole as there was no standing room. The old bombers rattled and shook as they made their way across the skies and the men tried to sleep or amused themselves by playing cards or even singing. Each man found his own way to allay the nerves and tried not to think about whether their parachute would actually open, what they might land on, or if they would be shot down before they even got there. Despite their natural underlying fears, they were fit, motivated, and prepared to go into action as part of the first paratrooper mission.

The first Whitley reached the DZ just after the designated time and the men dropped from the bellies of the aircraft into the freezing air and landed successfully within a few hundred yards of the target. However, due to ice on the release mechanisms, canisters containing weapons, equipment and most importantly explosives didn't drop over the same area and only one was found. Two planes were late because they had re-routed to avoid flak and the sixth plane carrying the demolitions expert, Captain Daly, a lot of the explosives, and six sappers missed the DZ all together, and they landed in the next valley almost 20 miles away. Lance Corporal Harry Boulter was injured when he smashed into a rock on his descent and broke his ankle. The boss, Major Trevor A. G. Pritchard, landed about a mile away and eventually arrived with the men from his stick (a term for paratroopers in a plane), and joined the other members of X-Troop, who had landed perfectly and had already secured the area. They continued to their objective with a reduced number of men and only just over a third of the explosives. On inspection of the aqueduct, they discovered that contrary to the intelligence they had been given, it was built with reinforced concrete and was much more difficult to destroy than the expected brick structure. In the distance they could hear bombs dropping on the railway yards of Foggia, hopefully creating the desired distraction.

Missing nearly two thirds of the explosives and the experts to set them, Major Pritchard put the responsibility of laying the charges onto engineer Lieutenant George Patterson, who informed him that they needed to adjust the plan due to the reinforced concrete and missing explosive charges. Major Pritchard told him, 'You're the expert now, and I'll stand by your judgement.'[5] Patterson went ahead and organised the placing of explosives around the base of one of the support piers. Covering parties led by Anthony Deane-Drummond secured the area and gathered a group of Italian men, who were forced to help. He and his guys then moved over to an adjacent bridge and laid some of the explosives under one end to prevent the enemy from pursuing them.

It was after midnight by the time the charges were ready, and all the men moved to safety before lighting the fuses. The bridge exploded but at the aqueduct nothing happened. Pritchard and Paterson edged forward to see what the problem was and flew backwards as the blast knocked them off their feet. Explosions and flashes of fire boomed into the darkness. The men waited, not sure whether they had been successful, but as the noise faded, they heard gushing water. Half of the aqueduct had collapsed, and water flooded down into the valley below. The nearby bridge had also been badly damaged. Job done. It was time for the men to begin their escape across hostile territory with the enemy now on the lookout for them.

The extraction plan was to make their way to the mouth of the River Sele, where they would be picked up by a submarine, HMS *Triumph*. The men now faced a 60-mile journey over mountainous, snow-bound terrain in freezing temperatures and knew that they should only move by night and stay under cover during the day, but they only had four days to get to the extraction point. Splitting up into three groups of roughly ten men and two officers, they headed west after burying their heavy equipment and rifles. Lance Corporal Harry Boulter was left behind with a local farmer. Still miles away from the DZ, Captain Daly and his stick heard the explosions and realised that they too should now head for the RV (rendezvous) point on the river.

The men had been supplied with no means of communication and could not relay the success of their mission back to Britain or even contact the extraction submarine. They set off with determination and a feeling of accomplishment but back in Britain the commanders called off HMS *Triumph*. Some reports suggest that an aerial photograph had shown the aqueduct to be still intact and it was presumed that the men had been taken prisoner or killed; others say that one of the bombers crash-landed near to the meeting point on the river and, not wanting the submarine to be discovered, it had been withdrawn. Either way there was no way of contacting the men to find out what had happened or to inform them that the submarine would not be there to meet them as planned. A basic lack of decent communication equipment was to be a recurring problem for the Paras.

As it so happened, it was irrelevant because the area was flooded with enemy troops and all the men were intercepted and taken prisoner. Fortunato Picchi was recognised as an Italian and taken to Rome, where he was interrogated, tortured, and finally executed by firing squad. The other paratroopers were all taken to prison camps, where most of them remained until Italy surrendered in September 1943. Despite constant attempts to escape by all the men, only two from X-Troop managed to get away and make their way back to the UK. Using guile, brazenness and tremendous determination, Alfred Parker and Antony Dean-Drummond escaped from their respective prisons and walked hundreds of miles across enemy territory dodging Germans, sleeping rough and relying on the kindness of strangers to finally get home.

Both these men displayed the indomitable nature of the guys belonging to this new elite force of paratroopers as they used their courage, intelligence, and supreme fitness to overcome tremendous obstacles to gain their freedom. All of the fledgling unit demonstrated grit and determination to get the job done despite so many setbacks, and set the bar very high for generations of paratroopers to come. The majority of the men got back into training and action as soon as they could and went on to fight again. These were the trailblazers; their spirit set the precedent for all who followed in this new specialist division of the British Army.

Former Regimental Sergeant Major of 3 Para in the mid-2000s, Pete Edgar Lane commented, on this first mission, 'Out-gunned, out-manned, and surrounded in unfamiliar territory, what more could a paratrooper wish for? Operation Colossus by name, was a colossal achievement. Targeting a fresh-water aqueduct in southern Italy was the first British airborne operation, which helped shape and set the benchmark for future missions. Paratroopers always a breed apart – then and now – Every man an Emperor!'[6]

The powers that be had wanted to see whether it was possible to insert men by parachute successfully and learned a few hard lessons about the planning of such operations. Once the success of this first mission was reported, it provided a huge confidence boost for the fledgling regiment and cemented their future as a force to be reckoned with. All of them knew the risks that they were taking and went in despite the dangers and the possibility of things going wrong. All credit to the character of the men. However, there were many questions remaining about the overall planning and ability to acquire accurate intelligence for these types of operations in the future.

## Operation Biting

It was another year before the Paras were tested again. The development of radar became a crucial issue in the course of the Second World War and so using aerial photography and members of the French Resistance on the ground to gather information, a daring plan was devised to steal advanced radar equipment being used by the Germans and to bring it back to the UK for analysis. After months of planning and top-secret training, airborne troops set off with the objective of seizing the German Würzburg radar installation at Bruneval, just north of Le Havre. With them was Flight Sergeant Charles W. H. Cox of the RAF, who was deemed an expert in radar. He had 'volunteered' for the role of taking the essential components from the radar installation and, having never parachuted before, he was given rapid jumps training before the mission.

The sticks of men dropped in on the night of 27 February 1942 for the combined mission, called Operation Biting. Choosing a clear night with a full moon meant good visibility for the pilots but it also meant that the planes could be easily spotted. The men jumped into the still, icy air praying that they wouldn't get shot on their descent, and landed on the cold, snowy ground. The Germans also saw the parachutists coming down and while the planners back home had reckoned on the men having over an hour before any support could be sent to back up the lightly armed numbers of Germans at the installation site, nearby reinforcements of around platoon strength were already en route. Adding to their difficulties, two sticks of men under Lieutenant Charteris had dropped off course and were lost. Radio equipment was damaged on landing and so the different sections could not communicate with each other. Under Officer Commanding Major General (Retired) Johnny Frost, the men came under heavy attack but got Cox safely to the Würzburg. The Paras held off enemy counter-attacks coming from all around while Cox dismantled the equipment and managed to gather what was needed very quickly and complete the task. They loaded everything onto trolleys and with German mortar capability arriving, the order was given to withdraw.

They now needed to get down to the heavily guarded beach for pick up by the Navy. Charteris's men had managed to orientate themselves and get into position; they stormed the villa Stella Maris, which housed several heavily armed German soldiers, took it over and provided covering fire for the others. Well behind schedule, everyone fought their way down onto the beach area, but they couldn't contact the Navy via radio or beacon. It wasn't long before German reinforcements arrived, and the Paras came under sustained fire from the top of the cliff from heavy machine guns. The situation looked desperate as they thought that nobody was coming to collect them, then suddenly, one of the guys spotted landing craft manned by Royal Marine Commandos with Bren guns heading towards them. The commandos aimed up at the Germans on the cliff tops, providing what covering fire they could as the paratroopers started to move onto the beach. All the rescue craft arrived together and with machine gun fire and grenades landing all around them, it was every man for himself as the soldiers scrambled aboard the boats with the radar equipment and escaped.

The raid was heralded as a great success and Frost's daughter, Caroline, remembered her father telling her, 'They arrived back in Portsmouth and all the ships were sounding their klaxon hooters and a Spitfire flew overhead and dipped its wings. The noise was terrific. Dad said that the hairs went up on the back of his neck and that it was one of the proudest moments of his life. Getting acknowledgement from the rest of the men was the best accolade he could get because only they really understood.'[7]

The current trustee of the Parachute Regiment Museum in Duxford, Warrant Officer 1 (Retired) Gil Boyd, summed up the raid, 'Operation Biting, the Bruneval Raid has to be one of the most precise, effective and accurate parachute operations of all time. Not only was it incredible and daring, but it was also the forerunner of what we know today as, the Parachute Regiment, and all it has come to stand for, with a motto befitting its role *Utrinque Paratus* (Ready for Anything). That's the military work the regiment does, at the tip of the spear for the British Army anywhere in the world at any time.'[8]

Major (Retired) Tony Hobbins said, 'The Bruneval Raid, was the Parachute Regiment's first battle honour on the Regimental Colours, and this has been immortalised in British Airborne Operations and in the ethos of past, present, and future paratroopers. There has been a lot written on Biting and to do it justice is extremely hard, especially as it dynamically changed the focus and came at a very dark time during the war. That being said, it was a complete success and Winston Churchill grasped the opportunity to sell its success to the great British public and the media, and to transform future warfare by evolving and expanding an airborne brigade.'[9]

The success of this mission was highly praised in the newspapers and was a huge boost to the country's morale. Volunteers from all over answered the call to join the airborne unit. They all wanted to see some action but not all of them met the high standards now set by this new and forward-thinking unit and didn't make the grade. With rough and inadequate facilities, the new men had to prove themselves at the training ground and those not demonstrating the required attributes were quickly RTU (returned to unit).

The training became more defined and provided the blueprint for the P Company (Pegasus Company) selection process still used today. The first fledgling parachute battalions were drawn up and emerged as a powerful force that influenced the course of the war. The new amalgamation and vastly increased numbers of paratroopers resulted in the official inauguration of the Parachute Regiment on 1 August 1942.

Chapter 2

# Defeating Nazi Germany, 1942 to 1945

The first major campaigns where the newly named Parachute Regiment was tested took place in North Africa, where they really set the tone for who they were and what they could accomplish, as well as earning themselves the famous nickname of the 'Red Devils'. The Denison smocks they wore had flaps of material to prevent them riding up during a parachute descent, and when not done up they hung down and looked like tails. The men landed in the desert regions and were covered in the red clay earth. Local tribesmen saw these men who had dropped from the sky with tails and red-stained faces and clothing and feared that they were devils sent to destroy them. As one story goes, the Paras had been watching local Bedouins herding their sheep and an older tribesman was shouting at a young boy called Mohammed, who was losing control of the flock. The Paras adopted the phrase as their new battle cry and when the Germans first confronted them in battle, they met these terrifying fighters covered from top to toe in red with 'tails' hanging down, roaring, 'Woah Mohammed!' as they charged forward with no fear in their eyes. The Germans held the Paras in awe; they began referring to them as the Red Devils and the name stuck.

For those readers who recognise the name, in 1964, the official parachute display team of the British Army and the Parachute Regiment was formed and quickly adopted the famous nickname, the Red Devils. Performing internationally, they are nowadays recognised as the foremost parachute display team in the world. The transition from paratrooper to Red Devil is not an easy one and involves a rigorous two-week selection cadre where candidates are sternly tested on all the skills that they will be required to utilise within the freefall team, and competition is intense. It is a huge honour to be selected and have this famous nickname bestowed upon them. However, all the guys are proud to remain serving members of the Parachute Regiment and as such can be called back to active service at any time.

In the Second World War, the 1st Parachute Brigade carried out three airborne operations and engaged in numerous battles in North Africa, where they captured or killed thousands of Germans. Often forgotten strategic battles were fought, with the Paras using their bayonets to overcome the enemy and take positions. More battle honours were awarded in North Africa than anywhere else. At Oudna, with veterans of Bruneval, the Paras found themselves isolated 50 miles behind enemy lines. Subjected to intense fire, they moved to take defensive positions around El Fedja farm, where they were surrounded by Germans. Rather than surrender, they held them off throughout the day and moving at night they fought their way back to Allied lines.

Much credit is given to Lieutenant Colonel Ernest 'Eric' Downe, who took over command of the Brigade. He brought in new officers, including Alastair Pearson and James Hill who instilled discipline into the men while at the same time encouraging what became known as ABI (Airborne Initiative). It was essential that the men had the ability to think on their feet and make decisions for themselves when necessary. The training of the parachute battalions was focused on the sole intent of turning these men who had passed selection and gained their wings into an elite fighting force. The commander of the 3rd Battalion, James Hill, had been seriously injured in North Africa and he and the others in command understood only too well the precarious circumstances the men would face on operations. They knew that chaos reigned when you first landed on the ground and that you needed supreme soldiering skills in order to survive.

The training regime put in place at the first depot at Hardwick Hall was specifically designed to push the men beyond normal endurance and to train them in the ability to move at speed. The guys were taken on long marches and various combat techniques were practised over and over again. Hill believed that the men would only be ready for action when they could TAB (Tactical Advance to Battle) 200km in three days carrying around 77lb of equipment.

The men needed to believe that they could survive and operate successfully behind enemy lines, despite being up against far greater enemy numbers, and knowing that nobody was going to come to their aid. They were trained to survive, fight and win with a never give up attitude. The ethos of the Paras was now firmly established. Some of the original guys who had joined 2 Commando couldn't keep up with the newly enthused pace of training and were returned to their units. Those that stayed formed strong bonds of Airborne brotherhood with the new volunteers joining them. JOE (Joined On Enlistment) was stamped on the documents of the new guys and the name has stuck for new recruits to this day. The men kept up their morale on operations by exchanging humorous stories and jokes and, as you can imagine, there were some real characters making up the Paras at this time. Dinty Moore was remembered as a man with a brilliant sense of humour who regaled the guys with stories and had them crying with laughter. As Major (Retired) Tony Hibbert said, 'Dinty was killed when his carrier blew up on a landmine in North Africa. I'm sure his driver was laughing when it happened.' A notable characteristic of the guys, which has never changed, was their ability to work hard, play hard and always find time to laugh. With the training now firmly established with a growing reputation for being demanding and tough, the men who made it were a new breed of courageous, fit, and intelligent blokes able to fend for themselves and work as a close-knit team.

As the war raged on, a daring and ambitious plan to invade German-occupied France got under way. In the lead-up to Operation Overlord, more commonly known as the Normandy Landings, the Paras were dropped into France to take and seize key strategic targets and cut off German reinforcements trying to reach the Normandy beachheads. In the early hours of 6 June 1944 around 7,000 British paratroopers and glider-borne infantry from the 6th Airborne Division, along with around 13,000 soldiers from the American 82nd and 101st Divisions, flew towards the French coast ahead of the main invasion force. The success of the landings lay first in the hands of these airborne warriors, who had to take out the German defences covering the beachheads and nullify the potential German response prior to the main force hitting the shores in the morning.

The drops were badly affected by the wind and incoming flak, which resulted in the men being scattered over a wide area. Some landed in deep water and drowned with their heavy loads dragging them under. With vital equipment lost and the first fatalities sustained, only about 40 per cent of the Division managed to land and form up in time to carry out their tasks. All of the men who landed safely gathered themselves together and endeavoured to join up with their main force. If they couldn't, they fought on regardless in small groups and caused mayhem behind the German lines as they went. The River Orne and canal bridges were successfully assaulted and bridges across the River Dives were put out of action.

The Merville Battery was a tier-one key target, a heavily fortified and well-manned post guarding the eastern end of the Normandy beaches. Surrounded by minefields, barbed wire and ditches, attacking it was a daunting but essential mission in the overall plan and one in which the Paras could not fail if the Allied ships were to come safely over the horizon in the morning.

Warrant Officer 1 (Retired) Jamie 'Nobby' Clarke, a well-respected and long-serving former mortarman and Regimental Sergeant Major of 1 Para (1st Battalion, the Parachute Regiment), recalled 7 June 2004, when he was presiding over the unveiling of a bust of Brigadier James Hill at the sixtieth anniversary of the operation. 'I remember discussing who should lead the parade and there was some argument between the various groups involved. Brigadier James Hill arrived, and I asked him if he could help with the decision. Without hesitation Hill told me that the 9th Battalion should lead.'[1]

Lieutenant Colonel Otway, aged 29, had been in command of the 9th Battalion for just a few months when he was shown a model of Merville Battery and told of its strategic importance. He had to take it at all costs. The guns in the battery were aimed directly at the areas into which the ships would be coming and also covered the Normandy beaches where troops would be landing in Operation Overlord. If these weapons remained in action, it was likely that the entire operation would fail. The reduced battalion of 150 men, who eventually managed to form up for the attack on that infamous night in 1944, were mostly around the age of 20 and had never seen battle before. With their vastly depleted numbers they were led by Otway into the taking of the Merville Battery. A frail old man at the time of the unveiling, Hill had been the one to give them the mission, which was nicknamed Operation Certain Death. It was with a heavy heart that he had sent them in, knowing that the battalion would most likely be decimated, but he'd had little choice due to the strategic importance of the target in the overall D-Day plan.

Planning for the assault on the battery began in the lead-up to Operation Overlord, and training took place away from prying eyes on a replica mock-up of the target built on private farmland in Berkshire. The battery and surrounding area were recreated down to every hedge and fence based on aerial photographs and human intelligence. It was essential that the training and information about the mission remained completely secret and, to test the men, a group of attractive WAAFs (Women's Auxiliary Air Force) were sent into the local town see if they could make the blokes reveal what they were doing.

In fairness to the men, not one said anything to breach security, but they certainly made the most of the female company that night.

Ahead of the 9th Battalion, a 'Troubridge' reconnaissance team went in to gather intelligence about the battery before meeting up with the rest of the men and confirming the attack plan. Bombers were intended to soften up the target by dropping munitions on the area before the parachutists landed, and gliders were due to come down inside the battery with more men and heavy equipment to support the mission. A taping party followed the reconnaissance team with the task of clearing the minefields and marking the route into the battery with tape. The 'Troubridge' party landed safely on the drop zone but had to dive for cover as the bombers missed their mark and the bombs fell on their position. Luckily no one was injured.

The planes carrying the battalion of paratroopers headed over the Channel and loud explosions filled the air around them as the men prepared to jump. The thirty-two Dakotas carrying around 540 men from the main body of 9th Battalion were thrown around by dust created by the bombing raid and strong winds; they flew in at the wrong altitudes and from different directions. A terrific amount of flak caused some pilots to roll the aircraft to avoid being hit. The guys getting ready to jump were thrown on top of each other and scrambled desperately to get themselves back up, out of the door, and into the air.

As the men descended it got no easier as they were shot at from below. Incendiary bullets pierced the chutes and the guys feared that they might go up in flames. Only seven of one twenty-man team made it onto the correct landing position, and nearly all of 9th Battalion were scattered over a wide area away from the DZ. What was not shown on the maps and photos that they had memorised were the deep ditches full of water. The Germans had opened sluice gates on the River Dives and the ground was flooded. Men landed in unforeseen water-logged trenches and were smothered by their chutes. Unable to get free and weighed down by their kit, many of them drowned. The Taping Party (men tasked with clearing and marking routes through minefields) also landed in wet ground and managed to get out safely, but unfortunately, they were not able to retrieve the tape.

The guys waded through water up to their chests and saw other men land and flounder in boggy ground. They made their way over to them as quickly as possible and grabbed hold of their harnesses but struggled to pull many of them up in time. The sinking mud sucked them under and out of sight in seconds.

The gliders carrying all the heavy equipment, including mortars, anti-tank weapons and mine detectors, struggled to control their landings. Going off course, they hit anti-landing poles, which resulted in several fatalities, and many other men were seriously injured. Two of the assault gliders had run into trouble; one managed to get back to land in England while the other struggled on across the Normandy coastline with damaged controls and part of its undercarriage missing.

The Troubridge party finally formed up into position and cut the outer wire fence. In front of them lay a huge minefield. With no detectors and no tape, the men bravely crawled forward digging for mines with their fingertips and then carefully making the devices safe. Sitting on their backsides, they moved along the path, dragging their feet to form two lines in the dirt to mark the cleared route. Reaching the inner belt of wire, they listened to the Germans inside the battery for half an hour before silently making their way back to the DZ to report their findings.

By 02.30 only 110 men had made their way to the RV, and so they waited. Otway recalled, 'I had no radio sets working, I had no engineers, I had no medicals. Damn all really. It did occur to me, yes, do I go ahead or do I not ... So, we went ahead. I was committed ... It would be true to say I went on and put all thoughts of failure out of my mind. It was a question of move off or give up. In the Parachute Regiment giving up is not an option.'[2]

Out of the darkness more men began to appear, and the number increased to 150 before they made their way to the lay-up area to form a new plan with their greatly reduced fighting force. The damaged glider finally arrived but miscalculated the target and landed in water east of the battery. With the mayhem continuing, the final glider made its approach unable to see the target and was hit by incoming flak, which forced it to land in a nearby orchard. The men clambered out of the stricken aircraft and heard Germans approaching. They got down into ditches, made themselves ready and engaged the enemy in a fierce firefight.

Near the battery, the men were not going to give up, and set off towards their goal, climbing in and out of holes created by the off-target bombing raid earlier, which made their progress in the dark even more difficult. They heard German troops marching up ahead and suddenly the craters proved to be very useful. The men jumped in and hid as the enemy soldiers marched right past them. They climbed out and were continuing on their way when all of a sudden there was a low groan. The men followed the sound and discovered one of their own lieutenants taking cover and smelling like shit. He had fallen into a well that was obviously used by the local farmer to dispose of all his household waste, and he was covered in sewage from head to toe. This broke the tension for a minute and put a smile on the blokes' faces as the para humour came into its own and the officer got very little sympathy as they continued with their task.

The men began to form up ready to cut through the wire and begin their attack when suddenly machine guns opened up on them. They had been spotted. Sergeant Sidney Knight leapt into action and led a small force to come up on the German gunners from the right flank. He and his men opened fire and counter-attacked with everything they had. Bravely throwing several grenades into the enemy area, they caused chaos amongst the Germans before attacking the position and successfully taking the gunners out. Knight then continued with his original mission and headed over to mount a diversionary attack on the main gate.

Despite the gliders not arriving to provide the support that had been planned, the order was given to begin the assault. A whistle blew and Bangalore torpedoes (explosive charges) were detonated to clear the wire in their path. The two assault parties streamed through the gaps and fanned out into formation, firing as they moved. Booby traps and mines exploded all around them as they came face to face with the German defenders and engaged in fierce hand-to-hand fighting. It was a brutal and aggressive onslaught as the paratroopers moved forward to achieve their objective of disabling the Merville Battery. The sun began to rise as the sound of shots, explosions and screams filled the air. Machine guns opened up all around and incoming shells were hitting men already lying injured on the ground. When the Germans inside the installation finally realised that they had been overrun and that their attackers were paratroopers, they dropped their weapons and surrendered. The Paras had killed most of the Germans, and twenty-three were taken prisoner. The main battery facing the beach, which was their primary target and posed the biggest threat to the invasion force, was successfully put out of action.

Despite the heavy losses and all odds against them, the men overcame adversity and successfully completed their tactically essential mission. The assault should have involved the original number of 750 men. Out of the brave 150 who had gone in, around sixty-five were still on their feet. The others were either dead or lay wounded. The seriously injured men were dragged on ammunition sledges to a Calvary Cross at a junction on the road to Breville. The remaining members of the 9th Battalion, joined by a few more men who had missed the assault, had a brief respite before heading to their next objective. Their work was not finished yet.

Jamie Clarke said: 'I will leave the military historians to debate whether the attack on the Merville Battery was a success. For me it showed everything that the Airborne Soldier is about. The Battalion, fully in the knowledge that high casualty rates were expected, with only 150 men making the RV, no heavy weapons, or explosives, still pressed home the attack. I was fortunate enough to discuss this operation with Brigadier James Hill and separately with my grandfather Sergeant Nobby Clarke, 'A' Company, 7th Battalion,

The Parachute Regiment, who also jumped on the Normandy landings. These were two men I held in great respect, both of whom had nothing but glowing admiration for the men of the 9th Battalion and their deeds that night. This for me, marks this action as nothing short of inspirational.[3]

The Airborne Division was tasked to take control of 24 sq km of strategic ground. Fierce fighting ensued as the men, with or without a leader, formed up in small groups and continued to attack and harass the enemy forces using the airborne initiative they became so famous for in the coming years. They engaged and held the Germans back from defending the beachhead landings, effectively buying vital time for the conventional infantry and mechanised troops landing on the beaches to gain a foothold and move inland. The Normandy Landings were successful, and the paratroopers continued to fight on to secure key positions ahead of the main landing force.

The Paras remained engaged in operations throughout the rest of June and July, and it wasn't until the end of August 1944 that they were finally withdrawn. The loss of men killed or injured was immense and the force needed to be reconstituted. The 6th Airborne Division had fought for eighty-two days of non-stop action. Six battle honours were awarded to the Parachute Regiment for Operation Overlord, of which three are borne on the Queen's Colour today.

It was the 1st Airborne Division, who had been impatiently waiting for their turn to get stuck into the action, who were used on the next major mission, code-named Operation Market Garden. The plan was to drop in the Division, along with the Polish contingent and the American 82nd and 101st Airborne Divisions, to secure the main canal and river crossings between Eindhoven and Arnhem. The airborne soldiers were tasked to take control of this stretch of river while ground forces breaking through the German lines came in to immediately support them. They would then move forward into the Ruhr and advance through Germany with a view to ending the war by Christmas.

The 1st British Airborne Division was given the most difficult target: Arnhem. Described as the jewel in the crown by Field Marshal Montgomery, the Paras dropped in a few miles away with the aim of getting into the town by last light and taking the road bridge over the River Nederrijn. Due to insufficient aircraft being available, the drops were staggered, leaving the three para battalions of the 1st Parachute Brigade to get into Arnhem and secure the bridge on their own before the rest of the division was dropped. The head shed (officer in charge) didn't want to delay and although there

Freepost Plus RTKE-RGRJ-KTTX
Pen & Sword Books Ltd
47 Church Street
BARNSLEY
S70 2AS

# DISCOVER MORE ABOUT PEN & SWORD BOOKS

**Pen & Sword Books** have over 4000 books currently available, our imprints include: Aviation, Naval, Military, Archaeology, Transport, Frontline, Seaforth and the Battleground series, and we cover all periods of history on land, sea and air.

Can we stay in touch? From time to time we'd like to send you our latest catalogues, promotions and special offers by post. If you would prefer not to receive these, please tick this box. ☐

**We also think you'd enjoy some of the latest products and offers by post from our trusted partners: companies operating in the clothing, collectables, food & wine, gardening, gadgets & entertainment, health & beauty, household goods, and home interiors categories. If you would like to receive these by post, please tick this box.** ☐

We respect your privacy. We use personal information you provide us with to send you information about our products, maintain records and for marketing purposes. For more information explaining how we use your information please see our privacy policy at www.pen-and-sword.co.uk/privacy. You can opt out of our mailing list at any time via our website or by calling 01226 734222.

Mr/Mrs/Ms .................................................................................................................

Address......................................................................................................................

Postcode.......................... Email address...................................................................

**Website: www.pen-and-sword.co.uk  Email: enquiries@pen-and-sword.co.uk**
**Telephone: 01226 734555   Fax: 01226 734438**
**Stay in touch: facebook.com/penandswordbooks or follow us on Twitter @penswordbooks**

were reports of enemy armour in the area, the decision was still made to go ahead.

Despite the initial element of surprise working in their favour, the Paras went unknowingly into a vipers' nest unsupported, and soon encountered the German II SS Panzer Corps. Only 2 Para, under the command of Lieutenant Colonel (Major General Retired) Johnny Frost, with a few other support elements, managed to reach the bridge, where they promptly secured the northern end.

Encountering issues with their radios, they had no way of knowing that no support was coming. German forces arrived with powerful tanks and artillery and began bombarding their positions with heavy fire. The men were cut off from the rest of their Brigade but fought back with fearless determination. Occupying burned out buildings with the injured sheltering in the cellars, the rapidly reducing number of men courageously held off the German offensive with their ammunition and supplies running lower and lower by the hour. Jon Baker, current Curator of the Airborne Assault Museum in Duxford, said, 'The German troops had been training in counter-airborne warfare using lessons learned from Normandy. They focused on cutting off the DZs and LZs (landing zones) and starved the division of resupply. It was still a close-run thing though, which demonstrates the fighting ability of the British Paras.'[4]

The entire airborne division was expected to hold the position for forty-eight hours before being relieved by ground forces but support in the form of 30 Corps could not get through and the para battalions failed to link up. Under constant attack from German forces, only 700 men had made it to Arnhem, and they held on for three days and four nights, battling on despite heavy losses and casualties. Major (Retired) David Collins said, 'What we call the Arnhem attitude is drilled into all paratroopers to this day. What you jump in with is all you've got. You don't know when resupplies are coming or if they are going to come at all, and you get on with what you're carrying on your back, using it sparingly and wisely. This was drummed into me, and it's drummed into all new recruits.'[5]

Finally getting the radios to work, they learned the truth of the situation in which they found themselves, and this was when the now famous, rumoured urban myth, but undeniably apt final radio message was sent by Major Digby Tatham-Warter, 'Out of ammo, God Save the King.'[6] When the brave blokes who held the bridge were eventually overrun, the Germans reported on the unbelievable bravery of the Paras and their total reluctance to surrender even when hugely outnumbered and outgunned by tanks and heavy armour.

John 'Johnny' Frost served throughout the war and became a legendary figure in the Parachute Regiment, not least because of his role in Arnhem. To this day men under his command remember him saying, 'If you can't run, you walk, if you can't walk you crawl and if you can't crawl, you pull yourself along by every tuft of grass.'[7] This was the mentality he took with him into battle and instilled in his men. His daughter, Caroline, said, 'For Dad the camaraderie and the bond between the men in the white heat of battle was deeper than blood. He never forgot Arnhem and every Sunday he would look up at a special painting of the battle and say, "No food, no meds, no water, no ammo, nothing left at all," before carving the roast. It is very poignant that although he rarely talked about Arnhem after he left the army in 1968, he bought a farm called North End.'[8]

The rest of the division lost many men as they tried to fight their way through to reinforce the bridge and found themselves trapped across the river at Oosterbeek. The Paras held on against overwhelming odds for nine days until ordered to withdraw across the river at night. The ground forces never managed to get through to join up with the airborne battalions and fewer than 3,000 men from the initial 10,095 that landed managed to get away across the river. For the returning guys, the flaws in the plan were obvious and avoidable. The intelligence on the presence of the Panzers should have been passed through; they presented a formidable enemy force to overcome, but more importantly, it was the decision to separate the air lifts of the men. The weather was fine on the first day and if more guys had been dropped initially, they would have had a far better chance of holding off the enemy and achieving their objective. On top of this, the failure of the radios and the lack of communication sealed the fate of these incredibly courageous paratroopers. We can't change history and as veteran Len Wright, who fought at Arnhem bridge said, 'We wanted and needed Operation Market Garden in 1944. We knew that there were risks and we were willing to take them. Now I know that there were even more risks than we were told about back then, but we would have taken them nonetheless.' This attitude is the bedrock of the Parachute Regiment and epitomises the never give in attitude of all who have served in the past, and still serve within it today.

Two members of the Parachute Regiment were awarded the Victoria Cross for their actions in Operation Market Garden and numerous other commendations were earned for what was truly a momentous battle. Veterans and paratroopers since the war still make what has become known as a pilgrimage to Arnhem to pay tribute to the men who fought and died there, and Parliament commemorates the events of those nine days every year. As ex-para, Dan Jarvis MP said, 'From the 17th to the 26th September each year, we remember the anniversary of the battle of Arnhem – nine days of some of the fiercest fighting witnessed in the Second World War, and one of the largest airborne operations ever conducted. Arnhem did indeed prove to be a bridge too far, but the story of those who fought there is one of immeasurable bravery and unspeakable tragedy. It would come to define our airborne forces, forging an enduring legacy.'[9]

The war was destined to continue for almost one year more and the Parachute Regiment took part in operations in the Ardennes, Norway, Denmark and Germany in that time. Due to the Paras' unique capabilities, in October 1944 they were utilised to drop into Greece. As the Germans withdrew to the north, paratroopers were dropped in and seized Megara airport before marching into Athens. Their training, skills, and ability to adapt to ever-changing situations were put to the test as they became embroiled in the struggle for power in the country. Along with searching out and destroying any German forces, they also had to face and control infighting between different Greek factions, restore local governance, provide humanitarian aid in the form of food and medicine, and ensure the availability of basic amenities to the innocent local population. There was no plan for these contingencies, the men had to think on their feet when they got there. As Colonel Terence Otway reportedly said, 'The scope of the Brigade's activities may be illustrated by the fact that at any one period during serious rioting they were feeding 20,000 Greek civilians, and on one day during the final battle in Athens they killed 170 rebels, wounded 70 and took 520 prisoners at considerable cost to themselves.'[10] It was a situation that became a common recurrence in the role of the paratrooper following the end of the war.

In March 1945, Operation Varsity, the largest airborne invasion in history, took place. Involving more than 16,000 paratroopers and thousands of aircraft, the 6th Airborne Division along with American and Canadian airborne forces were dropped near the banks of the Rhine to assist the troops on the ground in securing territory across the river in Germany. Learning from the lessons of Arnhem, all the paratroopers were dropped on the same day to link up with the ground forces, who had already begun the task of making river crossings. The massive airborne drops also took place in daylight, enabling the paratroopers to see their landing zones more clearly. However, this also meant that they were clearly visible to the enemy and came under severe attack from the ground. The Germans were shocked by the numbers of men dropping from the sky, which was thick and black with aircraft, and the ability of the British Paras to land and quickly organise themselves into a highly effective fighting force. Despite heavy casualties and fierce resistance from the enemy, including the 1st Fallschirmjäger now operating as normal infantry soldiers, the men succeeded in securing their objectives within six hours and linked up with the ground forces to continue the advance through Germany.

Following the collapse of the Rhine barrier, which was a huge line of defence for the Germans and the last real obstacle between the Allies and the homeland, the British airborne troops used their initiative to move on quickly and advanced north. As they made their way across the country, they engaged in fierce fights and overcame remnants of the German Army. They moved past Osnabrück, Minden, Celle and crossed the River Elbe. The 3rd Parachute Brigade rapidly covered 350 miles before reaching Wismar and many of the men completed the journey on foot. As R. W. Butcher reported, 'The Red Devils' superb physical fitness impressed even the Guards who supported them in Churchill tanks.'[11] Six days later, on 8 May, Germany surrendered.

In Operation Doomsday, the 1st Airborne Division, which had been sorely depleted during Market Garden, had been rebuilding its numbers and was made ready with only a few days' notice to go into Norway for the German surrender. Six thousand troops were sent in to deal with around 350,000 Germans, but the potentially difficult mission proved to be fairly easy in the end, and they were met by very little resistance. The task quickly evolved into maintaining law and order, securing airfields, and preventing the sabotage of vital infrastructure facilities. They also took care of the prisoners of war held in the country as well as hunting and arresting German Nazis accused of war crimes. The 1st Airborne Division retained control until the arrival of HQ Allied Land Forces in Norway and oversaw the return of the King of Norway from exile. The war in Europe was over and plans were in place for airborne forces to be transferred to spearhead the invasion of Japanese-held areas in Malaya and Singapore, but the atomic bombs dropped on Hiroshima and Nagasaki forced the Japanese to surrender.

By VE Day, the Parachute Regiment consisted of two divisions of 10,000 men in each. Over the course of the war around 80,000 to 100,000 guys volunteered and joined the Paras because the battalions had to be constantly replenished due to the high rate of attrition that they sustained. Thousands of men sacrificed their lives as shock airborne troops at the tip of the spear on the numerous operations they were tasked with during this period. Bearing in mind that aeroplanes were extremely new – very few people had ever been in one, let alone parachuted out – the men who volunteered for this role were brave and valiant men who were not scared of the unknown and embraced the challenges and risks that came with it.

Jon Baker perfectly captured the ethos:

> One veteran said that they didn't necessarily join just because they wanted to have a go at the enemy; they also got a nice uniform (maroon beret, Pegasus flash and wings), were paid a little bit more than normal soldiers and they were guaranteed to get the girls. This was the humour of the men. However, from inception in 1940 through to the Japanese surrender, the Paras fought in every theatre. They were joined by soldiers from Poland and Canada, and in India a whole division was raised. They were always first in and unlike foreign airborne forces were not immediately withdrawn but stayed on in an infantry role within the campaign – like in Normandy or after the Rhine Crossing. From little to no army parachuting in 1940 by the war's end two full divisions had been raised and were united by the symbol of Pegasus and the maroon beret. General Browning knew that this new force needed an identity, and a strong one at that, to fend off critics.[12]

The Parachute Regiment had proved its worth on the field of battle and was here to stay, but in the aftermath of the war they were faced with a variety of conflicts requiring all their skills.

# Chapter 3

# Post-War World

At the end of the Second World War, rather than the world becoming a peaceful place, it entered an era of utter turmoil. Empires crumbled, with uprisings and disturbances occurring in many areas across the globe. Millions of people were displaced, and the USA and Russia emerged as superpowers in direct conflict with one another, heralding the Cold War. The Parachute Regiment went through its own restructuring process with a drastic reduction in numbers and the amalgamation of the 1st and 6th Divisions into the aptly named 16th Airborne Division. The aim was to move all the paratroopers to Palestine as a staging ground from where they could act as a QRF (Quick Reaction Force) to any areas requiring support, and unbeknown to them, the men were going to get caught up in many emerging conflicts. The war may have been over and open large-scale battles a thing of the past, but the Paras were kept very busy over the next couple of decades and needed to use all the skills available in their toolbox. Some steely guile, robustness and adaptability was required to be able to deal with what came their way and they had to utilise a very different type of soldiering in the face of the new challenges that confronted them.

## Indonesia 1945–46

Thousands upon thousands of Paras were killed over the course of the war but for those that survived it had been non-stop action. They had been dropped into Normandy for operations associated with the D-Day landings, fought their way across France, dropped in Operation Varsity, and marched hundreds of miles through Germany, engaging with and pushing the enemy back as they went. After the end of the war in Europe, a number of paratroopers were immediately redeployed to the Far East in preparation for an operation to recapture the Malayan Peninsula from Japan. The 5th Parachute Brigade was training and preparing for jungle combat when the Japanese surrendered. The Brigade was now faced with the task of establishing law and order in areas that were quickly turning into bloodbaths as various factions fought over control of the region.

An air drop into Singapore was cancelled and the men went in by sea to meet the surrendering Japanese. Despite the clear evidence of Japanese atrocities such as the headless bodies of British personnel being found in ditches, the Japanese, somewhat surprisingly, laid down their arms without a fight. Paratroopers were attached to local police divisions and soon transformed the demoralised ex-policemen into a disciplined body of uniformed men acting with restraint and professionalism during very difficult times.

At the end of 1945, it became clear that the empire of the Netherlands East Indies (modern-day Indonesia) was out of control with widespread looting, murder and arson taking place. Dutch troops had not been able to get back to the islands and in the meantime the Japanese had surrendered all their armaments to the locals, who were now turning them on the Japanese and their own people. There was no government, and the islands were being torn apart by civil strife as rival political extremist factions fought for power. The rebels far outnumbered the British, Indian, and Japanese soldiers stationed there and they could not control the situation. It was a job for the Paras.

When the Brigade arrived in Jakarta on the large island of Java, they soon realised that the majority of the people wanted to live in peace. In a mobile offensive role, they began clearing the kampongs (villages) in the area. They swooped into the kampongs, sealed the outskirts, and then began systematic searches of all the houses for weapons. As Sergeant R. W. Butcher of the 12th Battalion recalled from his time there, 'A few nationalists were misguided enough to take on the men of the maroon beret. Most only had a brief period in which to reflect upon their silly mistake.'[1]

The Paras very quickly established a safe environment where off-duty soldiers were allowed to go about unarmed and they handed over to the arriving Dutch marines. The men were then quickly redeployed to restore law and order and civil government in Semarang in North Java, where anarchy now reigned. Gangs of thugs were roaming the streets attacking and murdering people, pillaging, and looting. The local population of Chinese, Japanese and Dutch lived in terror as the insurgents committed terrible atrocities and destroyed the city's infrastructure.

The men of the 5th Brigade had been previously blooded in airborne operations and as fighting infantry but now they had to use their skill set in a very different role in a very different environment. There were around 150 political and paramilitary factions fighting for control in Java, including groups with very bizarre names. According to the 5th Brigade War Diary they included, 'The League of Bearded Men Muslim Fighting Organisation' and 'The Black Buffalo Gangster Group'. No food could be imported into the area and the insurgents had cut off water and electricity supplies. There was no kind of governance in place and the city was in absolute chaos.

The Paras immediately took control of the situation by establishing a secure perimeter around the city, which they heavily manned with sentries to prevent insurgents infiltrating from outside. The nearby airport was secured, and only sanctioned patrols and special ops went outside the ring of steel they had created. In the city, they imposed curfews, carried out planned searches for weapons and munitions and set up checkpoints and security patrols around the streets. Butcher described the living conditions:

> The daily life of the men was a curious mixture of peacetime soldiering and active service. The men slept under mosquito nets on wooden and rope beds known as 'charpoys'. Most units made their own portable showers so that at least once a day the men could wash away the day's sweat because the weather was always extremely hot. Practically everybody suffered from ringworm sooner or later, which was irritating and unsightly. Its treatment, gentian violet, was even more unsightly. All around it was a pretty basic existence not lacking essentials but with few comforts or luxuries.[2]

Fighting insurgents one minute and installing order the next, the Brigade contained men with a wide variety of abilities, and they were all put to good use. They took over civil affairs and shared out the senior positions amongst the main segments of the population: the Dutch, the Chinese, and the Indonesians. Initially, they fed thousands of children who were starving because the scarce amount of food was being sold through the black market, but then the Paras began organising the food supplies. The entire population of several hundred thousand was registered and ration cards were introduced to ensure that even the poorest had enough to eat. Engineers began repairing vital communication links and restored water, electricity, and other public services. Medics set up their own version of a National Health Service even before it had been introduced back in the UK, a police force was trained and set up to take over from military patrols and they even got involved with criminal investigations and ran a prison as they constantly dealt with insurgent activity. As Butcher stated, 'The Brigade provided the basic framework of government to enable a more orderly life to be led by the population, in a remarkably short time.'

During the period of reorganisation, the Paras had to constantly contend with and fight against the various nationalist groups, often coming under artillery fire from heavy weaponry when they went out on patrol, but they soon overcame any opposition from the untrained, disorganised Indonesian rebels. Terrorism was virtually eradicated as the nationalists soon realised that it would be foolish to attack the city from the outside. 'They were no match for the skill, disciplined aggressiveness and fitness of the battle-hardened Brigade,' said Butcher.

In the few months that they were in Semarang, the paras improved the security situation and restored order to civilian life. Despite not being a rapid response force that was flown in and dropped into an area, on this occasion they still proved themselves ready to react to changes and to respond accordingly in the moment. Unlike the tasks they had been initially deployed to complete, dropping behind enemy lines and fighting sometimes to the death to achieve their objectives, they now had to ascertain exactly how to treat the people in front of them. Just as the Paras had done in Greece, one moment they were providing food and basic needs to the population and the next they were defending themselves from the very same people they were trying to help.

As a stabilisation force, the Paras faced a different set of decision-making problems to those faced in battle, but they got stuck in and after a very short time they had completely turned the situation around. The people knew that the Paras were tough and not to be messed with, but they also realised that they were protecting the population from the far worse murderous brutality of their own countrymen. Within a year the Paras established an ordered society and in March 1946 they were able to celebrate the anniversary of the Rhine Crossing with a huge parade.

In April 1946, they handed over to the Dutch and it was the end of the short but impressive existence of the 5th Brigade, which was then disbanded. In the not-too-distant future the Paras would be back to put their jungle skills to the test. Meanwhile, the men of the 5th Brigade were either demobbed and sent back to the UK or sent directly to Palestine, where another kind of civil disturbance was erupting.

## Palestine 1945–48

Dreaming of home after VE Day, many paratroopers were sent straight from Europe to the high temperatures of Palestine in the Middle East. These guys had been in the midst of ferocious battles leaping through flak-filled skies and using their fighting skills to defeat the enemy and survive despite having only brief respites. Now, instead of returning to their loved ones, just like the men deployed to the Far East, they faced a very different operating environment with a new set of rules of engagement.

For the veterans of the war, it was a stark difference to the full-on battles that they had been engaged in previously and they were now joined and bolstered by new recruits who had trained as paratroopers as part of conscription but had never been in battles of any kind, or earned their spurs as many of the older guys saw it. Following sixteen weeks' basic training and four weeks' parachute instruction at the jump school in Upper Heyford, the new Paras were sent out to Palestine to join the hardcore veterans of the Second World War. Despite their differences, the blokes all worked well together with the more experienced paratroopers helping to bring on the new 'crows' (a word derived from 'Combat Recruit of War' used in the First World War for new boys) and they all found ways of coping with the new environment with innovation and determination. The new recruits had passed the strict selection process and their training meant that they went to work knowing that they were ready for the job and confident about doing it well.

The, now named, 6th Airborne Division found some of the blokes living in basic tented accommodation, sharing communal showers, and surrounded by flies and midges. Their initial task was to help maintain a balance of peace between the Jewish and Arab populations without getting involved in internal security matters. That premise did not last long as tensions between the two races grew, and hostilities threatened the lives of civilians. The Paras were soon drawn into the escalating situation as Jewish factions began terrorist activities; the men were caught up in trying to find the perpetrators, protecting Arabs from Jewish attacks, and dealing with Arabs attacking Jews.

The background to the Israel and Palestine story is long and complicated but at the end of the Second World War the main problems were caused by the vast numbers of displaced Jews trying to leave Europe to find their homeland in Israel. After the Holocaust the Jews had the sympathy of the world, but their desire to create a Zionist state presented problems for the British, who were very aware of keeping good relations with the oil-rich Arab states who supported the Arabic Palestinians. With the world looking on, including the pro-Jewish Americans, Britain tried to restrict the number of Jews entering the country to avoid escalating trouble between the two races.

Early disturbances were mainly between the Arabs and the Jews and the personal security for the paratroopers was fairly light. In April of 1946, everything changed. A car park that had been taken over by the 6th Airborne Division became the target of the Jewish terrorists and sent a shockwave through the regiment. Seven paratroopers were killed in a rapid, well-planned, and violent raid and it was just the beginning of a catalogue of attacks perpetrated by Jewish terrorist groups.

Up to this point the soldiers had been unprepared for such aggression against British forces and immediately increased security levels across the board. As more attacks and sabotage missions were carried out, Britain launched Operation Agatha and the Paras became involved in a massive raid of Jewish Agency offices, where they found and confiscated arms caches and documents relating to terrorist attacks and sabotage missions. Offices, buildings, and whole sectors were cordoned off as the Paras supported police in the search raids. While they uncovered a huge amount of information and made thousands of arrests, they did not stop the terrorist movement and more atrocities followed in retaliation.

Much of the incriminating information and papers taken from the raids was kept at the HQ of British Troops in Palestine in the south side of the King David hotel in Jerusalem. Just after midday on 22 July, armed patrols went about their daily routine scouring the streets of Jerusalem in the searing heat on the lookout for the ever-present dangers. All of a sudden, a huge boom resounded across the city and clouds of smoke and dust blocked the sun as an explosion ripped through the southern end of the St David's hotel, destroying one side of the six-storey building. The bombs, which had been planted in the basement by Jewish terrorists desperate to destroy the papers that had been confiscated, tore up through the hotel wing to the roof. Floors, walls, and ceilings collapsed and the whole corner of the hotel disintegrated into a pile of concrete slabs and rubble, crushing people in the building or burying them alive. Passers-by in the street and people in adjacent buildings were affected by the blast and ninety-one people were killed. Paras raced in on red alert to King David Street to discover the chaos and devastation caused by the explosion. The guys immediately organised themselves into helping to lift and move the debris of concrete in a desperate search to find survivors and recover bodies, while others stayed on the lookout for further attacks. Para Alan W. Gauntlet described the scene, 'There appears to be organised chaos and we see horrendous scenes around us. Paramedics with stretchers and ambulances attending the dead and wounded. Our job is to help move and lift debris as required, to recover bodies. We must also be on the look-out for any other secondary attack. Not a very happy day but this was the start of terrorist action in the world.'[3]

The search for people trapped alive under the decimated hotel wing went on for the next few days and paratroopers working around the clock managed to rescue six survivors. Such scenes would be repeated many years later, on the streets of Northern Ireland.

Well-organised terrorist action increased, along with propaganda turning people against the Paras. They didn't let it get to them. Private (Retired) Tony Costello, who was sent out to Palestine in 1947 soon after passing the stiff selection process, remembered, '"Kalynot" was a nickname with which the Jewish children used to taunt us. It is a foul-smelling red poppy and, referring to our maroon berets, they called us, "The red poppies with the blackhearts". Rather than be insulted we adopted it as a mark of distinction, much to their annoyance.'[4]

The blokes went about their duties with self-discipline and ultra-professionalism under extreme provocation. It became normal for the men to be spat at and insulted on a daily basis, but they endured this in an attempt to maintain law and order. Over time they had to face much worse as the level of violence increased and they faced the possibility of being kidnapped and murdered, all the time restricted in their ability to respond due to the strict rules of engagement.

There were increasing attacks in 1947 and the Paras serving in the region had less and less chance to relax even on their time off as it was deemed too dangerous to go out and about. Dennis Edwards of the 6th Airborne Division described his experiences, 'We weren't allowed out of the camps, we didn't have any leisure time. It was like being in prison. Two or three lads got caught in the Jewish quarter and we woke up to see them strung up on trees outside our camp. It was a bad time, Palestine.'[5]

As the situation escalated, reinforcements were sent into the region. Vincent Leonard from 2 Para (2nd Battalion, the Parachute Regiment) described the role expected of the men and the situation they experienced, 'When we were deployed, patrols consisted of a full stick (ten to twenty men), a brick (four to six men) or, very occasionally a half-brick (two or three men). The patrols were intended to reassure and protect the local population from terrorist activity. It was common practice in these towns for terrorists to fire indiscriminately into the souk (market). Attacks on both British personnel and Arabs by the Zionist groups were now commonplace but there were also frequent attacks involving Palestinian terrorists. The British found themselves in the middle of a civil war and this post-war policing action was spiralling out of control.'[6]

The Paras relied on their resilience and quick thinking on many occasions as they came up against troublemakers on both sides. Corporal Laurence Soloman was on guard duty on a train when suddenly they came under fire from both Arabs and Jews fighting across the tracks. The train came to a stop and the driver ran away. A Palestinian police officer brought about a temporary ceasefire but now there was nobody to drive the train. Solomon took over. Without having a clue what he was doing, he stepped up to the plate without hesitation and drove the locomotive away from danger. Not knowing how to stop, the train came to a crashing halt at the station as onlookers stared in amazement. Nobody was hurt and he succeeded in keeping all the passengers safe.

One of the main causes of contention in the region was the number of Jewish immigrants coming from Europe. Escort troops from the Paras accompanied the illegal immigrants to detention camps in Cyprus, where they were looked after until it was determined where they would go. Costello remembered the boats that were 'rust buckets' coming in crammed with refugees. 'We had to go down to the beach at Nahariya where a boat carrying illegal immigrants had been deliberately run aground. We rounded up some of them but most escaped into the sandhills where a welcoming party was waiting for them.'[7]

In the middle of 1947, the United Nations sent a team into Palestine to consider a solution to the ongoing situation. During the UNSCOP (United Nations Special Committee on Palestine) visit, 4,500 immigrants arrived in a US passenger ship, which became known as The Exodus. Instead of sending the Jews to Cyprus to wait for legal immigration, the British leaders decided that the large number of immigrants would be returned to the place where they started, Marseilles in France, on three British boats. Over half the regiment was involved in escorting the refugees back to Europe on the ships, but their task was kept top secret.

The Paras on board assumed that they were going to Cyprus, and it was only once they were out to sea that they found out that they were actually heading for the south of France. The journey became even longer when the refugees could not land in France and were very controversially returned to Germany via Gibraltar, but the guys accepted the situation and quickly adapted.

On board the boats, the paratroopers maintained good relations with the refugees, playing with the children and chatting to the women, who were allowed up on deck. On arrival in Hamburg, the Jews put up great resistance to being moved and the blokes went down into the hold unarmed to persuade them to disembark. The soldiers slid down the ladders and came face to face with men wrapped in barbed wire and holding batons. The first man down, 22-year-old paratrooper, John de Grey descended at speed and let out a loud whoop, which caused all of the Jews to scatter, and he was then joined by the rest of his men. Up above, guys were ready with hoses in case things got out of hand. John recalled, 'While I was making a speech to the crowd, assuring them they would not be roughly treated ... Someone decided that the moment had come – turned the hoses on the platform and kept it up, sousing me and all the men so that we could not speak.'[8] This had the effect of making the Jews laugh and lightened the situation. All on board were then taken into Hamburg.

The Jews were not only coming to Palestine by boat; they were also being smuggled in on trains. Costello described the atmosphere as constantly tense:

> Between October and December, I was part of a team of paras taking Intelligence officers across the border into Lebanon. Some Jews were being smuggled into the country through Lebanon by train and I was part of a guard protecting British Intelligence officers going into Lebanon to interview Christians who had information about the trade in illegal immigrants. We cordoned the area around a house while the officers met with the informants and then brought them back over the border. I was also one of the guards at a large house on Mount Carmel where several foreign diplomats and King Abdullah I of Jordan were meeting. Our orders were to shoot anyone who approached from outside the perimeter. In Haifa we were billeted in a proper army barracks with a mess hall and even a cinema but even there we had to be constantly alert. One night a jeep drove straight through the barrier at the gate. The driver was shot but a bomb was discovered in the jeep. The vehicle was towed into an open space away from the buildings and I was part of an overnight team responsible for guarding the jeep. We had to stand with our backs next to the vehicle and then walk ten paces away from it. We stayed all night until a team came to deal with the bomb the following day.[9]

Costello was in Haifa with Private (Retired) Bernard Cribbins OBE, who went on to become a famous actor, and he remembered the night that the NAAFI went up in flames and they both formed part of a chain moving ammunition out of a burning hut. 'The ceiling caught fire and we were ordered to get out, just in time before the ceiling crashed in.' Cribbins and Costello, both in their 90s, are still friends to this day; the Para bond of brotherhood never breaking.

Britain was caught in an untenable situation but despite clearly predicting what would happen between the Arabs and Jews if left to their own devices, they announced that they were leaving. In November the United Nations revealed their decision to partition Palestine into two separate Jewish and Arabic states and both sides began striving to prepare for the partition by gaining ground and power. Throughout the country Arabs and Jews began attacking one another as the paratroopers tried to protect strategic communication links, oil installations and pipelines. Haifa became a focal point for fighting between Arabs and Jews, and the Paras were caught in the middle trying desperately to keep the peace, keep transport links open, protect the oil refineries and the port itself. Three paratroopers were killed in February and March, and in April 1948 a battle for Haifa took place. The Paras concentrated on protecting the port for their own withdrawal as the Jews and Arabs fought for control. Costello remembered boarding the *Empress Australia* ready to leave the country. 'We were being fired at from a block of flats and HMS *Penelope* shone a searchlight on their position and called out a warning that if they fired another shot, they would be targeted. The terrorists fired again, and the ship turned its guns on the window and destroyed them. The final withdrawal was by no means easy, but one of my best memories was listening to the FA Cup final on the radio on the journey back.'[10]

The British mandate came to an end on 15 May 1948, and before long the country dissolved into the Arab Israeli War, which marked the start of decades of unrest and never-ending conflict between the two states.

The Paras involved in Palestine had demonstrated their ability to adapt to a completely new situation and it was not the last time that the regiment would come up against urban conflict and acts of savage terrorism. The standards set during the Second World War remained firm in the years following. Only six years after their inauguration, the Parachute Regiment had established itself as a supreme fighting force demonstrating an intense and indomitable spirit in battle, and inspiring awe and respect for their tough but fair attitude in the midst of civilian turmoil.

# Chapter 4

# The Squadron

## Malayan Emergency, 1948–60

An escalating situation in the Far East during the 1950s led to a call for the Paras to join special forces in an arduous search for CTs (communist terrorists) hiding out in the dense jungle territory of Malaya. The situation required training for operations in a gruelling environment and put the mental and physical resilience of the men to the test. The jungle is commonly acknowledged to be the toughest operating environment in which soldiers can be asked to deploy.

In 1948, trouble began brewing in the jungle-covered country of Malaya as Chinese communists, who had ironically been trained by the British, saw an opportunity to gain power and began a campaign of terror. Using the jungle as their cover, they began attacking the workers on rubber plantations, raiding villages to get food and supplies and turning the people against the British with promises of freedom in order to get their support. On 16 June, a gang of CTs murdered the British manager of a rubber plantation and then two more Europeans at another plantation were executed. This came as a huge shock to the authorities and an emergency was declared by the High Commissioner.

Malaya (now Malaysia) was a British colony rich in many resources including rubber and tin, which were the source of great income. Many Chinese and Indian workers had been brought into the country to be employed in these areas. A relatively small nation in Southeast Asia with a high mountain ridge running down the centre, 80 per cent of Malaya's land area was covered in jungle. In 1941, Japan invaded the country and Britain made ready a special training centre in Singapore to train volunteers from the Chinese population, who were mostly members of the Malay Communist Party, to fight against the Japanese. The aim was to train these men in jungle and sabotage warfare to act as the MPAJA (Malay People Anti-Japanese Army) and organise resistance to the Japanese occupation. When the Japanese surrendered in 1945, a large group of these Chinese communists, well-armed and supplied by Britain, remained in the country, and believed that they could lead a successful insurgency against the return of the British colonials. The insurgency threatened the earnings from rubber and tin and so from a purely economic point of view, Britain did not want it to succeed but also did not want to declare a war. It remained known as the Malayan Emergency, but for all intents and purposes it was a war with thousands of troops involved.

The Malayan communists were not in a position to directly confront British forces and concentrated their efforts on attacks and sabotage; they killed civilians, soldiers and members of the police force and disrupted communication and transportation links. Committing atrocities, and horrifically executing victims in front of villagers, they spread terror throughout the communities and forced them to supply them with food, new recruits and information before disappearing deep into the jungle, where ordinary soldiers could not follow.

The SAS had been disbanded at the end of the Second World War and the situation in Malaya provided supporters of the 'Regiment' with the opportunity they had been waiting for that would enable them to gain a permanent position back in the UK forces' order of battle. Sabre squadrons from the re-formed Special Air Service (SAS) were deployed in a counter-insurgency, jungle-fighting role to combat the rapidly growing threat of the CTs, who were operating out of the dense and militarily challenging landscape. The situation on the ground evolved quickly and the three established SAS squadrons were stretched to their operational limit, so in 1955 the call went out to the Parachute Regiment as well as the New Zealand SAS to supply one squadron each to bolster their numbers and increase their effectiveness.

When the Parachute Regiment first heard the news that paratroopers were to be involved, the response to the call for volunteers was enormous and 200 men from across all three battalions were picked to go on an internal selection cadre. Sergeant (Retired) Fred Weaver, a serving member of 2 Para (2nd Battalion the Parachute Regiment) at the time, explained, 'Many of us put our names forward for the new squadron. We were keen to be a part of this exciting opportunity to get over to Malaya and get some action operating alongside the SAS. I was a corporal at the time with five years' experience under my belt and this was one of the criteria they were looking for. After a tough two-week course up on the Brecon Beacons being put through our paces, I was eventually selected and became part of the new Independent Parachute Squadron.'[1]

The fledgling squadron flew out to its holding base in Kuala Lumpur via Cyprus in February 1955 consisting of seventy-six officers and all ranks, including a couple of veterans who had gone into Singapore as part of the 5th Parachute Brigade in 1945. Their task, once trained and ready to go, was to penetrate deep into the harsh jungle environment in the hunt for the communist bandits, who were wreaking havoc in the towns and villages. Once the training started, the Paras showed they were up to the challenge and demonstrated their ability to learn new skills, assimilate information quickly, and cope with the huge mental and physical demands of jungle warfare. They went about the training with such enthusiasm that reportedly even the SAS instructors found it hard to keep up with them.

The final part of the training was parachuting, and each man did two jumps, one with a full rucksack and one with abseiling gear. The method for entry into deeper parts of the jungle involved parachuting into the trees and then abseiling down to the ground on ropes. The incredibly dangerous method of insertion known as 'tree jumping' meant that the men could be dropped into remote areas quickly and efficiently and take the insurgents by surprise. Unable to steer the parachutes, they dropped into the canopy hoping that their chutes would catch on strong branches from which they could drop a long cord and lower their rucksacks and then themselves to the ground safely.

Consisting of an HQ unit and four 'sabre' troops divided into four-man patrols, the Paras could insert into the bush by parachute, helicopter or, as on most occasions, by foot with two weeks supply of rations that were replenished by air drops in designated areas. With regular resupplies the men stayed in the middle of the dense vegetation for two to three months at a time. They were confronted by three types of jungle: primary has been relatively untouched by humans and contains high trees creating a canopy above clear and spacious ground, while secondary jungle has at some point been, cut allowing the sunlight to come through and encourage rapid growth of foliage and plants. This type is home to all kinds of nasty creatures, it is dark and humid, and very difficult to get through. The third form is bamboo, which is virtually impenetrable as it is extremely tough and grows close together.

Life in this environment requires an incredibly robust mindset and nowadays it is included in the selection process and training packages of all UK special forces units. Survival was a huge test of both mental and physical capability and a massive test of the men's capabilities. The guys coped with the extreme conditions without any of the modern advantages available today: there was no satellite navigation, the maps were inaccurate because they were based on aerial photographs that did not show the details of the land beneath the canopy – so the men had to rely on contours and pacing, radios were bulky and heavy, they carried tins of food rather than lightweight ration packs, and the technological support and weaponry was far inferior to modern-day equipment.

Even without an enemy who knew how to move and operate in the territory with skill and experience, there were dangers all around. In the hot, steamy climate, heat exhaustion and dehydration had to be avoided. Malaria-carrying mosquitos were in abundance, wasps, bees, centipedes, spiders, and scorpions could inflict painful bites and stings and giant ants would attack an injured man on the ground. Leeches attached themselves to their bodies as they moved and bites from tiger leeches caused painful ulcers or 'jungle sores' that could fester in the damp air. There were various snakes, crocodiles, and wild animals to be wary of, and also plants that stung and caused terrible rashes. Even the water was dangerous; often the carrier of disease, water from natural sources had to be purified with iodine or sterilising tablets. The men learned how to get water from bamboo stalks and other sources. Malaria, leptospirosis, and bush typhus were a real threat to all the guys and daily doses of anti-malaria tablets were essential. Hygiene and constant hydration were imperative to avoid fungal diseases and illness. Survival in the jungles of Malaya was as difficult and dangerous as finding and confronting the enemy. It was essential that the personal administrational skills of each of the blokes were always up to scratch. If not, they could well find themselves becoming a casualty before they had even had the chance to get close to the enemy. They risked becoming a burden and a danger to their own patrol and teammates due to the lack of medical support being available in the environment.

The men of the Parachute Squadron were up to the task and soon proved themselves as capable as the men in the SAS. It was reckoned that it took well over 1,600 hours of patrolling through the jungle for one kill and most of the time was concentrated on staying alive in the hostile surroundings. Their uniforms rotted and disintegrated on their bodies in the constantly wet and clammy atmosphere. Whenever they stopped, they removed blood-sucking leeches and stripped and cleaned their weapons to ensure that they were in perfect working order, and to prevent them from rusting. The whole time they had to remain aware of the threat of attack from terrorists using guns or blow pipes with poison darts that could kill a man in three minutes. After a normal patrol they emerged pale from lack of sunlight, a lot thinner and barely recognisable with long hair and thick beards. After a week or two on leave, generally spent in Singapore stuffing as much food as they could into themselves, drinking their own body weight in alcohol and partying the nights away, they then got thrown into another two weeks of refresher and continuation training. They learned new skills in such things such as tracking, booby traps and demolitions before going back into the dense undergrowth. In some operations they faced jungle covering the vast mountainous area of Ipoh and the Cameron Highlands, as well as Hula-Kinta, with the highest peak of Mount Korbu over 7,000ft high.

Fred Weaver recalled:

> It was New Year, and we were all looking forward to it, and we were due to head out on some well-earned and much needed leave. We had a system in place that if an emergency was to ever occur, we could quickly be called back at short notice and be able to deploy out into the jungle in support of the 'call sign' under attack. On this particular occasion we got the call to return to base immediately, and be ready to parachute jump into the jungle, as two of the Scottish patrols out there at the time were involved in what was perceived to be a fierce contact. After everyone got back and prepared ready to go, the jump was cancelled. It came to light that the two patrols had been bunkered down firing at each other for the last day or so in a 'blue on blue', not knowing that the two parts of their own unit were actually fighting each other! Luckily no one had been killed. This is a demonstration of what the jungle can do to you if you don't stay switched on at all times. Not that this stopped us from showing our total displeasure to those guys for messing up our New Year when they eventually emerged from the trees.[2]

Adding to the difficulty of patrolling through some parts of the region was the importance of moving stealthily and never leaving ground signs or clues as to their whereabouts. The guys from the Squadron used tracking skills to recognise the routes of different animals, and they listened to their calls as these could often alert them to the presence of people. In secondary jungle, they cut their way through the dense undergrowth using parangs, heavy but smaller versions of machetes, and in the evenings, they set up camp building A-frames commonly known as bashas, which they continually improved, so that they could sleep above the ground and were protected from rainfall. 'Basha' is the Malayan word for a hut with a thatched roof, but the guys adopted the name for their handmade shelters and is a term that is still used today by the Para Regt (recognised abbreviation of the Parachute Regiment), when stopping for the night on operations. They hung their boots on sticks to keep them off the ground and away from nasty creepy crawlies that had a habit of biting the guys when they put their hand inside in the morning, and their weapon was always, without exception, within arm's reach.

One saving grace of jungle life, and something to which every soldier looked forward, was the almost guaranteed full night's sleep. Once the sun went down it was pitch black and nobody could navigate their way through the undergrowth, and certainly not move more than a few metres without making huge amounts of noise, including the enemy. The men rose just before first light, which was signalled by the dawn chorus of raucous wildlife, and 'stood to', because this was when they were most vulnerable to a surprise attack. They then checked their surroundings and placed sentries out on duty before putting on a brew, having their breakfast and starting the day's briefing, known as 'morning prayers'. The camp was then completely removed, leaving no signs of it ever being there, before setting off once more on their vigilant patrol plan. Morale was of the utmost importance and the blokes supported each other throughout with witty banter, piss-taking and good humour; they demonstrated their unique characteristics by coping well with the climate and the stress of working in such an environment. Supplies were dropped in every two weeks, either into a safe area, a clearing created by the guys, or directly into the jungle where they had sent up a balloon to mark their position. The men carried Bergens (rucksacks) weighing up to 120lb including rations, but they often swapped their tinned food for the dried fish eaten by the Aborigines to give them some variety. Resupply days were good news because they included fresh food and letters from home.

The men made their way through the difficult terrain, going up and down hills often unable to see more than 20 to 30ft in front of them. The sunlight that barely made its way through the canopy of towering trees created shadows that could deceive as the men moved as silently as possible across miles of land and waded through mosquito-infested swamps and streams. The constant sweltering, green enclosure was uncomfortable and claustrophobic.

The communist guerrillas were adept at moving through this environment and often lay traps including punji pits: huge holes disguised with branches and leaves that had spikes of bamboo at the bottom so that an unsuspecting soldier would step on the covering, crash down, and impale themselves on the spikes. Pig traps consisted of flexible branches with bamboo spikes attached being pulled back and connected to a trigger wire; when the wire was touched, the branch swung round and smashed into the soldier's legs. Over time the guys learnt to understand the ways of the environment they were in and adapted their minds to cope with the demands of soldiering in the jungle. It wasn't long before they became just as expert as the CT guerrillas in negotiating the landscape and also learnt to lay booby traps of their own using explosives.

When signs of terrorists were discovered, they tracked them for days on end. If they came across a camp, they created an LUP (lying up point) and then quickly set an ambush and settled themselves in to watch and wait. 'Hard routine' was introduced, meaning that nothing could be heated, there was no smoking or using anything that had a smell: no soap, no toothpaste. They could make no sound; all messaging was done by Morse code on the radio or hand signals between the men. Those on duty sat for hours not moving a muscle and blending into the foliage as they remained focused on their target. Not only did they not want to alert the enemy but also the monkeys in the branches over their heads would scream and shout and give away their presence if they sensed anyone beneath them. Troops often waited, living in this way for two or three weeks in case the enemy returned.[3] Often nobody came and they moved on again. The Paras always remained alert, diligent and mindful, but in these kinds of stakeouts their mental fortitude was pushed to the absolute limit. Writer Chris Ryan gives a great analogy, 'Imagine waiting in your house and watching the front door, knowing that somebody is going to come crashing through it at some point in the next fortnight. And then having to sit there and not move a muscle for the whole time.'[4] On top of this you then had to be ready to react immediately when the opportunity did arise, moving fast and with aggression to win any firefight you may find yourself engaged in. The men of the Parachute Squadron spent a lot of time practising and refining their contact drills, making sure the four-man teams were sharp and ready for anything they might encounter during the long and arduous jungle patrols.

Their patience was finally rewarded when two kills were made by the Parachute Squadron in November 1956. Voices were heard coming from a small clearing up ahead of the patrol, the men approached silently and stalked the four men ahead of them before attacking. One CT guerrilla was killed, and another died of his wounds before he could be evacuated, the other two melted back into the undergrowth and escaped. Four more kills were later achieved in the highest mountain regions, with one troop consequently coming under attack from both blowpipe and shotgun at the same time but managing to escape with no serious casualties.

Although actual captures and kills were few and far between, the guys destroyed camps and further disrupted their enemy by clearing cultivation areas known as 'ladangs' to cut off food supplies. They also befriended the Aborigine tribes living deep in the jungle, often rescuing them from the oppression of the CTs. Getting these indigenous people onside was of great importance as they were used by the terrorists to pass messages to the different gangs throughout the region. Turning the natives against the CTs interfered with communications and weakened the guerrillas' operations. The main aim was to force the CTs out of the deep jungle areas and onto the fringes, where they could be captured or killed by other conventional ground forces. Combined with the political moves to provide the local population with better living conditions and to gain their trust so that they no longer could be used for supplies or support, the jungle patrols were successful in undermining the actions of the insurgents and they were gradually overcome.

The Independent Parachute Squadron, which became known as the Parachute Regiment Squadron, operated in Malaya for two years before being disbanded in 1957 when the Federation of Malaya was established, and the majority of CTs gave up the fight. The blokes had got the job done and they also proved themselves worthy of working alongside the SAS, which set a precedent for future co-operation between the two regiments.

Fred added:

> Once the two-year deployment was over and the Squadron was going to head back to Aldershot to be disbanded, some of us who had the will and skill set required had the opportunity to move over and join the SAS. So, eventually, around eighteen of us badged over to the SAS and I personally spent another five years in Malaya where I really enjoyed working as part of an SAS Sabre Squadron. During that time, I carried out numerous operations and was involved in many more adventures and enemy contacts.[5]

The men of the Independent Parachute Squadron were a credit to the ethos of the Paras: an elite and powerful group of men capable of enduring great hardship to achieve their goals and proving themselves to be worthy of working alongside and, as in Fred's case, transferring to the SAS.

Overall, the Malayan Emergency turned out to be one of the few successful counter-insurgency operations undertaken by Western powers during the Cold War. Meanwhile, other parts of the Parachute Regiment had been busy in Cyprus.

## Chapter 5

# Cyprus Insurgency

## Cyprus, 1955–59

In 1955, paratroopers posted in Cyprus found themselves facing a new and growing insurrection on the island and became embroiled in guerrilla-style warfare. Once again, their ability to react quickly to an emerging conflict was demonstrated as they turned their skills and focus towards the rapidly developing crisis. A terrorist campaign aimed at pushing the British out of Cyprus and becoming part of Greece was under way. The Paras took on the task of quelling the movement and learned how to master the challenging terrain of forests and mountains into which the insurgents disappeared after carrying out terrible acts of violence in the capital city of Nicosia and many other areas of the island.

At the end of 1955, 3 Para (3rd Battalion, the Parachute Regiment) were ordered to Cyprus in preparation for a mission to protect British residents in Jordan. By mid-January 1956 the majority of 3 Para were set up in tiny tents on a large football field outside Nicosia. Lieutenant Swann described the conditions, 'January 1956 was a considerably wet month. The difficulties of a Battalion living on a grassy field during a rainy period was quickly noticeable. Some men recall their mud-caked boots weighing more than the equipment on their backs due to the quagmire in which they were now living.'[1] While they waited to be deployed to Jordan, the men became involved in the internal security operations in Cyprus as rebels increased their campaign of terror.

A small island in the Mediterranean, Cyprus had been a UK protectorate since 1878 and became a Crown Colony of Britain in 1925 with a population of Turkish and Greek Cypriots. The Greek Cypriots, who outnumbered the Turks by four to one, were largely opposed to British rule and wanted 'ENOSIS', the union of Cyprus with Greece. The archbishop of the Cypriot church was the head of the Greek people and in the post-war period this was Archbishop Makarios. Makarios supported the growing agitation of his people towards British rule and brought in a retired Greek colonel, George Grivas, to lead a resistance movement: EOKA (the National Organisation of Cypriot fighters). In 1955, Grivas began his terrorist activities with a bombing campaign that started on 1 April and following further attacks, a state of emergency was declared in November. Operating from hideouts in the Troodos and Kyrenian mountains as well as the forests of Paphos, members of the terrorist guerrilla force went down into the towns and cities to eliminate their targets and then quickly disappeared with little trace back into the countryside.

As the EOKA attacks increased, the Paras assisted the police in setting up roadblocks, confiscating weapons and patrolling without engaging in full military action. The Jordan crisis was diffused but 3 Para were given new orders and remained in Cyprus to help contain the activities of EOKA insurgents. Quickly moving from their uncomfortable tents on the football pitch to a drier location on a rocky hillside, which they named Tunisia Camp, they then became involved in search and destroy missions against the EOKA members throughout the tiny villages of Cyprus and set up ambushes to catch them as they came out of their mountain hideaways.

The Paras patrolled the streets, guarded the camp, and went into villages searching for weapons, munitions and for key members of EOKA. They did as much as they could despite the added difficulty that many of the Greek Cypriots were involved with EOKA or certainly supported them. Villagers hid the terrorists in their homes, building secret rooms behind fireplaces and under floorboards and digging escape tunnels from the houses into the countryside. Talks to resolve the situation had broken down and 3 Para were given the task of arresting Makarios. They established a cordon around his palace and while members of 3 Para went in to search the house and make the arrest, the men creating the cordon were bombarded with stones thrown from a girls' school next door; it was just one example of the widespread anti-British sentiment. Makarios and the Bishop of Kyrenia were exiled to the Seychelles but Grivas continued with the EOKA campaign.

Demonstrating their versatility once again, the Paras soon became accustomed to the mountains and forests and could move about as easily as the guerrillas. In numerous operations they caught and imprisoned a number of the rebels and uncovered hidden stores of ammunition, documents, and photographs. The pictures provided valuable intelligence in identifying the key terrorist personalities and copies were sent to every unit to aid in the recognition of the men they were after.

During Operation Lucky Alphonse in June 1956, two parachute battalions, Royal Marines and five other units were involved in a massive search of the Troodos mountains. A 75-mile cordon was created as they attempted to flush out Grivas and the terrorist cells. Hidden camps and stores of arms and ammunition along with bombs were uncovered and two wanted terrorists were captured. Grivas was not found, and the decision was made to increase the pressure by firing mortars into the valley believed to be the location for his main base.

Despite the overall success of the operation, an ensuing tragedy marred the results. The forest area was tinder-dry from the summer temperatures and lack of rainfall and, whether it was from the mortars or terrorists trying to impede the operation, small fires broke out. The following day, strong winds fanned the embers and the fires quickly spread. The forest turned into a raging inferno as flames leapt through the woods and across valleys with trees exploding in the heat. Soldiers combing the area for insurgents were caught in the conflagration and while some managed to escape or shelter in rocky shelves, others were engulfed by the flames. Troops and civilian firefighters desperately fought the fire raging out of control across the land, but it claimed the lives of twenty-one soldiers, including one paratrooper, and injured several more.

The Paras continued their patrols across the island and discovered numerous cave camps and more stores of supplies, weapons, and bombs. On one occasion, the men of 3 Para sighted a group of terrorists and went in pursuit of the gang, who dropped their belongings as they made their escape. Some of the abandoned equipment belonged to Grivas himself and they recovered his diary and incriminating photos of him with other known terrorists.

Frederick 'Freddy' Crompton arrived in Cyprus just after his platoon had got really close to catching Grivas:

> I was thrown in right at the deep end joining 8 Platoon in the Troodos mountains. We searched through the mountain forests, sliding down the scree sitting on our packs. It was tough going carrying all our gear. We went back to camp for a short period of personal administration before heading back out again, this time patrolling the Troodos and Kyrenian mountainside. Sometimes we went into the forests at night and set up snap ambushes. We were dropped off by truck in the middle of the woods at dusk and lay in the bushes at the side of a track all through the night in the hope of catching some of the terrorists. Occasionally, we did manage to get to the most beautiful beaches for a swim but had our machine guns and rifles with us and someone on guard at all times.[2]

The Paras faced an arduous and difficult task as they scaled the steep slopes and patrolled the thick woods. Despite all their efforts, they struggled to win the confidence of the local people, who lived in fear of reprisals if they offered information. EOKA terrorists poured petrol over informers and set light to them, burning them alive.

The situation was tense, but the men got on with the job and maintained their sense of humour to keep up morale. When Freddy Crompton was stationed just outside Nicosia's main airfield, he described how the blokes lived in small tents that they had to crawl into and could only go out on their time off to bars outside the city walls, 'Even then, we went out in fours. With three rifles and a Bren gun and looking like Rambo we'd say, "Ready? Let's go and have a pint!"'[3]

In October 1956, the, now named, 16th Independent Parachute Brigade achieved the most success in Operation Sparrow Hawk. Identifying the presence of three terrorist groups in the Kyrenian mountains, the whole of the Brigade went in to destroy them. Over 2,000 soldiers scoured the hot, dry mountainside, tracking signs of the terrorists' movements and discovering caves full of weapons and supplies. Over the span of one week, they covered 200 square miles of remote countryside, searching by day and night. A 2 Para patrol investigated a remote farm and discovered a cave with a weapons cache and a wireless along with some clothes. Paratroopers Private O'Donnel and Private Pearce continued to search and found a hole in the wall of a fodder barn hidden by a coat. According to accounts, 'On seeing a head, a shot was fired into the cavity and someone inside shouted "Don't shoot! We surrender!" Nobody came out so another shot was fired into the hole. The Paras saw six men emerging from a trapdoor on the other side of the barn and quickly took them prisoner. They included highly sought-after terrorists with bounties on their heads and in their possession was a weapon that had been known to be used in several brutal murders.[4]

Fred Weaver was on patrol in the thick forest one afternoon with his 2 Para eight-man section when they came across a group of EOKA terrorists. 'We caught them by surprise and quickly captured them all without firing any rounds. Later we discovered that they were preparing a raid on one of the local villages.'[5]

Finally, with the help of some much-needed good-quality intelligence gained from locals on the ground, who strongly disagreed with EOKA's barbaric tactics, they uncovered more hideouts and managed to capture twenty of the most significant terrorist fighters, who had been using the remote local villages as communication and supply bases.

The men of 3 Para were also responsible for keeping law and order in Nicosia, which endured constant violent attacks from terrorists mostly aimed at police and military personnel. Ledra Road became known as 'Murder Mile' as snipers lurked on rooftops or inside houses and waited until their targets had walked by before shooting them in the back and disappearing. Often the victims were off-duty policemen and British soldiers with their families. Curfews were imposed and barbed wire separated the Greek and Turkish communities.

EOKA created mayhem with bombs and attacks and the Paras continued the hunt for the insurgents until talks began for Cypriot independence. The emergency ended in 1959 with the establishment of the Republic of Cyprus and independence was proclaimed in 1960. Unfortunately, animosity between the Greek and Turkish communities grew and the Paras were back there again with the UN peacekeeping force in the 1960s. This enmity eventually led to the 1974 war and the partition of the island that still exists today.

However, events in late 1956 had interrupted Cyprus operations and the paratroopers stationed there were sent back to the UK. Private (Retired) Freddie Crompton recalled, 'Suddenly we were sent back to the UK for training. We jumped every day for two weeks and were told that it was to help train pilots and then we were back in Cyprus not knowing what our next task was going to be.' The next task was going to be a daring and dramatic parachute assault into Egypt.

# Chapter 6

# Last Drop

## Suez Crisis, 1956

In Operation Musketeer the Paras engaged in the first battalion-sized parachute assault since the Second World War. Demonstrating their skills in parachuting and highlighting the ready-for-anything attitude, the Paras switched from trawling the Cyprus countryside looking for hidden terrorists to full-on battle against Egyptian forces. It turned out to be the last large-scale parachute assault to take place to date.

President Nasser of Egypt took control of the Suez Canal in July 1956, preventing access to all nations. The canal was a valuable route from the Mediterranean to Asia and the move was not acceptable to countries who depended on the free movement of shipping through the channel. Plans to reoccupy the canal zone were quickly put in place by France and Britain and, with the reputation they had established during the Second World War, it was clearly a task for elite paratroopers. Men of 3 Para were to jump in while the rest of the Brigade, along with marines, went in by sea. The initial plan was for a simultaneous attack, but in the event the airborne assault went in a day earlier. This gained the Paras the much-needed element of surprise, but, initially, left them without any recognised fire support elements from the ships, which were not yet in position.

Given the number of planes available to them, only 686 men from 3 Para could be dropped at one time. They faced a far greater number of Egyptians and the odds against them were considered to be five to one. The men from 3 Para in Cyprus continued with intensive training without knowing what their mission would be. Freddy Crompton said, 'We all thought we were going to be sent to cover the Hungarian Uprising until we were finally shown a model of El Gamil airport in Suez and training began for the assault.'[1]

The order came, and on 5 November the men set off heavily laden with personal equipment and ammunition weighing more than 150lb; in some cases, the loads were more than a man's own bodyweight. Tony Blake said, 'I had a heavy lead acid battery for the No. 62 radio set, a bandolier of ammunition and my own rifle, as well as my normal kit. When you lifted all that up in a weapons container it was damn heavy.' A number of vehicles, anti-tank guns, trailers, and signals equipment carried underneath Hastings planes were made ready for a heavy drop to provide extra support equipment.

Their mission was to secure El Gamil Airport, make it ready for use, and take control of the surrounding area. The jumps had to be below 700ft and so reserve chutes were abandoned, making the drop far more perilous but at the same time saving the men from carrying even more weight. Corporal Tony Lowe described how he felt, 'I was weighed down with enough equipment and rations to double my own body weight. I felt rather like a pregnant duck! The flight was crowded, hot and I remember sweating profusely with the amount of equipment wrapped around my body as the din of the aircraft's engines changed pitch in preparation for arriving at the hot DZ.'[2]

Despite the discomfort, Freddy Crompton described the feeling in the aircraft as being fairly calm, 'We didn't think about going into any sort of battle or trouble. In the plane everyone was yattering, talking; a bit of a singsong went on. It was just like we were dropping on an exercise on Salisbury plain.'[3]

The aim was to get the whole battalion on the ground in four and a half minutes and the planes flew in tight formation, the plane behind flying slightly higher than the one ahead to avoid mowing through the parachutists in front as they jumped out into the morning sky. Each company had been given different objectives to deal with and take control of, so they were split into smaller sticks of parachutists to go on each plane in a synchronised seating plan so that when each group jumped in order, they had the best chance of meeting up at their respective RV points on the ground. They could then quickly form up ready to move fast and aggressively to their respective targets and secure them before the enemy had time to react effectively. It took only twenty to thirty seconds for the guys to reach the sandy desert floor with knees bent ready to accept their landings. Some of the men dropped from as low as 400ft. It was imperative that the whole battalion dropped onto the airfield, which was on a tiny strip of land a mile long and 600 yards wide, so it was quite a challenge.

The jump was the most critical stage. The paratroopers were most vulnerable whilst in the air and then when organising themselves once they landed. Despite catching the Egyptians off guard, they were still met with a significant amount of flak as they came down, along with machine gun fire and mortars as they formed up on the ground.

Freddy described his own experience of jumping, 'We dropped at a very low height to get on the ground as fast as we could, and it was only on jumping that I soon realised it wasn't an exercise. They [the Egyptians] were shooting at us from the ground, all around the airfield. You could see the bullets coming up and as I was going down it looked as though they were all coming for me. I knew it wasn't an exercise then![14]

The blokes were well-drilled and knew exactly what they needed to do and where they needed to be; they quickly gathered up the equipment and brought their weapons to bear. Some of the containers were on fire but the men still bravely went over to get the important mortar bombs and ammunition from the burning boxes. Bullets whistled through the air and two men came down with their parachutes on fire; one landed safely but unfortunately the other broke his ankle. Lance Corporal Dickie Hudd remembered grabbing his equipment and preparing to head for the control tower when a mortar exploded 50 yards away, throwing another man up into the air and ripping his leg off.

The Medical Officer was hit in the eye by shrapnel as he came down but managed to deal with the injury himself and continue with his vital role. A parachutist blew slightly off course and landed in a palm tree at the side of the airport. Blokes rushed over to help him as he hung, swinging vulnerably from his harness. He looked up at the tree and said, 'Fuck me, get me out of here.' They quickly got him down and continued straight on with the task.

One man who injured himself badly was a war correspondent who had blagged his way on to a plane by saying that he had received parachute training but in fact he had never jumped before in his life. He sprained both his ankles and spent the whole time in the medical post. Paratroopers are not foolhardy mavericks, they are highly skilled, well-trained men.

Aerial photographs had shown numerous black dots covering the airport and it was not clear what they were; it was thought that they could be landmines. As it turned out they were large oil drums that had been put in place as anti-landing devices. They proved to be very useful for the men to take cover behind as they dodged the incoming fire spitting up the sand all around them. One group of Paras quickly took over the control building and tower. Private Clements aimed his rocket launcher at a pillbox and achieved a direct hit, thus silencing the machine gun fire, killing two Egyptian defenders, and taking nine prisoners. Men rushed into the tower as enemy tanks appeared, a rocket smashed through the wall and went out the other side, luckily missing everyone, but flying lumps of shrapnel were causing injuries all around. Shots were heard coming from some nearby houses, but these were soon dealt with when the blokes turned their weapons on the target. Within half an hour the airport was taken, and work began to prepare it for use. After an hour they managed to clear the DZ, and a French Dakota was able to land, albeit whilst still under some enemy fire. They quickly put the injured men on board, and they were safely flown back to Cyprus for further medical treatment.

Crompton was with 8 Platoon 'C' Company, 'We advanced towards the far end of the airfield coming under fire from enemy mortars, so we took cover on the ground for a wee while, and then carried on. We saw a lot of the opposition running. It was quite amazing; they were all legging it away. Over the next two and half days we found hundreds and hundreds of army boots, they couldn't run in their boots, they could only run without their boots on.'[5]

On the other side of the airport, air strikes softened up enemy target areas before the men went forward and engaged in battles around a sewage farm, where the desert sand turned into a mosquito-infested swamp, and in a cemetery with both Christian and Muslim headstones around them.

Night came and the men withdrew to the airfield to dig in, taking it in turn to take guard duties and happily watching Fleet Air Arm fighters destroy Egyptian MiG fighter jets before moving forward to attack the sewage farm. The men met with strong opposition and fierce close-quarter battles ensued. In the cemetery, the gunfire ripped into the ground, destroying graves, and fresh corpses now lay on the floor amid older, unearthed bodies. Vicious hand-to-hand fighting took place in and around the graves and in the middle of the firefight a funeral party arrived with wailing family members adding to the absolute chaos of conflict. The men advanced, carefully clearing the areas of Egyptian snipers hiding in the swamps of the sewage farm and in the tombs of the cemetery. The men of 8 Platoon came to a high wall with three tanks sighted on the other side.

Freddy was No. 1 on the anti-tank gun, and he was ordered to go over the wall with the weapon to take them out. 'I was told that there were three enemy tanks on the other side and that I needed to get over the wall. So, over I went, and the tanks were there, three Russian T34s, but they were dug in, and they were empty with no sign of their crews. The enemy had run off and left them, thank God!'[6] In typical Para style, Crompton did not question the need for him to go over that wall, whatever dangers he potentially faced on the other side. The men of 3 Para battled on and succeeded in securing the key targets of the cemetery and the sewage farm.

Overnight, there were talks calling for a ceasefire and the blokes made themselves as comfortable as possible in the circumstances. For those by the sewage farm it was not so easy as they spent the night bombarded by man-eating mosquitos and entrenched in the stink of raw sewage and shit. The peace talks were unsuccessful and the following morning the battle resumed as a low-flying enemy MiG strafed the area and injured two men. The seaborne invasion began and troops from the Royal Marine Commandos began their assault from helicopters as 2 Para hit the beach in landing craft with 3 Para providing covering fire with their heavy machine guns and support weapons.

A block of flats and coastguard buildings containing enemy snipers proved troublesome, but the men managed to take them over without sustaining any casualties. The Paras then moved forward towards two hospitals that were being used as a defensive position. When Freddy and his mates entered one of the hospitals, they found it to be empty. 'There wasn't a soul in the place. It had clearly been used as there was blood all over the sheets, all through the place, but they'd gone. As we came out, we were caught in crossfire, and we attempted to take cover behind a wall. The CO (Commanding Officer) and four other men including a guy called Lofty Read ran across the road into the shanty town and got caught in an enemy ambush. The CO lost three fingers on his left hand from a ricochet, but Lofty Read was badly hit and had been left for dead.'[7]

Fired on from all sides the remaining men in the shanty town were all wounded and barely able to defend themselves. Captain Malcolm Elliot, an anaesthetist, was on his way to the recently captured hospital to gather badly needed medical supplies when he saw the fallen Paras. Without hesitation, he drove straight into the firefight. Coming under heavy attack from all sides, he reached the men and managed to pull most of them away to safety. Elliot was later awarded the Military Cross for his actions.

'C' Company moved into an old coastguard station for the night and the following morning they spotted something moving some distance away on the beach. Freddy Crompton was there, 'Men warily went towards it, as the beach had been mined, and then they discovered to their surprise that it was Lofty Read. He had been shot right through his left leg and out of the other side of the right leg – just missing the family jewels. He wasn't dead and he'd managed to somehow drag himself back. It was incredible.'[8]

Political pressure from the United States and Russia forced an end to the conflict, and the next few days were spent on clearing up operations. In just two days the Paras had achieved the capture of El Gamil airport via an airborne assault, the clearance of Egyptian forces from the landing strip to the edge of Port Said town and the capture of major pieces of equipment and infrastructure. In just over four hours after taking control of the heavily defended airport, they had managed to turn it around and make it fully operational. The members of 3 Para achieved all their mission goals and more, in a very short space of time. On 6 November, Captain R. M. Smeeton, on board HMS *Albion*, arranged for 1,200 cans of beer to be delivered to the paratroopers who had dropped in the day before. In a note accompanying the beer he said it was 'a token of their admiration for the good work of the para troops'.

Freddy Crompton lost a couple of close friends, and one was wounded in Suez, but he said, 'I wouldn't have missed it for the world, a super crowd of people. When there are any problems anywhere, they always call in the Paras.'[9] Four men were killed in Operation Musketeer in 1956, thirty-two were injured and evacuated and four men were wounded but carried on fighting. Politically it may not have been well received but the Paras had proved themselves once again to be an elite force of courageous and determined men.

# Chapter 7

# Fighting in the Mountains

## Aden, 1963–67

In the district of Aden in the Middle East, insurgents fighting against the British were creating turmoil. Between 1963 and 1967 all three of the Parachute Regiment battalions, who were rotating through their central holding camp in Bahrain, saw action. Taking turns being deployed into the Yemen in a bid to maintain control of the area, they became engaged in some bitter fighting against the ever-growing threat of rebel groups. The battle took them up into the harsh and dangerous environment of the Radfan mountains and tested the Paras once again as they took on the rebel tribes on their home ground of rocky heights and deep gullies in blasting hot temperatures.

In 1937, Aden had become a British Crown Colony and after the Suez Crisis it became an important base for the British in the Middle East. Yemen consisted of a number of disparate states and in an attempt to unite them in preparation for independence, Britain instigated the formation of the Federation of South Arabia in 1963. This was against the wishes of North Yemen and an insurgency quickly grew in strength. After a grenade attack against the British High Commissioner, which killed one person and injured many more, a state of emergency was declared. Fighting between different factions including the two main groups of the NLF (National Liberation Front) and FLOSY (Front for the Liberation of Occupied South Yemen), as well as attacks on the British military, began to increase in intensity.

In 1964 hostilities flared in the mountainous region of Radfan. The main trading route running between the city of Aden and the neighbouring state of Dhala and on to Mecca, the Dhala Road ran alongside the inhospitable region of the Radfan mountains with no roads in or out. It was inhabited by numerous tribes, and it was usual for local tribesmen to collect tolls, under duress, from caravans passing through the area. This was stopped, and in retaliation members of the NLF based in the region began attacking travellers. Britain responded and forces including Para Regiment were sent in to clear the area of insurgents and bring the situation under control.

There were no clear maps, and the Paras were some of the first European troops to enter this region and be tested on this formidable terrain. It was a brutal challenge of their soldiering skills as they quickly adapted once again to a new and very dangerous operating environment. They expected to come up against a few, poorly armed, disorganised tribesmen, but in fact they were fierce fighters and skilled marksmen who had grown up with a gun in their hands. Constant inter-tribal battles had trained them well in how to use the terrain to their advantage, how to kill and then melt rapidly back into the local area without leaving a trace. Covering 400 square miles, the area was made up of high ridges of jagged mountains with loose scree and crumbling rocks. Deep wadis (dry riverbeds) fell away below the ridges, and watchtowers and fortresses had been built on the high ground. It was unbearably hot and there was little water available to the troops.

By the end of April 1964, a plan had been devised; the Paras were to go in with the mission of taking the rebel stronghold in the Wadi Dhubsan. The men of 3 Para, the duty battalion at the time, were based in Bahrain on standby to react to another possible flare-up between Iraq and Kuwait when they were given the order to prepare to parachute into the mountains. An SAS team had already deployed in to mark the proposed drop zone, but whilst nearing the area, the patrol was compromised. Surrounded by rebel troops, they engaged in an intense firefight and bravely battled their way out of danger. The parachute drop was eventually aborted, and the men of 3 Para went in on foot. Private (Retired) Brian Fleetwood, a tough scouser, joined the battalion in 1960:

> I was in 'B' company 3 Para, and we were warned off that we would be heading down to Aden as there seemed to be a bit of a scrap going on with the local Arabs. The next thing we were told to get all our equipment ready to drop into the Radfan, so we readied our kit in preparation to jump. Whilst at the airfield the news came through that the proposed DZ had been overrun and there were around three thousand rebels there waiting for us to drop in. One of the lads said laughing, 'What the fuck, there are only one hundred and twenty of us.' The reply came back, 'Don't worry they are just a bunch of goat-herders with muskets.' So, the plan was quickly revised, and we were instead flown down and then marched in on foot through the night with an aim of taking the enemy by surprise at first light. With the Marines coming in from the other side we would catch them in a classic pincer movement and drive them up to the top of the feature. Water was at a premium and we only had one water bottle to get us through the march.

We were told not to touch any natural water holes, as they had all been poisoned by the enemy.[1]

Carrying around 55lb of equipment, they embarked on the seven-hour march. Reaching the edge of the mountain, they started to move across the forbidding terrain, climbing up steep slopes and down deep gullies and back up the other side in scorching temperatures once the sun came up. For each 100 yards forward, they had to climb or descend 300, testing the guys' fitness levels to the maximum. As they moved, rebels hiding in the numerous caves or under escarpments attacked them using an assortment of weapons ranging from Russian-made and supplied machine guns to basic single-shot ancient muskets. The enemy may have been a so-called untrained group of rebels, but they had learned how to use guns from boyhood and were excellent marksmen. To reach their first objective, code-named 'Cap Badge', the men marched their way over the harsh terrain, continually fighting and responding to attacks, with the RAF providing much-needed air support. Finally, the Paras and supporting marines scaled the mountain to achieve their first goal and commanded the daunting Rabwa Pass overlooking Wadi Taym, where 'B' Company, 3 Para, dug in and held the position.

Brian went on to say:

My platoon sergeant at the time was Chay Blyth, a gritty Jock who went on to be the first person to sail single-handed non-stop westwards around the world. As we reached near to the top of the ridge line, we came under fire again and Chay shouted for us all to get down. We were exposed to the enemy with rounds landing in and around us and could see some of the guys getting hit, so a few of us dashed forward to a group of small huts where we took cover, and from there we returned some heavy fire before taking them out. By the time we got to the top and took the position, the entire group of rebels had disappeared using their local knowledge of the many caves and small mountain paths. By this point we had lost eight men. It was hard going and tough fighting such an elusive enemy; we killed many of the rebels, but a lot of the bodies were spirited away.[2]

The 10-mile-long Bakri Ridge was another target for the Paras. A sheer rock face ran the length of the eastern side, rising up to the top of the ridge at 5,000ft. A steep drop of around 3,000ft went into Wadi Dhubsan, which the rebels' thought was an impregnable position. The Paras were determined to prove this assumption wrong and whilst probing discovered that the ridge itself was lightly guarded and that there was a route up from Shab Tem.

They made their way up, this time carrying even heavier loads of equipment and weapons. In the oppressive heat, they moved on resolutely covering only about half a mile an hour as they journeyed up and down the steep slopes to get to their higher objective. Company Sergeant Major 'Nobby' Arnold led an advance group ahead of the rest of the force. Moving stealthily, they surprised twelve rebels and, capturing three of them, they drove the rest of them away with the use of fast, aggressive movement and firepower to claim the section of strategic land, which was soon renamed 'Arnold's Spur'. Still the men continued, clearing villages as they went and covering 11 miles in two nights until they reached Qudeishi. This village was heavily fortified and suddenly the guys found themselves under heavy attack. RAF support was called in and aerial attacks destroyed some of the fort defences before the Paras stormed the village and took it over. They now had complete control of the ridge and were looking down on Wadi Dhubsan, the main enemy base, and the location of their grain stores.

Well-hidden rebels with deadly precise snipers guarded the paths down and it was decided that the best way into the valley was by direct descent: abseiling down a 30ft rockface. Achieving complete surprise, a troop of Royal Marine Commandos descended into the wadi and the Paras managed to hold off the tribesmen who were attacking them from above. A full-scale battle ensued with RAF Hunters flying through the narrow gully to support the troops below. Finally, the rebels withdrew, and the grain stores were set on fire. The men of 3 Para along with the marines had a long climb out of the wadi to a point from which they were airlifted by helicopter and taken back to the city of Aden. A DSO, an MC, three MiDs and other commendations were awarded for their actions.

The comedian Spike Milligan, who came over to visit the Paras and perform on stage for them during a bit of down time in the main camp, described the battle as 'The Red Wolves taking on the Red Devils'.[3]

On what proved to be the final tour in Aden, 1 Para (1st Battalion, the Parachute Regiment) deployed to the city and played an integral part in the British withdrawal from the region. Colonel Mike Walsh was amongst them. A veteran from Suez, he was the Commanding Officer of the battalion and at that time the company commanders of the various rifle companies within the battalion, who became known as the Centurions, were rotating a month at a time to fight against the rebels in Radfan. The situation in Aden was tense, with the Paras patrolling the local area and making use of the semi-permanent sangars (temporary fortified positions) to keep a watchful eye on proceedings and dominating the Ash Shaikh Outhman district via these OPs (observation posts). OP4 was on top of a police station made up of breeze blocks and Belgian RL-83 Blindicide shoulder-launched, rocket-propelled grenades were fired at it on a regular basis. In the end, whilst making running repairs, the battalion organised for a helicopter to fly in and fit a huge mesh wire cover in front of it to give some protection.

The guys came under attack on a regular basis, and 1 Para lost three men on this tour, a figure that could easily have been much higher if it was not for some great work and a bit of luck. Two of the guys were killed by a sniper operating in the area, who was firing at the sangars through the concrete slits the blokes used to observe the city.

Lieutenant Colonel (Retired) Stuart Hepton, who was also the curator at the Airborne Assault Museum for a while, was a private soldier on this tour. He described the situation on the ground in Aden:

> I remember many incidents where we were really lucky, such as when one of the lads was taking cover in a doorway during a patrol and was shot right through the lanyard on his shirt. It would be difficult to get a much closer shave than that. I also remember being on duty at Check Point Golf, talking to local people as they came through the search bay. Suddenly a burst of fire ricocheted between my feet and some rounds ended up going through the latrine, which was fortunate for 'Paddy' who was sitting on the thunderbox [army portaloo] at the time. Another amusing story was when the CO was out on patrol; his signaller would give a code word over the radio network so the Centurions would know he was out and about. On this particular day, his vehicle came under fire as they reached a roundabout and the CO shouted to his driver to go right and try to break contact, so the driver calmly drove left around the roundabout, obeying the highway code, and eventually off the roundabout to the right, much to the dismay and anger of the CO. Luckily for all concerned, no one was hurt but I think the driver got a severe talking to from Colonel Walsh once he got back to Radfan Camp.[4]

By this time, 1 Para had pulled out of Ash Shaikh Outhman and was effectively manning the Pennine Chain, a fortified final defence line above the Radfan Camp in Aden. FLOSY and the NLF were now fighting each other for control, knowing that the Brits were soon pulling out, so the orders were given to keep things stable ready for the victor to take over when the British departed. In the end the NLF slaughtered FLOSY and took control of the state. The acronym SPOOSY (Send the Paras out of South Yemen) was written on one of the CP walls, which pretty well described the feeling of the Toms (nickname for ordinary soldiers) as they departed.

What was expected to be a short operation turned out to be a long and arduous campaign against an enemy who were long established, well hidden and knew the area like the backs of their hands; it was a proxy war against a communist-backed rebel force. After incredible feats of strength and endurance, and coming under heavy attack throughout, the Paras again proved their ability to rise to the challenges and overcome a determined localised enemy. They remained involved in the campaign until 1967, when the British finally withdrew from the country. Shortly after the departure of the High Commissioner, 1 Para boarded the new Hercules transport, which had just superseded the old Hastings, and flew out of country for the final time.

Meanwhile, other sections of the Parachute Regiment had been busy on another mission holding off the spread of communist-backed forces in Borneo.

# Chapter 8

# Secret Wars

## Borneo, 1963–66

While the Aden conflict was in full swing, the already overstretched paras were needed back in the Far East as President Sukarno of Indonesia began flexing his muscles and looking greedily at taking control of Borneo. It was going to be a testing and demanding deployment and jungle skills were honed in preparation for the task. The Paras proved themselves once again as a force to be reckoned with as they demonstrated the tenacity and unyielding determination of their forebears.

Sukarno was eager to impress Russia and China and, inspired by the success of the Viet Cong against the mighty US war machine, decided that he wanted to expand his territory and overrun Malaysia, which at the time was a British-backed federation including Malaya, Singapore, and Northern Borneo. Conversely, Britain, Australia, and New Zealand were attempting to suppress the spread of communism throughout the region. President Sukarno wanted to get rid of British influence and take over these territories for himself, and he began cross-border incursions into North Borneo. British forces were sent in to protect the border and between 1963 and 1965 there were occasional confrontations between the two forces.

A combined force of SAS and Gurkhas was joined by 2 Para in 1965. All of the men received training in jungle warfare, the skills previously learned by the men of the 5th Brigade in Java and the Independent Parachute Squadron in Malaya, and they faced the same difficult jungle conditions, which are still universally recognised as the truest and harshest tests of personal soldiering skills in existence.

The Paras set up base and sent in patrols to track down the enemy. The trips into the jungle were hard, gruelling trials of physical and mental ability as the men lay ambushes on likely enemy patrol routes and waited, sometimes for days, for any targets to come along. They had to utilise a huge amount of personal discipline, not doing anything that would create a sound or smell that might give their positions away, surviving on hard routine with cold rations and not smoking or even speaking. Their training provided them with knowledge of the local languages and medicine. These skills were utilised for communicating with natives in the remote villages and winning the hearts and minds of the local indigenous population, a factor that is imperative in conflicts such as this.

'B' Company, 2 Para, took over an already lightly fortified jungle base close to the Indonesian border and went out on regular ten-day patrols. Sent in as small four-man teams as well as platoon-size operations, they were trained and operated along tried and tested SAS lines. The men patrolled in bush so thick that they could not see someone 5 yards ahead of them. The majority of the blokes who had joined 4, 5 and 6 Platoons of 'B' Company were around 19 or 20 years old; they hadn't even finished training at the depot when they were sent over to finish off in the jungle instead of the Brecon Beacons, whilst the rest of 2 Para were called back on New Year's leave.

The intense tour of the region involved many patrols, skirmishes, and the odd confrontation with the Indonesian forces, but nothing encapsulated this conflict or determined the direction it took more than the ferocious surprise attack on 'B' Company's camp at Plaman Mapu. The rat-infested and overgrown position they had inherited from the Argyll & Sutherland Highlanders was far from ideal and already vulnerable before their arrival. Less than 2,000 yards from the border, it was situated on the slope of a small hill. It had a valley on either side and with mountains and high ridges above the camp it was easy for Indonesian forces to observe what the Paras were up to and gauge their strength and routine. Soon after arriving, the paratroopers got to work cutting the undergrowth further back from their perimeter. Giving themselves an extra field of fire, they surrounded it with barbwire and punji sticks to make it more impenetrable.

The Indonesian leadership knew that a decisive hit on Britain's elite Parachute Regiment would be a huge boost to President Sukarno's government and could turn the entire momentum of the war. 'B' Company was aware of a build-up of troops around their position but when the attack came on the night of 27 April 1965, they were caught by surprise. Two of the three platoons were out on an operation, leaving just the thirty-six men of 6 Platoon including attached arms, to defend Plaman Mapu. Some of the soldiers had only just come back from a long, hard patrol themselves and were sleeping when the attack started.

At 0500 hours, in the middle of a monsoon, the onslaught began. The terrific noise of the pounding, torrential rain hid the sound of 400 enemy special forces soldiers nearing the camp and suddenly they attacked with artillery, mortars, machine guns and RPGs. The men sleeping leapt out of bed, some of them just wearing their boots, trousers and belt order, others hurriedly dressing as they went into action. Suffering from exhaustion and malnourishment from their time in the wilderness, adrenalin and in-built training took over. In the documentary film *Return to the Jungle*, Private (Retired) George Averre described how he was in his bunker on his back attempting to get some sleep when he looked through the firing slit as the attack started and saw green tracer flying over his mortar pit. He realised quickly that it was enemy fire, as the British used red and not green tracer rounds.[1]

John (Drummie) Williams went outside to be confronted by the GPMG (General-Purpose Machine Gun) operator, who had been shot in the head and was seriously injured. The impact of the hit had also put the GPMG out of action. Williams immediately arranged for the gunner to be taken to the medical area and then began organising the counter-attack as all around him was being lit up by enemy fire.

Lance Corporal (Retired) Mick Murtagh, a 19-year-old private at the time, got onto the second GPMG and with Williams providing covering fire, they drove the enemy back into a gully. Murtagh, who received a MiD (Mentioned in Dispatches) for his actions on this day, said, 'I fired thousands of rounds that morning, with only one stoppage on my GPMG. What a fantastic weapon it was and if it was not for this, I think we would have been overrun. The Indonesians sighted the GPMG, and they counter-attacked the gun pit. The rain slashed down on the hillside, creating a wet and muddy slope which impeded their advance, and we were able to hold them off. I remember Company Sergeant Major Williams telling me to give him a go on the GPMG, but I ignored him, as it was my responsibility.'[2]

A mortar exploded next to Williams, but he carried on oblivious to the blood pouring out of a wound on his head. In pitch blackness with the rain pelting down, Williams ran around organising the defensive action. Ignoring the fact that he had been hit, he picked up wounded men and gathered ammunition to give out to the remaining blokes who were still fit to fight. During the deadly and close-quarter fighting, the young Paras forced the attackers back into the jungle. They knew that if they didn't win this part of the battle, they would all be dead before dawn.

Murtagh said:

> I was firing over the mortar pit where George Averre was stationed. The enemy was so close by this point that George was having to break all the rules in the book and was holding his mortar barrel near on vertically in the air with the secondary charges removed so he could

land the mortars in and around the enemy, many of whom were just twenty-five yards away by then. At one point I scarpered up the hill to get some grenades and extra ammo before sliding back down on my arse into my trench. Whilst gone, I heard the familiar sound of the GPMG firing down at the enemy and assumed that Drummie Williams had finally got his hands on it. Once down again, we primed the grenades and then four of us threw a salvo at the same time. However, only three of the grenades went over the lip, the other ended up on the floor of our own trench. Suddenly a cry of 'Grenade!' rang out and we all dived to the side for cover. The muddy, wet floor must have absorbed the blast and we quickly got back on with the task in hand. I never did find out who was responsible, but I have my suspicions.

They managed to hold off another attack and then Drummie Williams went forward in a patrol with three other men to clear the lines. He had asked for volunteers for the task and to a man they all said that they would go with him. They cleared the perimeter and then support began to arrive in the form of the QRF. Helicopters carrying more men and a doctor arrived to find the Para defenders of Plaman Mapu bleeding, covered in mud, and physically exhausted; many were wearing just their trousers and boots.

In a two-and-a-half hour battle, which has been likened to the 1879 battle of Rorke's Drift, the thirty-six men, many of them new recruits, had repelled a full assault by an elite Javanese battalion of reportedly around 400 men, killing at least forty and wounding another sixty. The enemy dragged their dead and wounded back into the jungle, leaving a distinctive blood trail behind them. It was a battle mainly fought by NCOs (non-commissioned officers) and Toms showing the ability of the men to act quickly, efficiently, and fight relentlessly using their own initiative. These young and inexperienced paratroopers showed courage and a will to win in the defeat of what was a far superior force on paper and who had the element of surprise in their favour. Two men were killed and eight were wounded; Company Sergeant Major John (Drummie) Williams had been hit on the side of the head when a radio set was destroyed by the mortar. Shrapnel had flown into his skull, and he was left deaf and blind on that side, earning himself the new nickname of 'Patch Williams'. He received the DCM (Distinguished Conduct Medal) for his actions, and many of the young Toms stated that if it had not been for his cool head, outstanding leadership, and unbelievable bravery that night, the battle would probably have been lost. The Military Medal was awarded to Corporal Malcolm 'Jackie' Baughan, and Private Mick Murtagh received an MiD.

On the fiftieth anniversary of the Plaman Mapu battle, three veterans, Les Simcock, George Averre and Mick Murtagh, as well as Lieutenant General James Bashall and some serving soldiers from 2 Para, held a service at a cairn erected on the top of the hill. This trip was organised and led by former 2 Para soldier Warrant Officer 1 (Retired) Gil Boyd BEM. It was Gil, as a passionate historian of the regiment, who brought all the various parts of this memorial visit together. He set his sights on building a cairn with a plaque at the site in Borneo and this came to fruition on 27 April 2015, marking the fiftieth anniversary of this largely forgotten battle, with Lieutenant General James Bashall, ex Commanding Officer of 2 Para, performing the unveiling. Gil also arranged to hold a military ceremony at Kranji Cemetery in Singapore, where the two fallen men of the Plaman Mapu battle now lay, and it was attended by other UK forces now based on the island.

Gil said:

> These young guys were unsung heroes, fighting what, at the time, was a secret war. The Indonesians had a clear view of the manpower depletion at Plaman Mapu, which was passed onto their command structure, and quickly produced an attack plan with what they perceived to be the best time to launch an overwhelming and decisive assault on these thirty-six paras and attached personnel. During the aftermath of the battle and the mopping up that followed, several hand grenades were found within the location with the pin removed, and only elastic bands were holding the handle on the body of the grenade. This formed a basic booby trap if the grenade was disturbed. These explosives were found on the ground outside the Command Post, Stores and Antennae. One can only surmise who placed them at these key locations, but from interviewing those that fought that day, they believe they were placed there by Indonesian 'friendly forces' or locals who were often inside the location on a daily basis, with an aim to help overthrow the location. Amazingly, none of these grenades were set off![3]

Raids and patrols in what was known as Operation Claret continued until March 1966 when offensive missions were stopped. The anti-communist General Suharto overthrew President Sukarno and withdrew Indonesian forces from the border areas. In August that year, he signed a treaty with Malaysia.

## Anguilla, 1969

During the 1950s and '60s the Paras were called up for deployment in various parts of the world including Jordan and Kuwait, where such was their reputation that even their mere presence prevented any attacks or invasions. In March 1969, troops were sent to the British colony of Anguilla in the Caribbean, where it was believed that civil strife had led to an armed insurrection.

In what was clearly a miscommunication, and then a slight overreaction by the UK Government, the Paras were mobilised to deal with what was believed to be a hostile uprising. Initially planned as a parachute insertion, the men were geared up and ready to deal with the so-called insurgents on the island. Luckily, the airlift was called off and the men went in by sea to discover that there was no opposition. Immediately adapting to the position that they found themselves in, the blokes soon turned the event into a hugely positive public relations exercise for the regiment.

In the process of de-colonisation, the island of Anguilla had been included in a Caribbean Federation with Nevis and St Kitts, about which the Anguillan people were not happy. Reports of gangsters and armed caches led to Operation Sheepskin, in which 2 Para were sent, along with 120 Metropolitan police, to restore order.

Numerous flashes on the beach were thought to be defensive fire as the forces went in, but in fact they were the lights of bulbs from press photographers. There was no Anguillan defence and not a shot was fired. Slated in the press for the 'invasion', the Paras along with the police, turned what was an embarrassing situation completely around. 'B' Company remained on the island and began improving the infrastructure of the local area with development projects and became very friendly with the Anguillan people. They played a lot of cricket on the beaches, and just like our national team, were beaten by the locals every time.

Mick Murtagh, a veteran of the battle of Plaman Mapu four years earlier, arrived on the second wave. 'Working as a rigger I had already had the misfortune of preparing one of their vehicles, which, for whatever reason, did not fit onto the assigned aircraft. I had a bad feeling about this particular operation, but the blokes soon got their heads around the situation when they arrived, and quickly adapted to their new environment and task in hand, which included helping with the census and supporting the local people with anything we could do.'[4]

The elite force of highly trained and tough paratroopers was unnecessary in this instance, but they revealed the other side of their nature: being excellent at using their initiative and reacting to whatever was in front of them with intelligence and diplomacy. They left Anguilla on a great footing to develop into a thriving community. Working with the police force, they maintained law and order, developed good relations with the residents and were eventually awarded the Wilkinson Sword of Peace, 'For their acts of humanity and kindness overseas'.

The 1960s were drawing to a close and had been a very busy time for the Parachute Regiment, who had seen many changes in their structure and manning levels.

The men who joined this versatile and elite regiment were up for any challenge, and they had proved themselves to be as successful in maintaining peace as they were in ferocious battle. The enduring success of the Parachute Regiment was without doubt due to the exacting and deliberately devised training and selection process.

# Chapter 9

# The Factory

Since the inception of the Parachute Regiment, training and selection have been paramount in establishing and continuing their reputation as a formidable force. The process, which is tried and tested to deliver the required results, is what makes the men different to other soldiers in the British Army. Each generation has written new chapters to create the legendary history of this regiment and the training sets the standards each recruit must achieve to earn the honour of becoming part of this elite unit.

In order to pass and become a member of this regiment, to have the honour of wearing the maroon beret, DZ and Pegasus flash and the coveted Parachute Regiment cap badge, and then to follow in the footsteps of their gallant forefathers, recruits have to pass the flagship test, known as P Company (abbreviation for Pegasus Company) test week. This deliberately gruelling and intense course pushes each potential paratrooper to their absolute physical and mental limits, only allowing the cream of the crop to pass and become a member of the airborne brotherhood.

However, before the new boys can even start to think about attempting and possibly passing P Company, they first have to navigate their way through what was known in my day as the Factory and was held at Browning Barracks in Aldershot. In the early days it was up at Ringway, then shortly afterwards established as an official training centre at Hardwick. Continuous evolvement and several moves followed, and today it is based in Catterick. The location may have changed, and the training has certainly been refined over time and as technology has moved forward, but the raw mentality and basic will to win has not.

The standard of training is high from the day you join, whether that be as a new recruit straight from civvy street or as a serving soldier transferring in from another unit. A six-month training syllabus is designed to weed out those undesirable applicants who are unable to commit fully in body and mind. The aim of the instructors, who are carefully chosen from the three regular battalions for their skill, experience, and mentality, is to completely break the guys down and rebuild them with a new in-built belief that they are stronger, fitter and all-round better than any other soldier they may ever come across. Tony Costello, who joined the Paras in 1947, said, 'I had a very tough upbringing; and I had no confidence, no self-esteem. For my National Service I applied to the Paras. People dropped out all the time as we went through training and selection, and I was very proud when I passed. Being a paratrooper gave me the self-confidence and independence which has carried me through life.'[1]

The training process is designed to nurture the exact blend of traits that any paratrooper will require. They must have the ability to drop in behind enemy lines with minimal supplies and light weaponry on a mission to take and hold key strategic locations and then fight and survive with little hope of reinforcement or support, in the short term, if at all. This is combined with the intelligence and initiative to quickly adapt to new and challenging environments where their role may well see them tasked with maintaining the peace and supporting the local civilian population through difficult and dangerous times.

Former 1 & 3 Para veteran Warrant Officer 2 (Retired) Steve Parker, who beat Covid after a forty-five-day battle on a ventilator, proved the Para philosophy of never giving up. Steve who joined in 1972, remembered how he had to fight his corner to get his posting to depot as a recruit instructor in 1983. He saw it as going full circle, giving him the opportunity to repeat the good work his own instructors had done for him all those years before, turning him from a scrawny junior soldier into the paratrooper he became. Steve said, 'I was very much of the mindset that our job as instructors was to bring these potential paratroopers through, teach them everything you have to offer and prepare them to the best of your ability for life in a parachute battalion. Of course, we are a robust regiment and had a firm but fair mentality. If they don't come up to scratch, then they go. We were not there to bully or break them, unless it was absolutely necessary, which of course at times it was, and that then becomes a good character-building exercise, which is what paratroopers are all about.'[2]

Steve also remembered his second time as an instructor, this time as a platoon sergeant at the Juniors training platoon in Pirbright. 'The guards officer commented on how the Junior Para instructors came across as these all-singing, all-dancing Para Regt hard men, but when he stood around and quietly observed how they conducted themselves and taught their recruits, he saw that these burly paras were more like big brothers when they were teaching the juniors.'[3]

For those who successfully navigate their way through the basic training phase and luckily avoid injury, then P Company awaits. This is the rigorous training and selection organisation that decides who is good enough to become a Para. Unless applicants for trainee parachute training have already undergone a tough training course such as one run by the UK Special Forces, they must pass the pre-selection course, P Company. Only then can candidates go to RAF Brize Norton for their basic parachute training and hope to gain their wings.

The following is based on my own experience in Aldershot in 1990. Now based in Catterick, there have been some modifications, but the principle is always the same: to find out if the candidates have got what it takes to join this elite group of soldiers. The age-old debate about which location and particular era had the hardest training syllabus and P Company test week rages on in the pubs where the current and former members of the regiment drink. Our society changes over time, so what was accepted before may not be anymore, but whatever method is employed it fortunately always seems to deliver the required end result for Para Regt.

The first half of P Company starts on day one with the steeplechase, followed by the log race and then the assault course. On day two is the legendary 10-miler, followed by a test of heights and nerve with an aerial assault course called the Trainasium, and then lastly the milling. Then it is up to Brecon for the second phase, which starts with a demanding 17-mile endurance march on day three. Day four commences with a 12-miler over Pen Y Fan and Fan Fawr, followed by a 6-mile speed march. P Company then culminates on day five with the fearsome stretcher race. If the recruits get through all of this without failing any of the key events, manage to amass enough points and are deemed worthy in the eyes of the P Company permanent staff, they then hope to hear that awesome word 'Pass' as their name is read out on the cattle grid and they receive the coveted maroon beret.

The steeplechase is not like you see on television or in the Olympics, a gentle run around a track in trainers with a few minor hurdles to jump over at regular intervals on each lap. This is an extreme cross-country course over 2 miles of uneven ground with numerous obstacles, mud and water to overcome and a mass of other men heading in the same direction, clambering over one another and pushing each other out of the way as if their lives depend on it. The course must be completed in nineteen minutes in order to gain the full ten points, and one point is docked for every thirty seconds over this time. Everyone aims to beat everyone else and to complete the course within the allotted time.

The gun fires in the background and everyone sets off. By the time they get through the first obstacle, their boots are full of water and mud.

It is absolute madness with guys pushing, shoving yelling, jumping over obstacles, and landing on top of each other. There are bodies everywhere and everyone tries to get away from the crowd and find some space where they can get into some sort of rhythm. This is an individual event, different to many others where they are encouraged to work as a team. The training is designed to find men who are good team players but also survivors who are able to operate alone if necessary.

They stumble through thick sludge and squeeze past the edge of trees as the branches cut and slash at their faces. Then they are splashing into a stream and confronting the water jump before scrambling through woodland. Leaping over wet and muddy obstacles, the lads slip, slide, and fall, struggling to regain their footing in order to continue and make up time. They have to get into the right mental zone, push on hard and keep the finish line in their minds. At the end of the first test some are injured and that is the end of P Company for them. For the rest it is a quick shower and change of clothing ready for the next challenge.

Later the same morning it is time for the second event, the log race. Fifty metres or so ahead of the guys are four shortened telegraph poles that weigh what seems like a ton. Toggle ropes are tightly secured on each side of the logs for their hands to slide through. One hand goes through and grips the two pieces of rope forming a loop, which enables them to lift the log and carry it. One bloke is at the front pulling the log with his rope wrapped around his shoulder and setting the pace. As a team, they have to carry the log, which is meant to represent a battalion anti-tank weapon, across 2 miles of undulating, sandy, sodden, and muddy terrain. They are in a team and each man takes his place on the log, holding the ropes as they race against other groups.

As a thunder flash goes off behind, a burst of adrenalin floods through each of them as they quickly rise up from a prone position on the ground and sprint to pick up the logs. The team lifts together and heads down the 2-mile course, across the sand towards the first steep hill, carrying the heavy log with the rope cutting into their skin. The P Company staff, dressed in their distinctive blue tracksuit tops and maroon berets, keep their beady eyes on everyone and Section Commanders run alongside shouting at the guys to move faster, to work as a well-oiled team, getting a grip of those who are not pulling their weight and encouraging their own particular sections to win the event. Their own pride as instructors, and maybe a side bet of a few beers, is on the line.

Going up sharp inclines and down the other side, slithering and sliding all over the place, the lads descend with some going headfirst but desperately making sure that they always hold on to the ropes. After the steeplechase in the morning, their bodies are already running on half-empty tanks. Around corners, through the mud, and then up the sand dunes they go. If anyone comes off and the balance of the log is lost, then the front man may have to change position to equal the weight out again. Encouraging each other to keep going, this time they are very much working as a close-knit team over 2 miles of pure hell. It is not unknown for just two members of the team to finish the log race, one at the back and one at the front, carrying the log on their shoulders to get over the line. All they can think about is staying on their feet as guys around them tumble and scramble to get up. If they let go of the rope and fall away from the log, they have one chance to get back on again, otherwise they are out. Sweat pours down their faces from under the helmets that seem at the time to serve no purpose other than to make them feel hotter and more uncomfortable as it flops around on their heads. However, they will be glad to have it on if they take a fall and fly into one of the logs, and it is what they will be wearing if or when they go into battle in the future. Their hands are bleeding, but they cannot give up or let go. Freddy Crompton remembered his P Company days in 1956, 'The log race was the worst and the hardest, running along tracks of churned up ground where the tanks had been. The sludge could be thick and deep, and you had to keep going. It was all timed, there were no second chances.'[4] At the end of the race, more recruits are missing. They haven't made it and that is only the second event of day one; the rest still have the assault course to go in the afternoon. It is time for another quick shower and change of clothes and then off to scoff at the cookhouse to refuel the body ready for the next event.

The assault course, another test of individual fitness and stamina, involves a combination of around fifteen high and low obstacles on a circuit that has to be completed three times within seven and a half minutes. The course is never dry, and the muddy conditions just add to the difficulty level of the energy-sapping test. They go round once, twice and by the third lap their legs are burning, working in automatic and only sheer determination will get them to the finish. The P Company staff don't tell them what points they have at any stage so that they don't get overconfident, think they have made it and relax too much in later events.

The day is not over yet. Now they go back to barracks and clean all their kit again ready for the following day's events. The candidates only have two PT shirts (red and white) so they must be washed and ironed and their boots, crusted in thick mud, must look as if they have just been taken out of the box brand new. Even though they are on P Company, their kit still has to be immaculate each day. This is all part of the test and reminds them of the self-discipline and dedication required to serve in a Para battalion.

The Parachute Regiment soldiers pride themselves on their personal skills and administration in the field, whether on operations, training exercises or promotion courses where they work alongside other regiments, and there are times when this intense training really comes into good use. When others are tired and just fall asleep, a paratrooper is getting his kit and weapons ready for the next day. When given fifteen minutes to rest on a long march, others just zonk out with their Bergens still attached to their backs, but a paratrooper is sorting out his feet or getting a much-needed brew on. These personal skills are highlighted and hammered home during the training phase and never leave the Paras throughout their careers; this is just one of the many things that stand them apart from other soldiers.

Finally, day one ends, and the recruits get the chance to put their heads down and get some sleep before the 10-miler. This is a tough but excellent preparation for marches on deployment and is a regular part of all training. The 10-miler is the flagship event of P Company and a test that the Paras like to do on a Friday morning usually after a heavy night out on the town to check their fitness levels. Hangover or not, everyone in the company takes part and it's a great overview on how fit they are at any time in their career. Today there are Paras 10 events, as they have come to be known, held in the UK each year that anyone can apply to do and match themselves against the Paras' fitness levels.

The 10-miler over various terrain and gradients is far from easy; with a 35lb Bergen on their backs, water, and a weapon in their hands they have to complete the run in one hour fifty minutes to get the ten points and pass.

A member of the P Company staff weighs all the kit at the start of the event to make certain that nobody is cheating and then leads the way making sure that the pace he sets will bring in the main pack exactly on the one-hour, fifty-minute mark. This means that the guys that keep up with him will get the full ten points for the event. There is a support team, as in most of the events, consisting of a medic and a wagon to pick up stragglers who aren't going to make the cut-off time, and these are always as close by as they can be.

The participants push themselves up the slopes with their calves screaming. Their legs feel like jelly from the sheer exertion, their hearts are bursting, and sweat is pouring out of them. At times, they are literally on their hands and knees getting up the steep and narrow hill. At the top of Flag Staff, there is a chance for a quick water break and then the P Company instructor checks which of them are still on the pace with him and designates other members of the training team to stay behind and mop up the stragglers. Then he is off again, and if the lads don't keep up with him, they won't get to the next much-needed water break on time or have a chance of receiving ten points. Their bodies are stretched to the limit, and they trudge through the sand and mud of Long valley using their mental resolve to keep going. Never really having any idea of time or distance left to cover, they will themselves to keep up and get to the end in time.

The event straight after this, the Trainasium, is the test to make sure that these wanna-be paratroopers have a head for heights and nerves of steel. This is the Para Regt confidence test. The course is purely designed to see how each of them will react when faced with a problem at high altitude whilst fatigued and under stress. There is not a great deal of physical effort or fitness needed for this event, however, a huge amount of mental strength, fortitude and nerve is required. The P Company staff are not only looking for confidence in the air, but total obedience to orders in stressful and scary moments. The test is designed to mimic the fear that the men will face when jumping from a plane in operational conditions with dozens of fellow paratroopers at their side. This aerial course has been well thought out and designed specifically to test candidates in this particular area with the help of psychologists, psychiatrists and not least the Parachute Regiment themselves. Hesitation or refusal to jump is not an option and it is quite obvious that none of them can expect to be a paratrooper if heights are an issue, or they cannot quickly overcome any hang-ups.

The Trainasium itself is a bit of a big children's playground and consists of a series of scaffolding poles and wooden planks built some 40ft above the ground in many places. The planks are wonky and unbalanced, all of them are placed in awkward positions and are replaced in many areas with wet slippery poles, which the trainees have to walk or shuffle over, and which are high enough to seriously injure or even kill them if they fall.

Scrambling up a cargo net onto the first scaffold platform, the recruits move along the planks until they reach a metal ladder. They climb up this until they reach the first of the confidence tests, the shuffle bars. Now 40ft above the ground, the metal is unsteady and slippery beneath their feet as the instructor below shouts at them to go and calls for their name and number. They shout out their details and then continue shuffling along the poles until they reach the two uneven metal stoppers, then they must lift each of their legs over one after the other, whilst still maintaining their balance. They inch over to where they might be told to stop and touch their toes before finally getting to the other side of the structure to climb back down to the platform below. Hopefully they successfully get through the first test of nerve, but there is more to come.

Proceeding to move along and over further parts of this difficult and testing obstacle, they reach the illusion jump. There is a large gap between the plank they are standing on and the next piece of wood, which is a couple of feet below and all that can be seen in the gap is the daunting distance to the ground. The narrow wooden platform and the other that they are supposed to jump onto has been designed and positioned in such a way that it creates an optical illusion and gives the impression of a long, impossible distance. In fact, it is not that far and is quite possible if they fully commit to the jump. The guys have to stand with their feet and knees together and jump exactly when they are told to by the P Company instructor, just as they would from the C-130 Hercules military transport aircraft with their parachute on and sixty-three other Paras around them waiting to jump. But this time the guys have no parachute. This is a crucial mental test to find out if they have the balls to do the job.

After making the jump, they continue around the obstacle, over a wooden seesaw and across more metal runners, with a rope swing into a cargo net. A standing jump is followed by moving across open bars before turning around, running up a slight ramp and springing onto a platform without stopping. This leads them to the final cargo net leap, or what is now known as the Superman Jump. The only way to ensure getting a safe grip on the net is to land sideways and to punch a fist straight through the ropes and grab on tight the other side. By aggressively punching through, the ropes are parted, and the arm goes through, creating the opportunity to get a firm hold. If anyone tries to dive at it or grab the rungs with their open hands, it is more than likely that they will miss and fall or bounce back off it. If this happens, the recruit is sent around again to complete this part of the course correctly. The jump used to be known as Leopard's Leap after a guy called Private Leopard missed by trying to grab the netting with his hands open and fell to his death. After that, P Company installed a safety net below, which made it only slightly less scary.

After lunch, the next event is the milling. Milling is a vicious fighting match, which takes place in 'The Factory' gymnasium. Benches are moved into the centre to form a small, tight square and when it's not their turn, the guys sit on these to watch the fights in the space between the benches. If someone falls backwards, then the recruits hold him up in the absence of ring ropes. The Officer Commanding of P Company sits on a raised platform flanked by the P Coy sergeant major, who is also looking for performance, and a P Coy sergeant instructor, who is the timekeeper and bell man. All wear their maroon berets and distinctive P Company attire.

Pairs are chosen carefully so that everyone is matched with someone of roughly the same height and weight. In cases where there has been a bit of a feud between two guys during the training, the staff take the opportunity to pit them against each other in a grudge match to get the situation resolved. For this event, half of the lads fight bare-chested, and the other half wear red, so that there is no confusion during the fight. Potential officers always fight in white. The instructors take the fighters into the block corridor in two lines before leading them over to the gym. Everyone stands opposite their chosen opponent and the pairs begin eyeballing each other and then shouting abuse and swapping a slap here and there. It is all designed to wind each other up and prepare them for the event.

The pairs get up to fight in the order they've been placed. They are already physically and mentally exhausted from running the 10-miler and completing the Trainasium, but this event is a test of pure determination, mental courage, and bravery. Milling is not boxing; boxing skills are discouraged, and the guys are not permitted to defend themselves. They just have to throw everything they have directly at their opponent's head, whilst keeping their own head up and fully focused on the target. All the P Company staff want to see is the will to fight, the guts to take a punch full in the face and keep moving forward. If anyone gets knocked down, they get back up and go forward again. Even if the person they are matched against is noticeably stronger and more skilled in the fight, combatants can still earn a good score by showing that they have the heart and resolve to continue moving forward and fight on, refusing to ever give up. Additionally, someone who is particularly strong or has boxing techniques and has won their fight swiftly might be told to fight a second time.

The gloves used to be 18oz, there was no protective headgear and there were no gum shields, but of course today there are. The bell rings and the first pair launch into each other while the rest cheer and yell and push them back into the middle when they fall on top of them. Blood flies across the ring. It is only meant to last one minute, but sometimes they let it go on for much longer if one of the fighters is not showing them what they want to see. If someone is knocked down, the referee stops the fight and then sets them off again. The aim is not necessarily to just win; what they are looking for is the determination to keep going in the face of adversity with the spirit of a warrior. There is blood everywhere as guys go at each other with no one taking a backward step.

It is an intense and often gruesome battle. The Officer Commanding of P Company does not mince his words at the end of each fight and if he thinks both fighters have given it 100 per cent, then he congratulates them. However, if he is not impressed then he will tell the offending recruit and leave them in no doubt about what a weakling he thinks they are. This can be a bit embarrassing for that person and leaves his chances of passing P Company and ever going to a Para battalion in great jeopardy.

Once the milling is over, they are told to stand down for the weekend with the wise words of advice not to drink too much because there is still a long way to go before passing P Company.

# Chapter 10

# P Company: Pass or Fail

Early on Monday morning, the diminished number of surviving candidates climb onto the army Bedford bus, the most uncomfortable bus ever designed, and are driven to the Brecon Beacons in Wales for the second phase of P Company. Of course, nobody followed the advice not to drink and in the proud traditions of the Parachute Regiment, many are suffering from very heavy heads. After a painfully long, four-hour drive, trying desperately to get some sleep the best they can, the recruits arrive in Brecon and debus on the old cattle market at the base of a large spur. Everyone puts their Bergens on and immediately prepares to set off on the 17-mile endurance march. They have to make their way up the track and over the Brecon Beacons to where they will eventually make camp that night. This is the sixth of the ten events to be completed, and the 17-mile endurance march is a very long and arduous test. A lot of the guys are already carrying niggling injuries; it is not going to be easy and will test all their resolve.

The Brecon phase is, in the eyes of the instructors, the most important part of P Company because it replicates the conditions in which the soldiers will, maybe one day, be expected to operate and fight. This was definitely put to the test in the Falkland Islands, which had a very similar terrain to Brecon and mirrored many of the hideous weather conditions.

As usual, the P Company instructor sets the pace; if they stay with him and get in within the allotted four hours then they pass and get their ten points, simple as that. The first leg is straight up the hill to the ridgeline from where they can see the Talybont Reservoir and valley below. They then hit the wood line and go down again, eventually coming out where the P Company staff will stop, carry out a head count and for those who are up with the pace there is time for a quick brew. Setting off again, they go up to Windy Gap, down again onto the metal road and around to Cwm Gwdi camp. Some guys will drop out at this point because of injuries that they can't overcome.

At the end of the march in the late afternoon feet start to show real signs of wear and tear with some huge blisters appearing. The medical staff pop them with a needle and then put iodine on them to stop infection and assist in recovery. This is unbelievably painful, but it clearly amuses the P Company staff as everyone gets the same treatment.

That night the guys bed down in the wriggly tin camp at the base of Pen y Fan mountain, known affectionately as The Fan, and get a delightful view of the next day's challenge. Here they eat their evening meal: an airborne stew knocked up by the chefs and delivered in a huge urn. They grab as much bread as they can get their hands on to go with the stew and wash it all down with a gallon of sweet tea.

The following morning, the trainees are up bright and early, go through some kit checks with their platoon instructors, wrap their blisters with zinc oxide tape and talcum powder and put on fresh socks in preparation for the day's two marches.

The first is the 12-miler over Pen y Fan. They head straight up to what the P Coy staff call the first ridge. In reality it is the fourth, because there are a few false ridges to overcome, which is a real killer at the start of the day. It's critical for each of the lads to make sure that they are with the instructor at that point, because if they are too far back, they will be taken out of the event for safety reasons and taken via Land Rover to the start of the Fan Fawr stage.

The 12-miler in itself sounds a lot easier than the 17-miler the day before, but the miles are now taking their toll, especially with the 6-mile speed march coming straight on the back of it in the afternoon. The second major climb of the 12-miler is up Fan Fawr, which itself is 2,408ft high with a cairn marking the summit. Again, there is another short water stop and head count before the steep descent down to the finish point. The hardest part of this for the recruits is staying on their feet as it is so steep and slippery, and in the back of everyone's mind is the worry of turning an ankle as they slip and slide on the way down. This would be disastrous with just two more events to go.

The remaining participants in this unforgiving trial stop for a quick break, get a brew on and some food inside them and have time to change socks and dress the blisters again. These get progressively worse and cause major problems for some of the guys, but nobody is going to allow blisters or minor injuries to thwart the charge to the finishing post of P Company.

Within the hour, they are off again on the 6-mile speed march, the final event of the day. Pushing their bodies to the maximum, emptying the tank of energy, every ounce of mental fortitude is required. The lads start to smell success and push their bodies to the absolute limits, ignoring any pain, to get to the finish line. At the end of this is evening scoff and another night's sleep, followed only by the famous stretcher race.

Dawn breaks. It is finally time for the last event, the stretcher race. This is a team event and one in which the recruits are also assessed individually. It is made crystal clear at the start that no matter how well anyone thinks they have done so far, if they do not perform on this final event, then it's a fail, and it will all have all been for nothing. The P Company staff goad all the lads by telling them that there are plenty of other regiments out there to transfer to immediately if they so desire.

Private (Retired) Paul Stoddart-Crompton, the son of Freddy Crompton, who dropped into Suez with 3 Para, followed in his father's footsteps and joined the Paras in 1990:

> For me P Company did exactly what it said on the tin, it selects only those who really want to be Para Regt or Airborne Forces because there's absolutely nowhere to hide. I thought it was going okay for me as I'd been up at the front for most of the events, but the real pressure came when one of my platoon staff, Corporal Danny Brooks, who was a fearsome character to us Joes, told me he had a tenner on me for Champion P Company Recruit just before the stretcher race and I'd better not let him down! I was awarded top student, but I never did find out if he got his tenner.[1]

The stretcher race, which is 6½ miles long and uphill for the vast majority of the distance, starts on the Talybont Reservoir. Weighing 140lb, the 'stretcher' is made up of scaffolding poles and metal sheeting. The recruits who are left are split into teams of twelve and all take turns to carry the stretcher or run alongside. They have helmets on, and the weapons slung over their backs are secured as tightly as possible to stop them from swinging around.

The instructors run alongside and if anyone looks as if they are not taking the weight or carrying it properly, they are out. If a guy trips over a rock or falls away from the stretcher, there is only one chance to catch up, or they are out. They will be back squadded, which means that if they want another go at joining the Paras, they will have to repeat it: all the training, P Company, everything.

By this point, most are verging on physical and mental exhaustion, and all are digging deep to squeeze that last bit of power out of their bodies to get through this final energy-draining test. The P Company staff are looking for those men who can up their game one more level in times of adversity, see who the strong characters are, and, on the other side of the coin, who cannot handle it.

When not carrying the stretcher, the men are expected to show encouragement to the ones who are and be ready and willing to take a turn at any time. The instructors are watching them like hawks and marking them accordingly. The Log Race and The Stretcher Race look like mayhem, but all the P Company staff know exactly what they are doing and are watching each individual to see how they react. Bodies ache, hands and feet are covered in blisters and blood, but the determination and desire to complete the race and win is all consuming for the potential paratrooper.

Everyone ends up finishing at the famous cattle grid, known as the Old Station, and it is quite a momentous occasion, to say the least. As the recruits come through, the instructors open the gate to the side, so that the exhausted guys don't break their ankles on the last few steps of the P Company challenge. All the vehicles are there with the Officer Commanding P Company and those who have finished the course can see all the berets, which they have already been measured for, lined up on a table. The final points from the stretcher race are added to previous scores and all of them stand at ease and form up in two ranks with nothing on their heads and wait for their number to be called. As each number is read out, which seems like an eternity when waiting to hear your fate, just one word is spoken: 'pass' or 'fail'. Each recruit comes to attention and acknowledges the result with a crisp 'sir' and, if successful, receives the famous maroon beret. Warrant Officer 1 (Retired) Richard Turner recounted, 'I did P Coy in 1986 and the last event was the stretcher race. I can honestly say I found it the hardest event of all. I appeared to be on the stretcher longer and longer towards the end of the race. After crossing the finish line, I remember sitting down on my own reflecting on what I had just achieved. It was an emotional moment; I was physically and mentally drained, and only later found out that I had completed it with a groin injury.'[2]

About one third of the candidates who make it through to the end and form up at the cattle grid, fail. Their kit is thrown into the back of a 4-tonne truck, they get on and are taken back to Aldershot. Those who pass get on a lovely, comfortable coach and are taken back in luxury to prepare for the next phase of the journey, No. 1 Parachute Training School, previously located at Ringway and RAF Abingdon but now based at RAF Brize Norton. At this point they are known as 'Baby Paras', and they still have to earn their Para wings. Instructor, Warrant Officer 2 (Retired) Steve Morris knows as much about the Parachute Regiment Training process as anyone. He joined Junior Para in 1976 and passed P Company as a recruit prior to joining 1 Para. He was selected for recruit company as a corporal instructor, and subsequently went back to join the renowned P Company staff, firstly as a sergeant, and then a second time as the company sergeant major. Steve knows exactly what it takes to pass this monumental test of fitness and mental aptitude, and what personal attributes and skills the P Company staff look for in potential paratroopers:

> The recruit training phase and P Company itself, has evolved over the years in line with operational conditions and what the regiment requires at any time. Whether that be adding the Brecon phase after the Falklands conflict, the days when the Trainasium was in the trees in Aldershot, or the decision to have the guys moving from bashas at night in between the marches to corrugated roof huts, or even the age long debate of the contentious move from the Factory in Aldershot to the Infantry Training centre in Catterick, all changes were made for a good reason and had real purpose. I don't buy into people's perception of that what they did was any harder than anyone else, it's a load of nonsense and must all be put into context.[3]

Recent changes have included the opportunity for women to apply and join the Airborne Forces. Steve recounted a story of when he was Company Sergeant Major in P Company, back in 1998 and was talking to the Brigade Commander, who was warning him that he may receive a call from a high-ranking marines officer at Lympstone asking him about the possibility of women attempting P Company, and what changes and preparations to the P Company tests had been made with this in mind. Steve said, 'I told him everything is sorted and in hand and the Brigadier asked me, "How do you mean?" So, I said there were going to be no changes to the tests, I've already got accommodation set aside for them to come on board, what more do we need to do? The Brigadier paused, and then laughed and asked me what I was going to tell the marines. I replied, "Exactly that, I have accommodation for women put aside, end of story."[4] At the writing of this book, one woman has passed P Company.

There is no way to describe the feeling of pride you have when you pass P Company. It is a truly exacting test of your physical and mental aptitude, and you feel as though you could conquer the world in that moment. It is difficult because it needs to be difficult, and it means that whoever attempts to join the Paras, whatever their background, race, or gender, they are judged equally to find out who has got what it takes to become a member of this elite task force.

# Chapter 11

# Jumps

While all other training continues to evolve, the basic process of learning to parachute remains the same. Four weeks at RAF Brize Norton lie in front of the men who pass P Company. Generally considered to be the fun part of training and something the recruits look forward to, it is still a stern test of your nerves and ability to overcome fear. It is certainly a time for the guys to relax a little and enjoy some good RAF food and a few beers in the Spotlight club in the evenings. First though, and far more importantly, is a week of ground training in the hangars under the watchful eyes of the PJIs (Parachute Jump Instructors) before the new recruits even get close to thinking about carrying out their first jump.

With enough side left, side right, backward, and frontal para rolls to last a lifetime, they leap around like a synchronised gymnastic team or run up and jump off the ramps performing various landings as they are called out by the instructors. They also learn how to fit their parachutes and pack their containers, which carry all their personal equipment and weapon when jumping. This container was attached to a parachute harness by two bulldog clips in the old days when I did my course, now it's done by a quick release strap system. When jumping and once in the air, the clips are released, allowing the container to drop on 10ft ropes and hang in the air below the parachutist. It then hits the ground just before you land.

A lot of time is spent in lift swings, which simulate being in the air. The swings help the men to learn how to exit the plane properly, and to check and deal with any issues the canopy might have once they are out of the plane. The trouble is they crunch their nuts up, at times raising the pitch of their voice, and definitely are not good if they have any expectations of fathering children in the future. The men practise how to steer the parachute into clear air space, which is not easy with hundreds in the air at any one time, and learn how to land and carry out the various para rolls safely and without injury depending on the angle and speed of the landing. A favourite exercise is the fan, which is 30ft up in the rafters of the hangar, and again it's nicknamed the nutcracker for obvious reasons. Designed to simulate the feeling of being in the air and then hitting the ground, Paras jump out of this, and very quickly learn how to exit the plane and accept their various landings.

The first jump is out of a massive hot-air balloon, which looks like an old Zeppelin with a metal-harnessed platform swinging below and metal bars around the edge to stop the guys falling out. The platform lands on the ground and loads up with the PJI and five would-be jumpers. The instructor gives the signal, and the balloon then rises to 800ft. From there the men can see the faces of all the people below and still make out who is who. It is totally quiet, not a sound and pretty scary. It quickly brings to reality just how low they actually jump and how little time the guys have in the air to get themselves sorted and ready for landing. There is definitely no time for taking in the views or even slightly enjoying the whole process; this is certainly not sports parachuting and definitely not for the faint hearted.

The trainees move along one by one and when called forward each man has to move in front of the gate, which is just a metal bar that lifts up and allows them to jump off. The instructor tells them to hook up, which means hooking the clip at the end of the static line parachute to the bar above their head. This automatically releases the parachute when leaving the platform and, from 100ft below, deploys the chute. There is also a reserve parachute in the event that the main one does not deploy by the time they have counted three seconds; one thousand, two thousand, three thousand, check canopy. The jumpers look up to hopefully see the wonderful sight of a full green canopy deployed above their head. If required, the reserve parachute, which sits on the front of their chest, has to be deployed manually by pulling the red strap away from the body, and this decision has to be made within seconds whilst dropping like a stone.

Once clipped on, the instructor raises the bar, tells the next person to come forward, adopt the position, and stand by. They have to cross their arms over the reserve parachute, get their feet into position and wait for him to say, 'Go!' As a paratrooper, each man is expected to jump immediately on 'go', or the green light when on the plane, with no hesitation at all. This is what a lot of the training is about and why the Trainasium is so precisely designed. Everything is aimed at preparing the men for that moment. If they are on the plane with sixty-four other fully equipped paratroopers jumping out at half-second intervals from a C-130 Hercules using port and starboard para doors, it is essential that no one slows down or even halts the process. Any delay endangers the lives of all involved. In the Paras, if someone at the door of the plane (or edge of the balloon) refuses to jump when told to go, they are pulled away, taken straight down and immediately kicked out of the regiment with no ifs, buts or second chances. Rick Wadmore recounted a story about a refusal on one of the flights:

> We had a platoon of baby paras going through their jumps course, who were joined by a couple of SF guys who had just passed selection, and like all guys who join the SAS who don't already have their wings, they have to come here and do their jumps prior to joining their Sabre Squadron up in Hereford. This particular guy was third in the port stick and hesitated at the door, then informed me he was not going to jump. I said mate if you don't do it, you will fail the course and he said, 'It's okay I've already passed selection.' I looked at him in amazement as I knew it would not make any difference. Sure enough, once back on the ground he went straight in front of the Officer Commanding and was then gone. A few years later I heard from a friend who said he saw him over in Northern Ireland back with his original regiment.[1]

The balloon jump is completely different to the noise and commotion of an aeroplane, and many say it is a far harder test of nerve for that reason. One way or another, it will certainly reveal if you have what it takes to do the job. For these unique soldiers, parachuting is a form of transportation to the field of battle, no more than that. This first jump is clean fatigue, so no container or kit to drop and take care of this time. During the ground training stage, the men learn about ground rush, a phenomenon that occurs when they get close to the landing zone. In the last hundred feet or so, the ground suddenly seems to rush towards them and there is a temptation to reach for it. However, if they do reach their legs out, then there is a good chance that they could break some bones, because their legs are too taught and rigid, rather than relaxed and bent. To avoid any injury, they have to stay in a good para landing position, accept whatever their landing is going to be, and perform the parachute roll required by the angle of descent.

After the balloon, the new recruits move on to jumping out of planes, with six daylight descents and a night-time drop to be completed before they can earn their wings. The ground training continues with the aim of improving awareness and skills in the air, the ability to steer the parachute and deal with any potential emergencies that may occur. In addition, lots of work is done on a daily basis on landing techniques and para rolls. These jumps also start with clean fatigue before moving onto jumping with equipment.

I remember my own experience. I had to pack my container beforehand, stand on the runway ready to load and then get it onto the plane. My adrenaline was rushing, and I could barely move. I sat down on a tiny, net seat fixed to the side of the fuselage with my parachute on and the heavy container with all my kit and weapon between my legs as we embarked on the first low-level flight. The pilot was also on a training flight and as we set off, following the contours of the land, some of the guys started being sick from the motion of the plane and the fumes we were breathing in. It was horrendous and just made you want to get out of the plane as quickly as possible. In my case this was a good thing and took away any doubt about jumping from my mind. I had the sick bag in my hands trying not to think about it. Twenty minutes out from the DZ, I had to stand up with my partner, attach my container, hook up to the wire and stand ready, with all the weight pulling on my shoulders and knees, waiting for action stations. The container itself weighed nearly as much as me in those days and I stood there dying from the weight and the smell of the fumes mixing with the stench of vomit. Finally, we got called to the door, the red light came on, shortly followed by the green light that meant go, and we had to get out, jumping at half-second intervals from both the port and starboard doors. I was desperate to get off the plane, to escape the burden of my kit and the foul smells, and to feel weightless. I was not thinking at all about the dangers ahead as we jumped.

Parachuting is scary and not a natural act, and so many things can go wrong. Sometimes chutes don't open: if a guy turns over or exits the plane badly, their parachute can get hooked up and drag them along the side of the plane or they can end up in twists where the rigging lines above them are so snarled that the canopy cannot fill with air properly. There can be air steals where one parachutist moves across another and takes their air, causing them to drop like a stone with no time to pull the reserve. A fellow para might drift into another man during the descent and get tangled up in their rigging lines, causing them to come down together, or a container can get stuck and not drop down properly. So many things can happen, and the men have to be ready to quickly identify a potential issue and then calmly deal with it. There is no one there to help once they are in the air.

Learning to parachute is not only a valuable skill to have in your armoury, but it is also a great test of physical and mental fortitude. While the equipment and facilities have improved greatly from the early days, jumping from an aeroplane at height with all the kit remains a terrifying act for most men, no matter how exhilarated they might feel once they have landed safely, or how many times they have done it in the past. Jumping out into enemy fire or behind enemy lines as they did in the Second World War and Suez requires even more courage and is what sets the Paras apart from normal infantry troops. It takes a huge inner confidence in your own ability as well as the others around you to commit to such an action, and, if we are completely honest, a fairly generous dose of luck, to come out of it unscathed.

After they have completed their eight jumps, with the final one being a night descent, they receive their wings, and the young recruits quickly sew them onto their clothing. Along with the beret and stable belt, this now signifies that they are qualified paratroopers, and it is a very proud moment.

Basic training, P Company and the parachute course is still just the beginning for these young Paras. They now have the fundamental knowledge, fitness levels, and skill set to be able to pass out from their training platoons to take up their hard-earned places in their respective battalions and this is where the real work and a steep learning curve will quickly begin.

Once in battalion, high-level, intensive pre-deployment training is likely to begin with operational tours coming in thick and fast. The new blokes need to quickly prove themselves and become accepted by their peers, who have generally been in the battalions for a while and have a fair bit of experience under their belts. The more seasoned men will not be fooled easily or allow any bluffing whatsoever from the new blokes. They expect the new boys to earn respect through their actions and personalities. Joining battalion is not for the weak-minded.

Beyond learning how to parachute, which is a paramount skill, there is then essential training for different scenarios. Always evolving and incorporating new elements into their programme to keep up with the ever-changing world, the Paras are highly trained to deal with all possible situations. Centres now exist all over the world to prepare the men for different soldiering environments. For a paratrooper in the Second World War or a serving paratrooper today, the standards have always been the same, the testing just as rigorous. To be selected for this superb force you have to prove that you have the physical prowess and the strength of mind to be eligible.

The Paras serving up to the end of the 1960s had proven that their unique ability to quickly adjust to each and every new operating environment stood them apart from other soldiers. The following decades were going to be as testing and demanding as anything that had gone before. The guys were going to face more diverse and challenging situations requiring their unique skill set as well as more innovative training and development to incorporate new techniques. By the end of the 1960s, Britain had already become embroiled in what turned out to be a long drawn-out deployment of the three para battalions, this time much closer to home.

## Chapter 12

# Troubles Closer to Home

### Northern Ireland, 1969–82

A stressful and onerous challenge presented itself to the Parachute Regiment as the 1960s drew to a close. This one really tested the all-round skills, flexibility, and resilience of the men. It forced them to quickly adapt to a difficult operating environment and brought them up against a savagely indiscriminate enemy. All of this was on our own doorstep, just over the water in Northern Ireland. The enemy did not show themselves on the conventional battlefield, nor did they fight in an honourable fashion. Hiding within the local population they eventually brought their wave of terror and bombings to mainland Britain. This conflict engaged the British Army in one way or another for the next thirty-seven years, and the Paras soon found themselves at the forefront of the long, drawn-out battle.

Historical tensions between Protestant Loyalists and Catholic Republicans began to grow in the 1960s, and the situation worsened as rioting and levels of violence escalated. Houses were burned down, and civilians were killed as Catholics and Protestants rallied their opposing forces. The army, including the Parachute Regiment, was first deployed on the streets of Northern Ireland in what was named Operation Banner in 1969. In the early days of what became known as the Troubles, the regiment lived in tough conditions packed into old factories and breweries with gaps in the windows letting in the wind and the rain, while others were accommodated at police stations, crammed in like sardines, and some were based in primary schools, where they sat on furniture and toilets designed for children. There had always been a Northern Ireland peacetime garrison but at this point the infrastructure to house a large number of troops had not been planned for and was not available. The role of the paratroopers was to keep the peace between both communities, not taking one side or the other. The larger Loyalist community was very much on the ascent and the security forces were tasked with manning the lines between the two groups and were mainly protecting the Catholics.

All three parachute battalions were operational in Northern Ireland between 1969 and 2007 on tours that lasted between four months and two and a half years, operating on the streets of the urban cities or in the rural countryside in areas such as South Armagh. Duties included patrols, during which they dominated the ground and allowed the RUC (Royal Ulster Constabulary) to carry out their normal daily routine to keep law and order. Checkpoints were set up so that they could stop and question suspected terrorists, known as 'Players', and house searches were carried out to find illegal firearms and munitions. Surveillance positions were established at various vantage points around the cities in high-rise blocks of flats, or covert rural OPs (observation posts) and guard towers in the hope of intercepting terrorists and bombers. It was a very new scenario for the regiment; although they had been involved in urban peacekeeping roles in the past, this time it was taking place on UK soil and involved British citizens. Completely different methods and skills were required to deal effectively with the rapidly unfolding and ever-changing events.

During the initial Troubles, the Paras attempted to get to know the local people, to reassure them that they were there for a good reason and set up facilities that were totally lacking in the impoverished neighbourhoods at that time; they tried to win hearts and minds wherever they could. Communities that had once mixed happily were now divided and pressure was put on individuals to stand up as Republican or Loyalist supporters and to shun the opposition. Names were distinctively Catholic or Protestant, and groups of friends made up of both Catholics and Protestants who were not interested in the politics changed their names according to which pub they went in, so that nobody would bother them. Feelings were running high, and a new branch of the IRA (Irish Republican Army) emerged in 1970. The Provisional IRA with members such as Gerry Adams and Martin McGuinness within its ranks were frustrated by the lack of progress achieved by peaceful means. They began a more violent campaign in their bid to end British rule in Northern Ireland and create a united, independent Republic of Ireland.

The security forces were caught in the middle of the opposing Republican and Loyalist factions and were very much restrained in their ability to respond or even protect themselves effectively within the rules of engagement. Training and experience were key in situations like this. Over time there was a definite shift in the overall picture as the Provisional IRA upped their activities and became the main threat to the troops and police on the ground, and the guys were soon under the constant daily threat of attack from the Republicans. There was a need for specific training packages to prepare the blokes for their deployment and these had to evolve to encompass the new and ever-changing challenges that the regiment found themselves coming up against. A programme for Northern Ireland was designed, developed and refined many times over the years as the threats and technologies changed. Initially it involved short intensive courses, but as the conflict continued, the NITAT (Northern Ireland Training Advisory Team) package was established.

In preparation for NI tours, the Paras began to be put through their paces on the much longer and more demanding courses run by NITAT and were tested in Tin City, where low-powered training rounds could be fired. Tin City was a mock town that was built with streets, houses, and even lifelike dummies of people with microphones and cameras attached. As they patrolled these streets, the soldiers were faced with various scenarios that they were likely to come up against in real-life Belfast. They were put under severe physical and mental pressure at all times, carrying out thorough 5 and 20m checks each time they stopped. It could be a wheelie bin bomb, someone opening fire on them from a building or something as simple as one of the dummies wanting to chat and offer up vital intelligence on an upcoming event. Around every corner lay a new provocation or threat and everything was filmed on CCTV. There was no hiding from the many cameras and microphones strategically located around the training area.

After each exercise, the blokes were taken back into a hi-tech debriefing theatre to watch the whole thing being played back from various angles, catching every move they made, or didn't make in some cases. A member of the NITAT told each of them exactly where they had behaved well and where they had gone wrong and could improve for the future. They banged home the point that it was essential that they all engaged with the general public and spoke in a polite manner. Winning the confidence and support of the local population was vitally important. It was drilled into the soldiers that they were not the enemy, that the vast majority were law-abiding citizens going about their daily business who could well become friendly and helpful towards the security forces if they were treated with respect.

The final stage of the training took place in a mock housing estate, this time with real buildings and people acting as the CIVPOP (Civilian Population), in which the Paras fine-tuned their skills. The CIVPOP, just like in Belfast, had 'known terrorists' amongst their ranks with certain roles within the organisation. Prior to each patrol, the men were shown photos of these 'terrorists' and they had to memorise their faces, names, addresses, and positions within the organisation. When they spotted them out on patrol, they had to report their movements to the control room and, if required, stop, search, and question them. It was intended to imitate life just as it would be when the soldiers hit the ground for real in the province.

The NI training camp package culminated in a live riot scenario held in the mock village. For this purpose, the NITAT acted as marshals, and they brought in another army regiment to act as extra CIVPOP. The Paras patrolled the village as normal and were instructed to react accordingly to any incidents that occurred. Whilst dealing with a mundane stop and search, tension began to grow with a crowd building up around them, and the brief was to carry out normal drills and only escalate the situation as and when the need arose. The NITAT marshals' role was very important and a degree of personal control from both sides was required. Suddenly, the situation escalated, got out of hand and turned into a full riot scenario. The CIVPOP had handy stocks of old rubber bullets, which were in replacement of the stones and bricks that were thrown your way in a real situation. Petrol bombs also became available for the crowd to throw at the paratroopers with the intention of creating a scene that was as real to life on the streets of Belfast as possible. Following protocol, the Paras called out the QRF (Quick Reaction Force), who turned up in full riot gear with helmets, shields, and wooden batons. They started to confront the raging crowd and attempted to take control of the situation. The whole idea of the training was to prepare the guys for the real thing. The petrol bombs were thrown in a reasonably controlled manner, but they were aimed at the base of the shields to give a realistic taste of what it was like to be on the receiving end of these devices. The flames roared up the shields and against helmet visors, creating unbelievable heat.

They also practised with baton gunners simulating firing plastic bullets at the pre-identified riot leaders and main troublemakers. This would, in reality, drop the individuals to the floor and enable snatch squads to run forward and drag them back behind the lines, where they were arrested and taken back to the police stations. The exercises were so realistic that sometimes the fights in training got out of hand and the NITAT training team had to diffuse the situation and end the exercise. However, even this was part of the training. Anybody who got too caught up in the moment, became enraged and lost their head, was taken aside and spoken to about the importance of keeping their discipline. The training was extreme and pushed the soldiers to the limit to ensure that they understood what these operations required. Restraint and self-control were drilled into them for operations such as Northern Ireland and other urban peacekeeping roles. The men of the Parachute Regiment are not ordinary soldiers, they are carefully selected and intensively trained to the highest of standards in all areas of possible deployment.

Operations in Northern Ireland were constantly monitored and were under extreme scrutiny by representatives from both sides of the Troubles, the powers that be, as well as the press, who were filming and recording everything. Even though the Paras were shouted at, spat at, assaulted with stones and petrol bombs on a daily basis, and came under armed attack, they had to keep a degree of personal control at all times. This is what they specialise in: keeping cool heads when all around are losing theirs. Assimilating the situation and understanding the rules of engagement, knowing the appropriate time and manner in which to respond to defuse a potential problem is their job. In Northern Ireland, when the time was right, they acted fast with controlled aggression in response to a live threat to the civilian population or fellow security forces on the ground. This is what the regiment is all about, and upon which their great reputation has been built.

Techniques were developed to covertly insert patrols onto the ground and set up OPs. The COP (Close Observation Platoons) had overwatch of known terrorist group members and reported on their movements and known associates. With the aid of night vision devices, they were able to keep an eye on activities that took place under the cover of darkness. Given some staunch Republican areas to cover, they went in to search flats and houses known to be used by terrorists for keeping weapons and bomb-making equipment. However, with the help of supporters in the local community, the IRA managed to set up their own warning system, which gave the men involved time to escape or move the weapons and munitions. The IRA grew in strength and numbers; receiving support from America and other countries, they made bold statements promising to push out the British by bullet or bomb.

Both 2 and 3 Para came into the province on short tours, and it was soon established that the constant changeovers were preventing a lack of continuity, so 1 Para set up in Palace Barracks, just outside the Belfast city centre, near to Hollywood, for a twenty-month tour. It was one of many long tours the battalions carried out over the coming years. They were given better equipment and vehicles and prepared themselves to deploy to any trouble spots at short notice. Riots were generally met with soldiers moving forward behind shields, but 1 Para brought in their own style of driving straight into the mob, piling out of their vehicles, and confronting the troublemakers face to face and making sharp arrests. The method worked as they went into crowds of as many as 3,000 people using this method and, subsequently, large-scale riots began to decline.

The new Provisional IRA were now well armed and well equipped. With skilled military-style fighters among their numbers, they began copying the army with their own covert manoeuvres and training of new recruits, which resulted in an increased number of attacks against security forces. The lack of intelligence about who was involved proved to be a highly frustrating problem and led to the creation of specialist British Army units that eventually became highly successful in infiltrating these organisations and keeping close tabs on the terrorist movements and operations throughout the province. It was initially very difficult to garner information and even those people who were not militant were too frightened to pass on any information. Informants were regularly killed, or seriously harmed by kneecapping or tarring and feathering.

On 6 February 1971, Gunner Curtis was shot dead by the IRA in Belfast; he was the first British soldier to be killed since the start of the Troubles, and the Prime Minister of Northern Ireland declared that the Province was 'at war' with the IRA. The UK government decided to get tough, and troops were sent in to quell riots with CS gas (tear gas). However, British soldiers were still liable for prosecution and were limited in their legal activities. They were to use minimum force at all times and could only fire at a terrorist if they were positively identified as carrying a weapon and about to use it to endanger life. Decisions had to be made in a split second by the young men entrusted with this responsibility, and it was a heavy burden to carry if they got it wrong.

The violence increased as the terrorists, unwilling to confront soldiers directly as in a conventional war, began to use craftier guerrilla tactics and utilised the use of hidden IEDs (improvised explosive devices) as weapons against the security forces and the innocent general public.

Several police officers and two civilian adults with two children were in the reception area of the local police station in Springfield in May 1971 when a man came in and placed a suitcase on the floor before running outside. Suddenly someone spotted the burning fuse sticking out of the side of the case. Shouting and yelling, the policemen organised the evacuation of the hall, and Sergeant Michael Willetts of 3 Para, held the door open, making sure that everyone moved through to the safety of the rear passageway. In a selfless act and in the pure spirit of the Parachute Regiment, he was not required to be in that area, but he remained in the doorway shielding those behind him as they hurried away from the danger zone. The bomb went off and debris spun through the air; a flying chunk of metal embedded in Willett's head in the huge explosion, and he was mortally wounded. As he was carried out to an ambulance, people in the street jeered and spat at him as he lay dying on a stretcher. Seven RUC officers, two British soldiers and eighteen civilians were also injured in the attack that day, but Willetts sacrificed his life to save civilian adults and children alike. He acted without thinking twice about his own safety whilst protecting others, including people from both sides of the divide, some of whom hated and despised his presence in the country.

In August 1971, the highly controversial system of internment was brought in. Proposed by the Northern Ireland leadership, and approved by the British government, anyone suspected of terrorist activities or supporting them, could be arrested without charge, and taken in for questioning. Bombings, riots, and shootings increased, and barricades were put up by militants to create no-go areas for the forces. The men of 1 Para went in with determination to clear these barricaded areas and restore control. At the Ballymurphy estate a barricade had been booby trapped, and in the move to take back the area, the Paras became engaged in a prolonged firefight with IRA gunmen before finally clearing the barricades.

Not only did internment prove unproductive because most of the suspected ringleaders and prominent terrorists escaped and took refuge across the border, but it also increased the level of unrest within the local communities as hundreds of innocent people were arrested, and consequently, the ranks of the IRA sympathisers swelled.

In 1971 there were just under 7,000 violent incidents in the province, including attacks on police stations, and over 1,000 bombings.

The Para Regt found themselves being deployed into hardcore terrorist areas where the control had often been lost by other army units or the police. It was a theme that continued for years. They were tasked to work with the RUC to bring a sense of order to the situation and restore control as fast as possible. During these missions and as they entered the hostile, and often no-go areas, they found themselves coming under multiple types of attack and had to constantly evolve and develop new ways to overcome these threats as they went about their business. The men of 1 Para had been in Belfast for eighteen months up to the beginning of 1972 and had established a reputation for being extremely tough and professional. Moving hard and fast into volatile situations, they made it very clear that they had a job to do, which they did as safely as possible.

One of the first car bombs to be used was in Donegall Street. A warning was given by an anonymous caller, but they gave the wrong location and hundreds of people moved into the adjacent street to get away from the area under threat. The car bomb detonated in the road that they ran into, killing seven and injuring scores of people including school children. Many lost their limbs as the terrific blast shattered windows, damaged buildings, and tore people apart. Paras were involved in dealing with the aftermath, helping the seriously injured, checking that the area was clear and that there were no further attacks.

Sunday, 30 January 1972, has become an infamous date in the history of the Troubles and the Parachute Regiment itself, and it still causes controversy today. The events are still not completely clear, and I don't think that the truth behind what really happened fifty years ago can ever now be proven beyond doubt by either side. The soldiers of 1 Para were tasked with a very difficult and dangerous mission to clear a no-go area in the city centre of Londonderry called the 'Bogside'. The area had been barricaded and was known to be guarded by armed and hooded IRA members. Police and security forces had not been able to get into the area, which was known to the local occupants as 'Free Derry' and had stood as a symbol of defiance for nearly two years. The IRA had several ASUs (active service units) based in the Bogside. They ran sideline businesses involving protection rackets and drugs, and provided training for some of their new recruits in the area. During an organised civil rights march, which went by the no-go zone, a plan was devised that involved 1 Para going in to gain some control by separating the troublemakers from the innocent marchers, detaining them where necessary, and clearing the barricaded area.

Shooting began, with a number of rounds fired from both sides, and resulted in the deaths of thirteen Republicans, and another fifteen injured. In response to the shootings, an angry mob burned down the British Embassy in Dublin and the IRA began a bombing campaign in both Northern Ireland and mainland Britain. In February 1972 they detonated a device at the officers' mess of the 16th Parachute Brigade headquarters in Aldershot, causing the deaths of the Regimental Catholic Padre, Gerald Weston, a gardener and five workers, including the mother of a member of 1 Para, and injuring seventeen others. Bombs went off in pubs and often there were multiple attacks on one day. On 'Bloody Friday', 21 July they set off numerous bombs across Northern Ireland, including well over twenty in Belfast city centre alone. Nine civilians were killed, and more than a hundred others were injured. The paratroopers witnessed the consequences of these attacks as they again went into the streets, caring for the injured and clearing bomb sites.

The men of 2 Para joined a large, combined force just over a week later in Operation Motorman as tanks and bulldozers went in to clear all the no-go areas. A few hours after it had finished, nine civilians were murdered in a terrorist car bomb attack in the village of Claudy. The bloodiest year of all in the Troubles was 1972, with hundreds of people killed and thousands injured, as the IRA increased their use of car bombs in crowded areas.

Despite the shadow of Bloody Sunday hanging over the men, they still carried out their duties with resilience and professionalism.

Steve Parker said:

I first joined the battalion in 1974, a couple of years after Bloody Sunday and because of what happened in Londonderry in 1972, 1 Para was persona non grata at that time. However, a good few of the blokes were still getting time in the Province reinforcing the ranks of 2 & 3 Para, who were deployed on numerous tours during this period. I eventually first deployed to NI in 1978 to what we called bandit country in South Armagh and Crossmaglen, covering the border areas and the town centre. We were supposed to be going by ferry to NI. However, when the word got out that 1 Para was returning to the Province for the first time since Bloody Sunday, huge demonstrations took place around the port, so in the end we had to abandon that plan and fly in direct from Brize Norton instead. When we first hit the streets, it was a strange feeling and the local population just completely ignored us; they didn't get involved in any sort of conversation. However, as time went by, the guys tried their best to win some of the more open-minded elements of the local population around, and sure enough we did manage to get on and get the job done with some level of success.[1]

The Paras continued at the forefront of operations throughout the decade. By the end of 1978 they had lost seventeen men on duty; one killed by a sniper was shot in the head whilst out on patrol, others were victims of IEDs. There was worse to come.

On 27 August 1979 there was not only the IRA assassination of Lord Mountbatten, but also an atrocious attack on members of 2 Para near the village of Warrenpoint. A patrol was on its way from Ballykinler Barracks to take over duties at Newry near the border with the Republic of Ireland. Unfortunately, the routes between the barracks and Newry were limited and while the soldiers varied the journeys as much as possible to deter possible attacks, they were always vulnerable. The convoy of a Land Rover and two 4-tonne trucks carrying men from 3 Platoon, 'A' Company, made its way along the road beside the shore of a lough marking the border. Thick woods lined the Republican side of the stretch of water, providing a perfect place for terrorists to watch the road without being seen. As the vehicles moved along the road, they passed a trailer parked in a layby loaded with bales of straw. The Land Rover and the first of the trucks went past but just as the second truck went by, a massive explosion blasted out. Underneath the straw were milk churns packed with incendiaries and surrounded by cans of petrol; as the convoy passed, 700lb of explosives were remotely detonated. The blast tore into the rear vehicle, killing or injuring the men on board. The front vehicles accelerated to get away and under cover, as burning bodies from the last truck were scattered across the road. Steve Taylor, who was 18 at the time and had been in 2 Para for six months, reported the events of that day.

> I was in the second truck but the wagon I was travelling on began to develop some mechanical problems. As was the procedure, the vehicle with difficulty took up the forward position. We moved onto a dual carriageway onward to Newry with a gap of 100 yards or so between us. On the side of the road on the left-hand side was a trailer packed with straw. As the rear vehicle came level with it, there was a huge fireball and explosion. The brakes were slammed on and for a split second, in what seemed an age, we stood mouths agape. The sides of the truck were gone. Protected only by makralon, able to stop 9mm ammo and Molotov cocktails, it was little if any use against an IED. Bill Kearns, a senior Tom (nickname for an ordinary soldier), screamed 'Move!' That broke the spell and as per our drills we deployed into fire positions. Black acrid smoke burned, there was little left of the truck.

The men rushed around trying to help their fallen comrades, reinforcements including Royal Marines and helicopters arrived, and an Incident Control Point (ICP) was set up outside an old gate house a few hundred yards away. A Wessex helicopter prepared to leave with two casualties, the Commanding Officer arrived with his signaller in another helicopter, and they raced towards the gate house. Suddenly, another explosion, of greater magnitude than the first, blasted outwards. Another even larger device concealed in the gatehouse had been detonated. The terrorists had anticipated the ICP location. Huge boulders of granite blew in all directions and men were torn asunder as the gatehouse disintegrated.

Taylor continued:

> I recall feeling uncomfortable and started to move away from the area. As I did, the secondary device exploded. I was thrown through the air,

bowled over by a huge chunk of spinning masonry like a bowling pin, and I landed with a thud, smacking my right elbow hard. Time seemed to slow down; everything was in slow motion. I had entered 'The Zone' where super adrenaline kicks in. I looked up and saw tons of masonry, wooden beams and debris coming down on me.[2]

The explosion demolished everything around it and killed twelve more men as well as injuring three and damaging the Wessex helicopter. It was the British Army's largest loss of life in a Northern Ireland incident. Devastatingly, sixteen paratroopers and two Queen's Own Highlanders were killed that day, and six more Paras were seriously wounded. Many of the blokes were young recruits like Taylor who had only recently started their first twenty-month tour. None of the survivors, including Taylor, will ever forget that day or the friends they lost. Catholics in the local area feared a fierce backlash from the Paras, but they totally underestimated the self-discipline and control of the regiment; there were no reprisals.

The Troubles continued throughout the 1980s and '90s and into the twenty-first century, with 1, 2 and 3 Para all deployed on short six-month stints or longer two-and-half-year 'roulement' tours of the Province. On many occasions two of the parachute battalions were in theatre at the same time.

Whilst the Troubles were still ongoing, a national crisis erupted in 1982 when Argentina invaded the Falkland Islands. While 1 Para continued their duties in Northern Ireland, 2 and 3 Para went into action defending the British archipelago in the South Atlantic.

## Chapter 13

# Maggie's Boys

**Falklands War, 1982**

The men of 1 Para were still deployed on Operation Banner in Northern Ireland when Argentina launched a surprise attack on the Falkland Islands on 2 April 1982. The population of this territory considered themselves British and did not want to be put under Argentinian control. Britain's government, led by Margaret Thatcher, was not going to let them down and while peace negotiations got under way, a task force was immediately set up. Within the next few weeks, a fleet of ships including requisitioned merchant vessels was sent on the 8,000-mile journey to the South Atlantic. The men of 3 Para, who were on Easter leave when the call came in, immediately returned to barracks, and set off on the SS *Canberra*, a luxury cruise-liner, as part of the spearhead battalion. They were followed by 2 Para shortly afterwards in the MV *Norland*, a North Sea car and passenger ferry, and the men prepared themselves for a possible invasion.

When most of the colonies in the British Empire regained independence after 1957, The Falklands remained a British Crown Colony. Argentina had long claimed sovereignty over the islands but the Falkland Islanders themselves wanted to remain part of Britain and the situation was never resolved. In 1982, the Argentine government, a military junta led by Lieutenant General Leopoldo Galtieri, was not popular and he saw the retaking of the Falkland Islands as a way to garner support by promoting patriotism. In March 1982, Argentine scrap metal workers raised the Argentinian flag in South Georgia Island and on 2 April, Argentine amphibious forces quickly overcame the small garrison in Port Stanley. The following day Argentina seized the dependent territories of South Georgia and the South Sandwich group. Britain was outraged by the actions and with similar aims of raising patriotism and uniting the people in her favour, Margaret Thatcher assembled a task force.

On the long journey to the stop-off point and forward mounting base on Ascension Island the troops kept up their fitness by running around the deck, fine-tuned their weapon skills and checked their equipment in preparation for war. Time was spent on medical training as the men knew that in the heat of battle they would have to administer first aid and sustain the lives of those around them whilst waiting for support, which in that terrain might take some time. There was an air of excitement among the many young troops who had never experienced any form of battle and were eager to fight and put their training to the test, but everyone fully expected the peace negotiations to avert any conflict. On board the ships the mood was light-hearted and fun as they trained intensively and partied hard in the evenings with music and singing, competitions. and hilarious drag shows. On board the *Norland* the famous and recently deceased 'Wendy', the gay pianist entertained the guys of 2 Para. The 'two can' rule was in place and as usual the blokes found some novel ways of getting around this and drinking more. On reaching the Ascension Islands, the men of 3 Para sunbathed a little and relaxed on the beaches between live-firing training exercises. They felt sure that talks for peace would work, but then news came through about the sinking of the Argentine *Belgrano*, followed by HMS *Sheffield*. There was no doubt in anyone's mind now that the war had started. There was no way back for a negotiated peace settlement; this was going to be for real. The Paras were excited about the opportunity to put their skills to use and get stuck into some action.

The orders came through and the ships moved on towards the Falklands, which consists of two large islands known as East and West Falkland with well over 700 other smaller islands. Both 2 and 3 Para prepared to land in the San Carlos Bay Waters area on the west coast of the predominantly mountainous and hilly East Falkland with the main objective of taking back the capital Port Stanley, which lay on the opposite side of the island.

The men of 2 Para landed on Blue Beach on 21 May.[1] The men had stacked up in platoon lines in formation on the huge landing craft. When the ramps were lowered, the words 'Troops Out' were shouted by the coxswain and the men of 2 Para jumped out into the water ready for war and formed up on the beach in all-round defence. They then had four to five hours of darkness to get to Sussex Mountain before first light, where they would be holed up for the next few days. Slogging over wet and soggy terrain and carrying huge loads of between 80 and 100lb, they tabbed across the inhospitable terrain in freezing temperatures. It soon became apparent that their army-issue boots were useless at keeping their feet dry in these extreme conditions and, subsequently, several men got trench foot. Reaching their defensive position, some managed to dig in easily or build sangars, which offered some form of defence and overhead protection, but others lower down found that when they tried to dig trenches in the boggy ground the holes immediately filled with water.

Then 3 Para followed in and landed on what was known as Green Beach. As the landing craft drew closer to the shore, the section GPMG gunner covered the beach to the front in case the enemy lay in wait. As the ramps lowered, the blokes, high on adrenaline, piled out into ice-cold water, which came up to the waist of the tall men and nearly engulfed the shorter ones as they waded, soaking wet, onto the shore. The freezing climate and continual, intermittent rain and snow meant that they would not be properly dry again for a while. Luckily, they were met by members of the SBS (Special Boat Service) rather than an Argentinian Defence Force as they struggled to unload and gather their equipment. The battalion then moved off and dug in on a nearby feature whilst waiting on their orders for the long march to Mount Longdon to begin a few days later.

Camped out on Sussex Mountain without a clear idea of what they were to do next, 2 Para could only watch in horror as ships were attacked by the Argentinian air force. Not only were the losses tragic, but it also meant that vital support and supplies for the land forces were being greatly depleted. What resupplies they were getting mainly consisted of cigarettes and Mars bars, but there were no spare socks, which were in great need. The men waited, feeling ineffectual without orders, shivering, and huddling in the atrocious piercing cold, wet and windy weather. With inadequate and substandard cold-weather gear, they were joking and generally taking the piss out of each other, attempting to keep their own morale high.

Finally, 2 Para were told that they would be moving south to capture Darwin and Goose Green settlements and airfield, which were located on a heavily defended isthmus to the south. With the attacks on the ships and the time the men had now been stagnant, it was felt that the task force needed to make a decisive move on the enemy, show them who they were up against and take a key strategic position before the momentum of the landings was lost.

On 26 May after one false start, the men of 2 Para finally set off south in light order, just carrying ammo and rations for three days and leaving behind on Sussex Mountain their Bergens, sleeping bags and all other personal kit. Proceeding on foot due to a lack of helicopter assets, which had been exacerbated after the loss of the *Atlantic Conveyor* on 25 May, they headed for their first objective and form up point of Camilla Creek House, which was a 13-mile march away. The battalion with its support arms was ready on the start line by 2 am on the morning of 28 May with sore feet and wet gear.

However, any discomforts faded from their minds as they mentally prepared themselves for the impending battle.

As the preparations were finalised for the attacks on Darwin and Goose Green, it became apparent that they were vastly outnumbered. One of the section commanders was briefed on enemy numbers in the 'thousands' and was told that the Argentinians had dug in very well all around the area. They already held the high ground and were well-prepared with interlocking fields of fire for their heavy machine guns, backed up by mortars and artillery. It was going to be a hard slog clearing the enemy lines and then, to make matters worse, the BBC reported on their World Service on the imminent attack by British paratroopers on Goose Green. As expected, Argentina responded to this announcement with further bombing raids and by raising their alert readiness.

The men of 2 Para were ready, the battle plans for the rifle companies' attack and support from HMS *Arrow* were in place. *Arrow* bombarded the enemy target prior to H-Hour but then the gun jammed. They were unable to fix it and after a delay of thirty minutes, the men started. With a fire base set up by Support Company at Camilla Creek House consisting of air and naval fire controllers, mortars and snipers, as well as the three guns from 8 (Alma) Battery, 29 Commando Regiment Royal Artillery, the two-point rifle companies moved forward towards their targets until coming under contact.

It was pitch black as the order came and the men went into the fray. The red light of tracers filled the sky, the noise of machine guns rattled their bones and mortars boomed out, thudding into the ground all around. The soft earth cushioned the full impact, but mud and shrapnel still flew in all directions and men were blown off their feet. Harriers were unable to come into the area at night, and 2 Para had to go it alone with only their own support-arms-weapons covering their movement forward.

'B' Company moved up unopposed towards their target feature axis, which was an Argentinian .50-calibre Browning machine gun post on top of the hill. Sergeant (Retired) Martin 'Scouse' Margerison was a corporal at the time:

> It was pitch black, no one could see fuck all. All of a sudden, I spotted what looked like a figure in the distance, what I first perceived to be a haystack, then it moved, so I challenged it using my limited Spanish, and it responded in like. It was an enemy sentry. My gut reaction was to take him out, but I was wary that if we opened up on him, it may well bring some heavy fire from the enemy machine gun post above onto

the rest of our company. Time was moving in slow motion at this point. Rather than putting his hands up, the sentry turned towards us, looking like he was moving his weapon in our direction, so I initiated contact and the rest of the section lit him up. We then continued up the hill in what was now an advance to contact. Shortly after reaching the top, we were engaged by another position to the left, illume was put up in the air and we went left flanking, eventually taking out eight trenches and going into a re-org. The rest of the company was also in contact and taking prisoners. We could see in the distance that 'A' and 'D' Company were also in battle, fighting hard to take their own targets.[2]

Onwards and upwards 2 Para pushed, the soldiers filled with trepidation and adrenaline flowed as the reality of the situation sank in; this was not an exercise, it was the real thing. They closed in on the enemy positions, threw in grenades and followed them in with bayonets ready for savage, bitter fighting to the death. All was pandemonium as screams, shouts, yells, explosions and the metallic smell of blood filled the darkness.

Training took over as they blocked out the sight of their mates and fellow paratroopers being cut down in front of them. Instinctively they moved hard and fast with aggression and control, stepping over the dead Argentinians strewn across their path. Stopping to help a wounded comrade often resulted in both men dying, and so men who had been hit were often left as the battle raged. In some cases, the injured could not be reached for hours on end, as the incoming heavy fire continued. As is well-known, no plan survives contact with the enemy, and in the madness and confusion of battle, the companies got split up, the reserve company ended up in front when they should have been behind, and the point company got held up in an area where there were no points of orientation. Chaos reigned as the well-entrenched and well-armed foe unleashed their fire down on the advancing troops and enemy snipers took out men with deadly accurate shots.

Hour after hour the men fought on through the bleak night. Nobody thought about the cold or the wet now; this was the do or die brutal reality of war. As daylight broke, the rifle companies found themselves held up and exposed, in many cases on flat ground offering little cover, and they desperately moved back under the cover of smoke into safer positions and reorganised themselves for the next phase. Scouse Margerison's section, along with most of the rest of 'B' Company, were short of ammo and artillery support and found themselves pinned down on top of the feature by an enemy heavy machine gun post around three hundred yards away. He recalled:

When we came under fire, 'B' Company was split. Half of 6 Platoon, including the platoon commander, Lieutenant Chip Chapman (Major General Retired), took cover forward in the gorse line. This gorse ran across the full frontage of Goose Green and was the only foliage cover we had in the whole of the advance. In a bid to break contact and regain some momentum, it was 'B' Company Officer Commanding John Crossland, an icon, ex-1 Para and SAS, who managed to get us some smoke, and said, 'A surprise is coming, be prepared to move.' The smoke landed between the gorse and the rest of the Company, giving us some cover, and it was then Chip who said, 'Prepare to move,' and Manny Eissermann who actually told us to go. He said on 3, but the fucker started on 2! I passed the info on to my guys, gave the lads the order to move and we all got up and ran for the smoke. I stopped halfway to shout to the gun team to come and join us, and all of a sudden, I was hit. I initially thought it was the back blast from one of our own eighty-four anti-tank weapons and then started to see stars. Now lying on the floor, covered in blood, I realised not only had I been shot through the face, but also through my shoulder. I could hear the blokes saying, 'Scouse has been hit,' and I was trying to tell them not to fuckin' move, to stay down, as the enemy gun was still firing short bursts at my position. Shortly afterwards, Baz Bardsley and Manny Eissermann came bravely running down the hill, grabbed my webbing yoke and dragged me to the top. Whilst I was being patched up, drips put in and given some morphine by the medic, Ged Peatfield came over and asked if I wanted to press the button which would fire the Milan Missile Post which had been set up ready to take out the enemy machine gun nest which had hit me. I said I was a bit fucked, so he pressed it for me. Off it went, whizzing to its target and destroyed the gun post as I lit up a fag and watched smoke coming out of the hole in my face.[3]

Frustrated by the lack of progress and knowing that any faltering would result in defeat, Commanding Officer Lieutenant Colonel H. Jones charged forward to take out a machine gun up ahead of one of the rifle company objectives. Warnings were called out to him and his support team as it became clear that he had not seen the enemy trenches on the other side. As he charged up the hill, a machine gun opened up and caught him full on the back. He was thrown forward, got up once more and was hit again. This time he fell just short of the enemy trench, mortally wounded. Lieutenant Colonel H. Jones was posthumously awarded the Victoria Cross for his bravery that day.

Following the death of their commanding officer, command of the battalion initially passed to Major Keeble. With the attack getting bogged down and losing momentum, Keeble quickly assessed the situation, reorganised the troops and prepared to resume the advance. The men of 2 Para were galvanised and encouraged by the bravery of Jones, and throughout that day they found ways forward through pure guts and stubborn resolve, with the support of the mortar crews who fired hundreds of rounds into the enemy positions. Despite being blocked by minefields, having a napalm bomb dropped on them, surviving the strafe from a fighter plane, and facing an overwhelming number of well dug-in Argentinian soldiers, by early afternoon, 2 Para were starting to turn the battle. They had taken the key terrain and positions around Darwin Hill and opened up the route to Goose Green.

At last, air support came in and destroyed crucial targets, and the men pushed forward again. As night came in once more, the paratroopers were soaking wet, exhausted, and hungry with very little ammunition left. Men went out to forage whatever ammo and food they could find on the dead Argentinians littering the ground until, finally, helicopters came in to evacuate the casualties and bring much-needed supplies. The men took stock of the previous day and night and braced themselves for the final taking of Goose Green. They thought about the dead and injured and wondered if they would survive the following day. Some prayed, they thought about their loved ones and promised to be better people when they got home.

The following day, after being offered the opportunity to unconditionally surrender by leaving the township, the Argentinian garrison commander surrendered and his men formed up, removed their helmets, and lay down their weapons. It soon became apparent that 450 paras had overcome a force of over 1,000 Argentinians during the battle for Goose Green.

While 2 Para were in the midst of battle on the isthmus, 3 Para began to make their way on foot from San Carlos to Port Stanley, stopping off to regroup on their way to their first objective, Teal Inlet, around 30 miles away. Waiting near Port San Carlos, they had nicknamed the area 'Bomb Alley' after witnessing the aerial attacks on the port. As they waited, they prepared for their mission with gritty determination to succeed. Due to the distinct lack of air transport, the men had to TAB (tactical advance to battle) across the breadth of the island, encountering appalling uneven, rocky terrain and contending with the miserable weather conditions. Carrying huge loads on their backs, one guy stated that his Bergen weighed so much with the ammo and personal equipment that he was unable to get up on his own and had to be pulled to his feet by his mate; this was a familiar tale. They set off with enough supplies to last them three days.

Known to the men as the Long March, many were exhausted, others sustained injuries on the ankle-breaking ground, and some were suffering from exposure. They didn't encounter any Argentinians; for now, they were battling the elements. It was more like something from the First World War than modern warfare. The sodden, marshy ground seeped into the impractical boots and both trench foot and frostbite got to some of the guys. The warm kit they were issued, consisting of hand-me-downs from a previous operation, was totally inadequate for the climate, and usually fell to pieces. All of the men had experienced the Brecon Beacons, a tough and testing locality where men have died from exposure, but that was nothing compared to the numbing, whipping winds, blizzards, and incessant rainfall that these men had to endure even before they began fighting. The battalion pushed on across the hideous terrain, making rapid progress and hell-bent on getting to their goal. They made it through sheer will power and dogged determination, not knowing what was to come or when the ordeal would be over. Teal Inlet was undefended, and they moved on another 20 miles to make base at Estancia House and waited for their assault on Mount Longdon in the range of mountains surrounding Port Stanley.

They were shattered, their bodies aching and shivering, their clothes permanently damp or wet. Hunger gnawed at them after surviving on half rations for the march and they had the constant niggle of what lay ahead. In the back of their minds was the knowledge that they would soon be required to fight. During the march, word had spread through the ranks of 2 Para's victorious battle for Goose Green, the death of the commanding officer and the number of casualties they had sustained. They had also heard about an appalling incident when the Argentinians had not honoured their own white flag, and consequently three members of 2 Para had been shot dead and one injured whilst going forward to engage in negotiations. This news only made the men of 3 Para even more determined to win their own impending battle at Mount Longdon and gain revenge on behalf of their sister battalion for this cowardly act.

After a few cancelled moves, the order was given for the attack and the rifle companies of 3 Para moved off to get to their start lines at the base of Mount Longdon in the darkness of night with their objectives clear. However, the start time was delayed as the companies struggled to cross the Murrell River. A makeshift bridge had been laid down over the crossing point consisting of ladders with a board on top. The men were slipping and sliding across the board with their heavy loads; some guys fell into the freezing, fast-flowing waters below and had to be hauled out, half-drowned.

Using their characteristic ability to improvise, they got rid of the boards and made their way along the ladders more successfully. The spearhead company reached the start point and were ordered to fix bayonets. Knowing what this meant, the men filled with adrenalin and fear of what lay ahead. This was it; this was what all the blokes had been trained for. This was the ultimate test. The mountain range was teeming with Argentinians waiting in well-prepared defensive positions protected by rocky walls and occupying the high ground. The men prepared to start just after midnight and strode silently towards the mountainside to get as close as possible to their various targets without being noticed.

Frost lay on the ground and misty clouds of breath hung in the cold air. It was -10°C, but the vicious wind gave a chill factor of almost 30° less as the men tried to control their breathing and moved stealthily forward under the cover of darkness. Suddenly, an explosion followed by an agonised scream broke the silence as Corporal Brian Milne from 'B' Company, the lead in the assault, stepped on an anti-personnel mine. The silent advance to contact immediately erupted into a cacophony of mayhem. The men in the minefield froze, those further away ran for cover in the rocks at the base of the mountain as the Argentinians reacted and opened fire with all guns blazing. Contrary to previous reckoning, the Argentinians were well equipped, and their response was intense and aggressive. In the minefield, a medic arrived for Milne, whose leg had been torn off, while the other men moved quickly in single files to the relative safety of the rocky slope ahead. There were no further detonations.

The Argentinians began putting down effective fire; it was clear that they had the benefit of night sights. The men in the lead sections found that they had inadvertently passed by some of the Argentine positions prior to first contact being initiated, and now found themselves fighting in both directions, desperately trying to gain a foothold in the battle and clear the enemy positions closest to them. Fire ricocheted off the rocks and mortars pounded and churned the earth all around their positions. Machine guns blazed and snipers got to work cutting down the men at every opportunity. When they caught sight of a guy out in the open and away from hard cover, or even just a body part sticking out from behind a rock, they fired bullets that ripped through unprotected flesh. There were stories of guys holding helmets up on rifle barrels trying to draw the snipers' fire, then when the helmet was blown away, their muckers could home in on the enemy muzzle flashes and take them out. None of the Paras had body armour, and the airborne helmets they were using had no Kevlar on them and were about as useful as a bicycle crash helmet, offering no real protection from high-velocity rounds.

Despite the confusion with men getting separated from their sections and platoons in the mayhem of battle, the blokes managed to team up with each other and pushed on, moving back and to the side as they came under fire from all angles and fought to find a way through and up the mountain towards their objective.

Held down by enemy fire but knowing that eventually they would sustain casualties if they stayed put, Corporal McLaughlin, commander of one of the lead 'B' Company sections, stood up on the mountainside in the face of incoming fire. 'Follow me lads, I'm fucking bulletproof,' he called out to his guys and bravely led them forward in a charge to successfully take an enemy position. Spread across the slopes, the Paras fought valiantly as red and green tracers bounced off rocks and shouts and calls were lost in the deafening roar of guns and mortars. Men were prepared to sacrifice their own lives to protect the brothers by their side or help the injured as they pushed relentlessly on, sometimes barely able to see a few feet in front of their hands.

The men of 3 Para finally took the top of the mountain but there were Argentinians holding out on all the surrounding ridges and they were met with heavy artillery and SF (Sustained Fire) machine guns. Often, they found themselves in exposed ground and ran for shelter, but their cover didn't last long as they were identified and targeted again. On occasions this cover was in the areas they had cleared. Colour Sergeant (Retired) Colin 'Taff' Edwards was a lance corporal and Corporal McLaughlin's 2iC (second in command):

> Somehow in the mayhem, I got separated from my gun team, but met up with two guys from other sections, Terry Mulgrew and a young lad called Tony. The three of us found ourselves up against a rock face with a big gap and a large sloping rock. From the other side of the rock and about fifteen metres away we could see gunfire being directed towards 4 Platoon who were still making their way out of the minefield. Me and Terry crept as far forward as we could, and we could see the bunker where the muzzle flashes were coming from. I had one grenade left (we were all issued with two). I pulled the pin and threw it and I heard it go off, but the firing continued. I asked the other two if they still had their grenades. Tony said he still had his, so I told him to get up where I had been and to throw them at the bunker. He replied, 'You do it Corporal, you're a PTI and got bigger arms,' at which all three

of us had a chuckle. I climbed back to the gap in the sloping rock and threw the two grenades, one after the other. As soon as the second one went off, we dashed through the gap and took cover in the rocks which formed the front of the bunker only to find that me and Terry were in the 'shit pit' that the occupants of the bunker had been using as their toilet. It stank and we were both covered in toilet paper. 'For Fuck's Sake!' I spluttered, and chuckled. Terry mentioned that he was gasping for a fag, so we crawled into the now silenced bunker where there were two dead Argentinians inside. We took this opportunity to have a quick smoke until we heard Scouse shouting for us to re-org on him, so we doused our fags and made our way to the voice.[4]

Once again, they were all together as a section, but they were still pinned down. Taff followed Scouse to see if they could find a way forward and as they passed a rock concealing another bunker, an Argentinian soldier pointed his weapon out towards where the rest of the section was trapped. Taff said, 'Scouse shot him in the head at point blank range and I was splattered with blood, he was that close. So, in the space of ten minutes, I had been covered in shit and blood.'[5]

On a recce to ascertain the position of an enemy .50-calibre machine gun that was preventing the men from moving, a platoon commander was hit and taken out of action. Now in charge, Sergeant Ian Mckay made a snap command decision to go in for the attack and take the enemy post. Knowing that he was running into oncoming fire, he bravely continued forward and managed to throw some grenades, but he was killed as he came to the lip of the trench. The men behind rallied and pushed up under a barrage of bullets, and despite sustaining further casualties, they kept on going under covering fire and took the position. Sergeant McKay was posthumously awarded the Victoria Cross for his actions that night.

The platoons pressed on, engaging the Argentinians over and over again as they emerged from everywhere. The men moved and cleared, overcoming areas despite the Argentinians having the advantage of the upper ground and their snipers with night sights picking them off with fatal accuracy. Voices shouted out across the booming light show announcing someone was down. Swearing and taking the piss out of each other, they fought on, even laughing when one cried out that he'd first been hit in the arse by a sniper and then again by shrapnel from a grenade. Talking to their mate one minute, they turned to see him take a bullet through the head and slump over, dead. They risked their lives pulling or carrying injured men to safety with bullets bouncing off the rocks around them before returning to their task. It was a gruesome, drawn-out battle as the men engaged in close-quarter fighting and bodies lay strewn across the frozen, stark, and desolate hillside.

With discussions and plans being made and changed constantly, communications sometimes went down when radios were hit, or signallers were lost. There was confusion and chaos, men were separated from their teams in the pitch black, the platoons were held down by incoming shells and terrific firepower from all around the mountainside, but they never lost control. Strong support from HMS *Avenger* offshore initially ripped the enemy apart but that came to an end when it was called away to assist two ships that had been hit. The Paras continued to fight on, aiming their guns at muzzle flashes and eventually a Milan team came in and fired missiles at the enemy targets that had been causing carnage.

Medics set up first aid posts and were immediately called in for the mounting casualties. Some had to skirt around the minefield to get to 'B' Company and all of them came under fire on the slopes as they made their way towards their fallen comrades. Flashes and bangs, the thwack of bullets hitting solid bodies, tracer lights tracking across the sky and the interminable clatter of machine gun fire mingled with shouts of anger and screams of pain as they ran up the slopes to where injured men lay dying. With bayonets fixed, they fought their way up the ravaged mountainside to get to their airborne brothers and then fought their way out again. Men lay with their limbs torn off telling the medics to tend to the mate next to them first. Drips were put in and morphine administered but they had to watch as the life faded from the eyes of a few they couldn't save, and they listened to tough men calling for their mothers. It was heart-breaking stuff, but this was what the blokes had signed up for and their training and skills took over.

The fighting went on throughout the long, dark night, the tremendous noise of fire and shells seemingly endless as the shattered and depleted lead platoons stood firm. Under covering fire, guys carried the injured and dead back to the temporary base sheltered by rocks, and more were injured and killed as they risked their lives to help their fellow men. The numerous wounded struggled to cling on to life and not all made it while they waited hours for casevac (Casualty Evacuation). The rest of the blokes looked worn and years older; they wiped away tears and tried to keep warm as they came to terms with the deaths of their mates and the reality of war.

Paras from the other platoons came through and began to put heavy fire down on the opposition. They moved forward clearing positions, lobbing grenades into trenches or bunkers and then jumping in with bayonets ready. The Argentinians realised that they were overwhelmed and began to surrender Mount Longdon. When the first light of morning came, the men pushed forward to the final objective, skirmishing all the way up the slopes until the Argentinians turned and began running down the hill. The Paras went in hot pursuit, but they were abruptly called back as it became clear that the Argentinians had given up and were not going to counter-attack. Through pure implacability and bravery, 3 Para had won out against the odds and finally had control of Mount Longdon.

However, it was not over, and it was not long before a bombardment started that was to last for the next two days. As soldiers, we know that when you set up a defensive position you automatically set up DF (Defensive Fire) locations. When you are forced to retreat, your support weapons, such as heavy machine guns, mortars and artillery can quickly hit these pre-defined areas as they are taken over by the enemy. This is what then happened on Mount Longdon. Once the Argentinians had left their defensive positions and had run back towards Port Stanley, their support weapons began attacking their previous posts now occupied by paratroopers.

The guys were told to quickly dig in and make use of what positions the Argentinians had left, if safe to do so. This feature had been hard won and a lot of the men had given their lives in the taking of it. The men of 3 Para would be damned rather than give it up, even if they were being heavily bombarded. At this point the Guards had still not taken Mount Tumbledown, and enemy heavy artillery positions and rockets from Tumbledown as well as in and around Port Stanley were still in range to fire at Mount Longdon. One of these rockets tragically killed Corporal Stuart McLaughlin and the battalion sustained several other fatalities and injuries during this forty-eight-hour period of heavy bombardment.

Further south, as 3 Para started digging in on Mount Longdon, 2 Para moved up for a second full-on battle on Wireless Ridge. Joining 3 Para in the mountains with an aim of establishing clear routes into Port Stanley, this time they had much more support and the advantage of a troop of light armour Scimitars and Scorpions with night sights.

On 11 June, 2 Para flew up from Bluff Cove and Fitzroy on choppers and now under the command of their new commanding officer, Lieutenant Colonel David Chaundler, they tabbed into an assembly area and arrived on 12 June in preparation for the assault on Wireless Ridge. Those in 2 Para were also on standby to support their sister battalion on Mount Longdon if the situation should warrant it. Their mission was to join 3 Para in the mountains with an aim of establishing clear routes into Port Stanley. In all likelihood, the Welsh Guards would have been tasked with this attack, but they had been tragically decimated at Fitzroy when their ship, *Sir Galahad*, had been blown up. The men of 2 Para were ready and keen to get involved again and wanted to be there when they moved into Port Stanley.

First orders were cancelled, and the men of 2 Para spent a night in the raw, stinging cold watching and listening as 3 Para fought through on Mount Longdon, and waiting for the go-ahead to move on Wireless Ridge. They moved onto their start line, ready to go into action once 3 Para had secured their targets, with the aim of obtaining four positions consecutively. They were to come into each position from different directions to confuse the enemy and supporting fire was meant to add to the distraction by putting down a huge amount of shelling before the men went forward.

During the final set of orders and just before H-Hour, it became apparent that a minefield was blocking their route, but it was too late to change. The non-commissioned officers were told not to tell the Toms about this. As Colour Sergeant (Retired) Paul (Bish) Bishop, a lance corporal in 'B' Company at the time said, 'We went straight back and told the Toms. There is no way you're not going to pass on info like that to the blokes. Either way we were still going through it, but the guys needed to know what they were walking into.'[6] Now knowing that a minefield lay in front of them, the decision was made to advance in single file, each guy hoping that the path they had chosen was away from any anti-personnel mines, and if they were honest, that they would not be the one to be blown up.

With 'A' and 'B' Companies on the left flank, 'D' Company moved forward to take their first objective, which was just under Mount Longdon and which in the end was taken without too much enemy resistance. The 12 Platoon Sergeant, John Meredith (Captain Retired), explained, 'The Argies had legged it, so we moved through quite quickly and then went onto the ridge itself with an aim of moving down and clearing it of enemy as we went with artillery and mortars in support providing fire missions out in front of us.'[7]

'B' Company moved up to their target feature supported by the Scimitars firing into likely enemy positions and came across what looked like an Argentinian sangar, which they were ordered to clear. As Bish said, 'When we went firm at our first objective, we were tasked to clear what looked like an enemy HQ position. Several grenades were thrown in, and guys, keen to get involved, were continuing to lob more and more into the target until someone got a torch out and shouted, "Stop!" There were loads of 105mm shells lying up the side, which were likely to go off at any time if they were not careful.'[8] 'B' Company then went firm and attempted to dig in, this time with tools that had been binned for the Goose Green attack in a bid to lighten their loads. They ended up being shelled for the rest of the night by enemy artillery based in Stanley. The men could hear the rounds being fired, then the whizz in the air followed by the loud explosion as they landed in and around their positions. In the end, the guys managed to judge the time it took for the rounds to land after being fired and perfectly timed their fag breaks between the barrages of fire.

'A' and 'B' Company went firm in their positions, and it was 'D' Company, this time with less support than they had been promised, who started to move down Wireless Ridge, and the real chaos and confusion, which are the trademarks of war, came into play. Supporting artillery logged incorrect co-ordinates and fired on the wrong target, landing in and amongst the Paras, killing one man and injuring another; it could have been much worse. New co-ordinates were entered but they were wrong again and this time the fire just missed 'B' Company. A pause in fire left the men waiting anxiously for the guns to be reloaded with the proper adjustments. As they carefully moved forward, an illume went off and the Argentinians were alerted to their presence in the west, and not the north as they had been expecting. The enemy turned all their weapons and let rip on the Paras, killing one and injuring others. The men of 12 Platoon dived for cover, returning fire, but they didn't stay down for long. They got back up and charged forward down the ridge with such energy and aggression that when they reached their target and LOE (Limit of Exploitation), they saw the Argentinians hotfooting it away. They were told to go firm at this point as SF were supposed to be making their way up the other side of the isthmus. However, due to not being able to land, they never arrived.

John Meredith said:

> We took the enemy position, occupying what cover we could find, and I told our GPMG gunner who had a night sight to take a look over the ridge to see if there was any more enemy. He said with horror that there were fuckin' hundreds of them! So, I told him to open fire and all hell broke loose. We fought off three counter-attacks before dawn broke. One got so close that the enemy were throwing grenades at us, so we brought artillery fire in, which dropped just in front of our positions. In the morning the blokes quickly assessed the fire positions that they found themselves in, and hastily moved to more suitable cover. When the officer commanding came round on his own during a lull between counter-attacks, I politely told him to fuck off, as he would only draw unwanted fire down onto us, so off he trotted.[9]

The men of 2 Para continued to put fire down on the fleeing Argentinians and any opportune targets that were in range, such as an enemy helicopter that was on the ground near Moody Brooke. A Tom who had carried a heavy 84mm on his back the entire conflict, put a round straight through the doors of this chopper, which drew a loud laugh from his muckers and got him some stick. Cease fire was eventually called as it was obvious that the Argies running away were not fighting back and the fire was now attracting heavy shelling on their own position from the enemy artillery in Stanley and what was left around Tumbledown. The Paras now looked down on Port Stanley and realised that the next mission would be to move down quickly and take the capital before the Argentinians could reorganise themselves. The greatest fear now for the men of 2 Para was that they just didn't have enough support, supplies or ammo to make another assault and could well get drawn into a protracted FIBUA (Fighting in Built-up Areas) battle for the capital. However, as the sun came up, they were greeted by the welcome sight of dejected Argentinian soldiers flooding away from their positions, and they knew that it was all but over at this point. The enemy had lost too many of their comrades and their will to fight had been broken. Once the official surrender of the Argentine forces had been confirmed, the race to Port Stanley was on.

The men of 2 Para on Wireless Ridge were the first to make a move, shortly followed by their brothers in 3 Para on Mount Longdon, who had removed their helmets and replaced them with their maroon berets as they made their way down the slopes past the half-frozen, twisted, broken bodies of their foe lying across the mountainside. They walked slowly into the devastated capital of Port Stanley to be met by surrendering soldiers, the smell of cordite and burning buildings.

The Para Regt played a pivotal role in the conflict with two battalions fighting, and eventually winning the momentous, bloody, and heroic battles at Goose green, Wireless Ridge and Mount Longdon. Despite being vastly outnumbered and outgunned, they were finally able to enter Port Stanley. Both battalions had achieved victory through pure aggression, skill, and that never give up Para Regt attitude after engaging in some of the bloodiest and toughest hand-to-hand fighting since the Second World War. Ultimately, they had physically and psychologically destroyed the spirit of the much larger enemy force and written themselves into the history books forever. 'A' Company, 2 Para were the first troops into Stanley and proudly raised the Union Jack once again, officially reclaiming the Falkland Islands.

Whilst waiting for the move home to commence, the paratroopers spent the next few days bunkered up in the houses in Stanley and enjoying a few well-earned beers when the local pub reopened. Toasting their fallen brothers, they quietly breathed a sigh of relief. Over forty men were killed, and numerous others injured during this conflict.

John Meredith was awarded a DCM for taking charge and continuing the attack on Goose Green after his platoon commander was killed, combined with his efforts on Wireless Ridge. In total, two Victoria Crosses, two Distinguished Service Orders, five Military Crosses, five Distinguished Conduct Medals, twelve Military Medals, thirty-four Mentions in Dispatches and an MBE were awarded to men both living and dead. Boys had become men in this baptism of fire; but in reality, the guys didn't want medals or acclaim, they just wanted to honour and remember their mates who had made the ultimate sacrifice on behalf of our great country. Once again, the Paras reminded us of their true worth, and the Class of '82 cemented their own place in the history of this famous regiment.

The soldiers arrived home to tremendous celebrations but there was little time to rest as the Troubles in Northern Ireland persisted.

# Chapter 14

# The Troubles Continue

## Northern Ireland, 1982–2007

The men of 1 Para were mightily disappointed not to be involved in the Falklands War and got some heavy stick from the other battalions for not being there, but the situation in Northern Ireland was still keeping them very busy and 2 and 3 Para were soon back on tours in the Province. Terrorists continued to cause havoc throughout the 1980s as the soldiers went out on patrols and put their lives on the line every day. Towards the end of the decade and moving into the '90s the Paras were thrust into a period of sustained activity in Northern Ireland.

In 1989, 3 Para deployed to West Belfast to take over an area called Woodbourne. This was the start of a continuous period of operations by Para Regt in a bid to take control of the area, which had got out of hand and had become a hotbed of terrorist activity. The unit was followed by 1 Para two years later and then 2 Para after them. Eventually, over a seven-year period, the regiment achieved their aim and reduced the terrorist activities exponentially.

The longer tours meant that soldiers brought their families over to live in the country and although they were well-protected, they were still living with the threat of IEDs or being caught up in an attack when they went about their daily lives. Added to the stress of the job was the worry about the safety of their family. A lot of the single men got Irish girlfriends, attracted by the need for some love and home comforts when off duty. Some even went on to get married, often for the reason that they could move into married quarters that were more comfortable. However, the long hours and the stress of the job often tested the strength of these relationships, and a large percentage broke down. A soldier's marriage is a difficult one. They can't tell their wives about what they are doing or what they are experiencing due to operational secrecy and when something happens it is the other guys that they want to be with because only they can truly understand.

During these postings for an average of two to two and a half years, a battalion, broken down into four separate companies, split its time between specific roles, in a four-week cycle: Operations – Woodbourne – Leave –

Guards & Duties. Operations were run by the battalion ops room at Palace Barracks with a typical notice-to-move period of two to six hours and were mainly for carrying out escort details or short-term surge operations. Woodbourne was their bread and butter and on this rotation the men were based in the RUC station patrolling their primary AOR (area of responsibility) and supporting the RUC in maintaining law and order in West Belfast. Leave period consisted of R&R (Rest and Recuperation) for home leave and continuation training. Lastly, there was a Guards & Duties rotation around Palace Barracks, something that none of the blokes typically enjoyed as it entailed stagging on the camp, which was mind-numbingly boring.

West Belfast was the TAOR (Tactical Area of Responsibility) for Woodbourne RUC station and the rotational company was based there with the task of dominating the region. The station was responsible for the Lenadoon, Poleglass and Twinbrook estates, and Andersonstown, which was the area where signallers Howes and Wood were executed by the IRA in 1988, and they were all hardcore Republican areas. However, just outside the RUC station was the small Suffolk's Estate, known as 'The Oranges', which was made up of staunch Protestant families who refused to move or be intimidated out of their homes. Up until 3 Para arrived in the late 1980s, the area had been a stronghold for the Provisional IRA terrorist groups, and they had been able move around the area freely. Thanks to 3 Para some control had now been achieved over the district, but it was still rife with danger, and the police required close military support when carrying out day-to-day community policing to enforce the rule of law. At times there could be up to twenty soldiers securing the area for one policeman to complete his patrolling duties. Woodbourne Police station was heavily fortified and protected due to the number of attacks it had come under over the years, but it was still very exposed, particularly when patrols were going in and out of the station.

On 18 November 1989, the men from 'A' Company 3 Para had been deployed down to the Rathfriland area and were making their way through Mayobridge in a two-vehicle patrol, not far from Warrenpoint. As the lead vehicle passed an old chapel, a massive command-wire-initiated device believed to be a 400lb bomb in a gas cylinder was detonated at the side of the road. An RUC sergeant at a nearby checkpoint reported hearing a dull thud followed by a cloud of dust and then a huge blast. Everything went into slow motion as the armoured Land Rover lifted up into the air and flew off the road. The men inside were ravaged by the explosion and three were killed but the fourth survived. Thrown out the top of the vehicle by the force of the blast and seriously wounded, he was kept alive by members of the patrol from the second vehicle.

On the same tour, Richard Stacey was based on rotation in Woodbourne. Stacey is a well-respected and typical old-school Para, now owner of the famous, and last remaining, Para pub in Aldershot called the Trafalgar Inn, he is also one of the founders of the Parachute Regiment and Airborne Forces Memorial Group, who do such good work supporting ex-Para families within the airborne community. He was on duty in West Belfast when he fell foul of the IRA tactics:

> I was on foot patrol along the Suffolk Path linking with the Poleglass estate and at the time I was giving a new NCO some ground orientation during a handover. I was just pointing out the Gallic Football Club, when I heard what was like a click, and thought oh fuck! I found out later it was the detonation of a command-wire IED. As the blast hit me, I was blown around forty feet to where I landed on the ground. Before the realisation of my injuries hit me, the first thing I told the guys was to get some photos, a typical Para Regt reaction. Shortly afterwards, I felt myself slipping away down what I remember as a white tunnel and saying to the guys, 'I'm going now.' Next thing I remember, I was smashed on the chest, which brought me round. I opened my eyes and said, 'Who the fuck are you?' and he told me he was RUC. He was there along with my mate Stef, who was also looking down at me. I clearly remember that the blokes brought a stretcher down and as they carted me off towards the ambulance, I could hear the screaming and banging of dustbin lids as the local people came out onto the doorsteps to cheer and clap that they had got one, i.e., taken out one of the Paras! So, despite my injuries I was annoyed with the chanting, so I shouted, 'Fuck off, you ain't got me,' and then I started singing the national anthem, banging out the line, 'God save our gracious queen, you haven't got me you IRA bastards!' in defiance. I sustained shrapnel injuries to the legs, arm, arse and balls, and the back of my head was blown out. I know that if it was not for the Airborne helmet I was wearing, I would not be here today. The lid held my skull together until they could get me to hospital where they operated for twelve hours on my injuries and miraculously saved my life.[1]

After a hard year of rehabilitation at Headley Court, Richard Stacey felt as though he was now malingering but then the opportunity was presented for him to go to the Para depot in Aldershot as an instructor. He grabbed this

Second World War parachute training at Hardwick Hall.

North Africa 1943, Vickers machine gun team.

Arnhem September 1944, fighting through the streets.

June 1944, briefing prior to Normandy jump.

Indonesia 1945, at the halfway house.

Palestine 1946, peacekeeping duties.

Malaya 1954, crossing a river on jungle patrol.

Cyprus 1955, observing the ground situation in the search for EOKA.

Suez 1956, last airborne assault onto El Gamil airport.

Radfan 1964, deploying in by Wessex helicopter onto a high feature.

Borneo 1965, Plaman Mapu the day after the battle.

Aldershot 1987, P Company log run.

Catterick 2018, P Company Trainasium recruits look up at the shuffle bars.

Parachuting from a C-130 Hercules, port and starboard para doors.

Northern Ireland in the late 1970s, early days of the Troubles.

Belfast 1989, Corporal Stacey receiving treatment after being blown up by an IED.

Northern Ireland 1990s, 3 Para Tom on top cover.

Belfast 1995, First beret patrol as the peace process commenced.

Falklands May 1982, coming ashore in San Carlos Bay.

Falklands June 1982, 2 Para on Wireless Ridge after taking the feature.

Kosovo July 1999, 1 Para on patrol in the capital, Pristina.

Sierra Leone May 2000, Op Palliser with 1 Para, plus elements of 2 Para.

Sierra Leone 2000, Op Barras hostage rescue mission, reorg on Magbeni village.

Kabul 2002, Op Fingal 2 Para observation post on TV hill.

Kuwait Fort Pegasus March 2003, 1 Para training prior to crossing the Iraq border.

Iraq 2003, Paras taking control of the British Embassy in Baghdad.

Afghanistan 2006, Musa Qala Pathfinder outpost.

Afghanistan 2006, Herrick IV, Kajaki Dam team a few days prior to the minefield incident.

Afghanistan 2008, Herrick VIII, Bruneval Company, 2 Para defending FOB Gibraltar.

Kabul 2021, Op Pitting 2 Para assisting the local Afghan people.

Kabul 2021, Op Pitting. The iconic sign used by registered evacuees to attract the Paras' attention.

Baghdad Crossed Swords 2005, ABF get together for private security contractors.

with both hands and achieved a distinction on his acceptance cadre. He took two platoons through training before returning to 3 Para to hit the streets of Belfast once again.

In 1990, shortly before the end of the 3 Para tour, there was a tragic incident, which resulted in the shooting and killing of two teenage joyriders on the Glen Road, West Belfast. Joyriding occurrences were becoming more and more frequent around this time and in March 1989, 3 Para had lost one of their own when he was killed by a joyrider while on foot patrol on the Falls Road. Youths were stealing and driving cars at fast speeds towards the checkpoints, testing the reactions of the soldiers, and thinking it was fun. Generally high on alcohol and drugs, they raced towards police and military checkpoints late at night and failed to stop when clearly challenged to do so. Several soldiers had experienced close shaves in the weeks leading up to this incident. On many occasions, the cars appeared to swerve towards the paratroopers as they passed through the clearly marked checkpoints. The security forces had no idea who was driving these vehicles, it could be terrorists looking to ship weapons and munitions around late at night under the cover of darkness, high-profile IRA personalities attempting to avoid detection, a player using the vehicle as a weapon, or, as in this case, just youths joyriding.

One of the paratroopers who opened fire on this night was subsequently convicted in 1993 at Belfast crown court for murder. The Para, who fired four shots at the car, said he had done so because he had feared for the safety of his fellow soldiers. The judge at his original trial convicted him of murder based purely on the fact that he had fired his final shot through the back of the car when 'the joyriders no longer presented a direct threat to the Paratroopers as it passed through at high speed'. The case became one of the most politically sensitive in Northern Ireland at the time, and a campaign was launched in 1994 to exonerate him. He was finally cleared of all criminal wrongdoing over the shooting of the two joyriders and went on to continue serving his country. Making a split decision in a moment of duress and believing that the people in the car were a clear threat, the soldier acted to defend himself and those around him.

The Paras were never really safe, even when off duty. The savage and cowardly murder of Private Tony Harrison was proof of this. On 19 June 1991, Harrison was watching television at his girlfriend's home in East Belfast. Happy and relaxed, he was there on leave to make plans for their wedding. All of a sudden, two IRA men burst into the room and shot him in the back five times as his fiancée, her mother and a 10-year-old girl looked on in horror. His cowardly murder demonstrated the lengths that the terrorists would go to kill a Para. There was no boundary of morality or honour that these people adhered to in this so-called 'war'.

Needless to say, tensions were high when 1 Para took over from 3 Para in 1991. On the anniversary of internment, it was traditional for Republicans to 'demonstrate' and on this particular night, nearly a year into the 1 Para tour, a platoon was patrolling the Lenadoon area near what was known as the Big Five. This was five tall blocks of flats at the top of the hill that dominated and overlooked the entire local area. Lenadoon was a staunch Republican and IRA-supporting estate and had become famous way back in 1972 when 'The Battle of Lenadoon' took place. This was a series of gunfights over six days from 9 to 14 July between the Provisional IRA and the British Army in and around the Lenadoon Avenue area. Twenty-eight people were reported to have been killed during this time, ending a two-week truce between the forces of the British government and the IRA. Since then, Lenadoon had not changed much and was home to many known, high-ranking IRA terrorists and was a tough and dangerous place to patrol.

A huge bonfire had been built down the hill on the waste ground above a community centre and it was just a case of when, not if, it would all kick off. As the teams of paratroopers moved down the avenue towards the community centre, a mob started to descend on them carrying wooden pallets and throwing stones and bricks. The Paras moved quickly down the avenue to where they managed to RV around the community centre building.

The light was fading as more and more local youths joined the crowd, which was becoming increasingly aggressive towards the soldiers. Molotov cocktails began raining down on the guys, along with an assortment of bricks and other missiles. The mob used the wooden pallets as protection as they strode forward to get in range of the defensive line held up on each side of the centre. The rioters were organised, and they advanced as one well-drilled unit holding up the pallets as shields and then opening them out to throw their chosen missiles at the Paras before retreating with the pallets back in front of them. Colour Sergeant (Retired) Justin 'Sam' Salmon, a corporal in 5 Platoon 'B' Company and a highly experienced and respected junior non-commissioned officer, was out on patrol that night:

> I clearly remember that as we battled with the rioters alongside the guys from 4 Platoon who joined us at the community centre, the local drunk was walking down Horn Drive. He walked right through the riot, which by this time was in full swing, with bricks, rocks and petrol bombs raining down all over the place. I remember watching as he passed through the middle of the melee, and not a single missile,

Molotov cocktail or plastic bullet hit him, nor even came near. It was as if he had a protective force-field around him. It was quite funny at the time, took the edge off the situation for a few seconds, and is still engraved in my memory![2]

The situation became more tense, and the decision was made to utilise the baton guns. Plastic bullets were fired in volleys at the wooden pallets with the aim of stopping the rioters from getting any closer, and to disperse the crowd, but it wasn't working, and they were getting low on ammunition. Just in the nick of time, the QRF from Woodbourne turned up, consisting of more paratroopers as well as the RUC special response units who were known as The Blues.

Following their training in the UK, the Paras worked as a well-drilled team to fire volleys of rubber bullets at the mob and when the main perpetrators went down and the mob retreated, snatch teams bravely rushed forward, grabbed hold of these individuals, and dragged them back through the lines. The RUC then arrested them and shipped them off in the wagons to the police station.

The Paras and police held their lines for around five hours with the constant threat that at any time the IRA could open up with live ammunition. This had happened many times in the past in the Province and one of their favourite techniques of attacking the army and the police was using their own crowds and people as cover. Finally, the rubber bullets and mounting number of arrests deterred the attackers, and the crowd started to slowly disperse. More rubber bullets were fired that night at the Lenadoon Community Centre than in the previous five years of the Troubles.

In 1993, Richard Stacey joined 2 Para on their tour of the Province, and eventually took a job in the HQNI (Head Quarters Northern Ireland) Int cell, where he put his previous experience and knowledge of the area to good use in the New Lodge AOR:

Whilst on patrol with the 17th/21st Lancers on Spar Mount Street, Belfast, we came under fire from the window of a house, and the RMP (Royal Military Police) girl who was with us got hit three times by AK47 rounds. Within seconds I was close enough to react, and cocking my SA80, I dived through the window of the firing point, landed on a sofa and then ran out the back into the alley way. I apprehended a guy attempting to lock the back door and get away. I also got hold of a second suspected terrorist and handed them both over to the RUC. They were subsequently charged and convicted as part of the terrorist operation look out system, commonly known as dickers. I then secured the AK47 which had been used in the attack and began clearing the area as the incident support agencies started to turn up. The most bizarre thing then happened. Out of nowhere, I spotted a guy hastily walking towards me wearing a Para Helmet. I recognised him and said, 'Davis, is that you?', 'Yes, Stace,' he replied. He was an EOD (Explosive Ordnance Disposal) officer and came from the same part of London as me. He quickly made sure that everyone knew not to go near the building and firing point again and helped to establish a cordon. Within what seemed like seconds, bang! A secondary device went up covering several of us, who were still relatively close, in dust and rubble. Luckily, and thanks to Davis's warning, there were no injuries. The terrorist plan was clearly to lure the security forces into the building where the shooting took place. The second device had been planted on the sofa that I had landed on in front of the window. On a timer, it was expected that a number of personnel would go into the building after the shooting and the bomb was designed to cause maximum fatalities and injuries.'[3] Stacey was to later be Mentioned in Dispatches for gallantry, with regards to his actions that day.

The IRA continued with their campaign both in Northern Ireland and on mainland Britain with more than 10,000 bomb attacks between 1968 and 1998. They killed over 2,000 soldiers and civilians and maimed many more before peace negotiations began to make progress. However, while in the 1970s and '80s the mission was 'to kill or capture the IRA', in the 1990s events led to changes in the overall atmosphere of the region and the success of a tour began to be measured not only by those killed or captured by front-line forces, but by the number of complaints against a unit.

In 1995 1 Para were in Belfast when the word came through that they were to move from hard-patrolling techniques to a softer approach. The number of troops in the region decreased after the Good Friday Agreement in 1998 and after the final decommissioning of IRA weapons in 2005 the forces gradually moved out, with the last troops leaving in 2007. Due to both the Good Friday agreement and ceasefire, helmets were swapped for the famous maroon beret and the British press covered these first, and now famous, patrols on the street as the start to the end of the Troubles commenced.

Lance Corporal (Retired) John Campbell was raised in the staunch Protestant area of Shankill, East Belfast. A battalion personality well-liked by his peers, he was on patrol with the Anti Tanks Platoon on the Falls Road:

> We didn't really know exactly what was going on at the time of the peace agreement. The intelligence and briefings we were receiving were not keeping up with the pace of the quickly evolving situation, and the locals seemed to know more about what was happening than us. A few of the locals stopped us, asked why we were still patrolling the street, and said, 'Mr, you should not be here.' Apparently, it had been reported on the news that troops were to cease daytime patrolling. As paratroopers we still felt we had a job to do and were told to swap helmets for berets in an effort to soften our profile. I was as surprised as anyone when I walked around the corner to be confronted by a horde of tabloid press and news reporters, snapping away at us. The guys' view on the situation was simple, we were worried that all our hard work and risks taken over the years, could be for nothing if the terrorists were now to be given carte blanche to roam the streets again with no active deterrent to stop them.[4]

The Parachute Regiment was one of the British government's most used assets throughout the Troubles in Northern Ireland. The Paras became stalwarts throughout the campaign and were an ever-present pillar of strength and unbreakable support. Even after some of the horrific attacks and losses sustained by them at the hands of the Republican terrorists throughout their thirty-seven years of service within the Province, they remained steadfast and resilient.

The Paras are highly trained in prevention and pre-emption tasks, as utilised within the region. Professionalism, resilience, discipline, versatility, courage, and self-reliance sum up the regiment's philosophy when operating in Northern Ireland and saw them receive over forty gallantry awards, including the George Cross for Sergeant Willetts, 180 honours and commendations, and sixty MiDs (Mentioned in Dispatches), in this, the longest campaign in the history of airborne forces.

There have been many criticisms of the Paras' methods, particularly regarding Bloody Sunday, with a few uninformed people making comments suggesting that paratroopers were unsuited to the conditions in Northern Ireland because they are trained to be 'aggressive killers' and cannot control themselves in these types of environments. This shows a complete misunderstanding of who the Paras are and their ability to adapt to the environment in which they are deployed, their amazing self-discipline, personal honour, and empathy for the civilian communities around them. I can personally testify to this as I was a member of 1 Para in the 1990s in Northern Ireland and witnessed first-hand many of the events detailed above.

## Chapter 15

# Ethnic Cleansing

**Kosovo, 1999**

With tours in Northern Ireland still ongoing, 1 Para got the sudden call to deploy to Kosovo in the Balkans in June 1999. Bolstered by men from 3 Para to bring them up to full battalion strength, they headed off to the Macedonian border to begin preparations as the spearhead battalion ready to deploy into the neighbouring war-torn region under Operation Agricola. It was the only operation that the regiment carried out as part of the 5th Airborne Brigade, but they were ready for the task and began training with cool and professional heads. At this point they didn't know if events might lead to a full-scale invasion, and they prepared for all eventualities.

At the end of the Cold War, ethnic tension in the Republic of Yugoslavia raised its ugly head and during the 1990s horrific crimes against humanity were committed as separate regions fought for independence. Kosovo existed as a virtually autonomous province in Serbia with a large Albanian population living alongside Serbs. The President of what remained of Yugoslavia, who was based in Serbia, Slobodan Milosevic, not only wanted control of Kosovo but also wanted to get rid of the Albanian, largely Muslim, population in the province. Around 200,000 Albanians fled the country as a campaign of terror began. The KLA (Kosovan Liberation Army) rose up against the Yugoslav Army, Serbian paramilitary groups, and police but they could not prevent the programme of ethnic cleansing being put into force. Massacre, rape, and the total destruction of whole villages was taking place, while other Albanians were told to leave their homes, with no time to pack or prepare, and get out of the country. As many as 10,000 Albanians were killed and over a million were displaced. The world watched on in horror as war crimes including genocide were committed and streams of refugees made their way into neighbouring countries with barely more than the clothes on their backs. It was a humanitarian disaster.

After initial talks to persuade Milosevic to withdraw his troops failed, the UK government urged NATO to act and a bombing campaign on Serbian installations began. It was expected to take only a few days to force Milosevic to back down but, in the end, it went on for two and a half months. Over 1,000 planes carried out 38,000 missions over a period of seventy-eight days while Milosevic refused to stop, and in fact the oppression and brutality against Albanians increased.

The call went out for the Parachute Regiment to stand by and the men from 1 Para prepared for deployment. Demonstrating the ingrained Para Regt characteristics of tenacity, and the will to be involved, a small number of 1 Para had been sent to Bosnia earlier in the year and when they found out that their battalion was going into action in Kosovo, they wanted to be a part of it. Lance Corporal, at the time, now Sergeant (Retired) Andrew (Ghandi) Rutherford described how they managed to get themselves from Bosnia to the Petrovic army base in Macedonia where the rest of 1 Para had been sent to start preparations for mounting operations into Kosovo:

> We asked for permission to leave and head back to 1 Para, and the General in Bosnia called us and said that if our battalion gave the OK then we could go. Well, we had no way of communicating with the battalion, so we just told him that we'd been given the go-ahead. We then had to work out how to get there, as no support or transportation were forthcoming. We were in Banja Luka, and I knew it wasn't just a walk down the road and would take some major airborne initiative to get us there in time. There was a regular convoy taking troops to Split in Croatia for R & R but that took two days. A couple of us went into the quartermaster stores and I blagged myself some captain's pips. I put them on my uniform and then masquerading as a captain, I went to talk to the RAF. To my horror they e-mailed 1 Para HQ, enquiring about a certain Captain Rutherford, and we thought our cover would be blown and I could instead be heading to the prison, but to my surprise the reply came back saying that we could go. A Chinook came in and we got a lift straight down to Split. We now needed to get across to Macedonia, so I went into the ops room at the old, tiny airport in Split and in my best officer's voice I asked if there was any transport to Petrovic. They said a Puma was just coming in and so we jumped on that. Once the aircraft was up in the air, I took off the captain's pips so that I could resume my normal rank when we arrived and re-joined the battalion. I was hoping to get away with the blag once we had landed. One of the crew asked me what I was doing, and I came clean and told him that we had bluffed our way on. I knew that they would never have taken us if they knew we weren't officers. They looked at us in amazement and

shot a few choice words in my direction, but it was too late by then. I'm sure they saw the funny side; we definitely did. In Petrovic there were a few puzzled faces when they saw us back, but then I just slipped back in with 'C' Company and got on with the task in hand. I remember when the six of us involved were back in Aldershot after the Op had finished, General Jackson had heard of our exploits, and came down personally to present us with our medals. Nice touch, I thought.[1]

As part of the KFOR (Kosovo Force) in the NATO Joint Guardian Operation the Paras were training and preparing for what could be an invasion. They were soon given orders to move and were inserted by helicopter into a cornfield near to the border on fifteen-minute warning. They spent a few days checking their heavy equipment, carrying out exercises in the hot June sun, and waiting to get the go-ahead. Plans kept changing and they still didn't know if they would be going in to fight, keep the peace or just have the operation cancelled, which was not an option that the blokes wanted to hear. Talks continued and contingency plans were in place for the possibility of a full-scale invasion when Milosevic finally agreed to withdraw all Serbian forces from the region.

The Pathfinder Platoon is an integral part of 16 Air Assault Brigade, acting as its advance and reconnaissance force. Its role includes deploying prior to the main force, often by use of high-altitude, free-fall parachutes, then locating, marking, and securing drop zones and helicopter landing areas in preparation for airborne operations. Once the main force has landed, the Pathfinders then often deploy out in front of the parachute battalions providing tactical intelligence as well as specialist offensive action roles. As you can imagine, the selection process to join the elite Pathfinders is extreme and even though it is open to anyone to apply, the Pathfinders are predominantly made up from paratroopers serving in one of the three front-line battalions.

Small teams of Pathfinder troops, acting as the Brigade's advance and reconnaissance force, went in ahead of the main deployment to keep an eye on the departure of the Serb forces from small towns and villages. Sergeant (Retired) Tom Blakey recalled being inserted by helicopter into the middle of nowhere:

As the chopper rose up and disappeared, we suddenly realised that Serbian troops had been hiding in the trees. They emerged with heavy weaponry, tanks and armoured vehicles and we all held our breath. There was no way that we could take them on, so it was a bit of a balls in mouth moment. Luckily, they came forward in a friendly manner and soon began sharing their drink with us and laughing. They actually wanted to be with us for protection from any more air attacks. We reached a town and stopped but they carried on through and we began to get reports that they were setting fire to houses and buildings as they left. Before we knew it, there were US Apache helicopters flying over the area with guns pointed down at us. One of the guys quickly waved a British flag and we managed to avert a possible 'blue-on-blue' incident. We were getting some rest, taking turns to stag on, when we heard the crack of AK rounds going over our heads. We immediately went into a contact drill, breaking possible contact and setting up a snap ambush in a hedge line. This time it turned out to be KLA and fortunately we didn't execute the ambush, because we would have wiped them out. They claimed to be pursuing and shooting at Serbs and we got orders to check the village and clear out any remaining Serbian soldiers. I was lead scout as we made our way down the streets. I had no body armour and ahead of me were dark windows and doorways. I was literally waiting to get opened up on or shot, but luckily the gods were with me, and they had all gone by then.[2]

In all the villages they went through, the Pathfinders were greeted with smiling people, relieved to see them. The tragedy and horror of what these people had experienced was marked by numerous mass graves along the way.

The men of 1 Para made ready and waited for the green light to go in; their task was to clear the main road leading to the capital, Pristina, ready for the thousands of KFOR ground forces to follow them into the country. The route into the country was through the Kacanik defile. It was bordered by steep mountains with numerous tunnels and bridges, all of which could be hiding Serbian snipers, soldiers or booby traps. The whole area also contained minefields. The first task for the Paras was to make the route safe and contain any hard-line resistance fighters who had chosen not to give up the battle.

As the majority of Serbian forces withdrew to Serbia in the east, the Paras went in from the south into the Kacanik pass with an air-mobile helicopter insertion using Chinooks and Pumas. Pathfinder teams secured the landing zones and sappers began clearing the route of mines and checking tunnels and bridges for explosives. Andy Rutherford remembered carrying a Milan anti-tank weapon up a steep mountain to where they were going to set up a fire base, and then being called back down to a small village where they were then told they were going to spend the night. 'The village was completely empty, it was bizarre. Not a soul anywhere. We went into houses and saw signs of a rapid departure: pieces of food on the end of a fork, chairs tipped over where people had jumped up and rushed out, smashed glass was everywhere. Then, after we had been there for a few hours, all these people started descending from the mountainside. Once they realised that we were British and not Serbs they knew it was safe to return.'

Another force of paratroopers made rapid progress along the very basic, dusty road passing a few Kosovans in clapped-out motor cars or still using horses and carts. They passed fields in which they saw the simple, wooden posts poignantly marking mass graves, and villages with burned out houses still smoking. In one village a tactical team was called in to check out a local mosque for booby traps. Corporal at the time, Warrant Officer 2 (Retired) Joey Madden from 1 Para, said, 'It was a beautiful building, stunning. We took our boots off as a mark of respect and when we went in, we could see that it was a gorgeous old mosque with all the mosaic designs but there was blood splattered all over the place. It had been used as an aid station and that was when it really hit us: it had been really grim there.'

They kept to the road for fear of mines but on one occasion a soldier's beret blew off his head and landed in a field and without thinking he automatically chased after it. He retrieved it and returned to his section safely as the men stopped for a brew. The next minute there was a loud explosion; a cow had stepped on a mine in the same field and was now lying on the ground screaming in agony with one leg gone. After that the men kept their sacred berets safely in their smock pockets.

Suddenly news came through that the Russians based in Bosnia were coming in from the north and were making a move on Pristina airport. The Russians were old allies of communist Yugoslavia, and the Americans, in particular, were worried that they were there to support the Serbs. It was imperative that NATO forces got there first. The Paras were ordered to get to the airport as soon as possible to prevent the Russians from taking over the runways and using them to bring in reinforcements. Brigade Commander Adrian Freer ordered a group of men, to move quickly north.

Leaving their heavy Bergens behind with HQ, these paratroopers immediately began commandeering Pinzgauer military vehicles and, picking up various groups of men along the way, they raced towards Pristina and its airport. In the pouring rain they arrived to find that they were too late, and their path was blocked by Russian tanks placed across the roads leading onto the runways. The men stood, weapons made ready, staring down the Russians guarding the route, not sure whether everything was going to kick off. Suddenly, Brigadier Freer stepped towards the Russian soldiers on duty. Without fear or hesitation, and in a bizarre moment of comedy, he ripped open his smock to reveal a T-shirt that said 'Spetznaz' – the Russian word for Special Forces – and began talking in fluent Russian. The men of 1 Para gripped their weapons more tightly, identifying individual targets and stood ready as the rain pelted down on them. Watching the Russian soldiers standing around the Brigade Commander, they were all on tenterhooks aware that things could go wrong at any moment. A false move or misinterpretation from either side could easily initiate a full-on firefight. Suddenly, the Russian soldiers laughed, and the tense atmosphere broke as one offered the Brigadier a bottle of vodka. He told them that he didn't want their drink, he wanted to see their boss.

The Paras stood guard as talks went on with the Russian general long into the night. Joey Madden was there:

> We commandeered this block of flats, the Russians had the bottom floor, and we took over the top two floors. We were all stagging on our kit, twenty-four hours role and patrol with the Russians doing the same. It was proper tense; we were all giving each other daggers knowing that it would only take one trigger-happy nutter from either side, and it would all go off. We were all stood ready and good to go. Ninety of us were there and half slept while the others were on watch in or around the wagons. It was an edgy time; we didn't trust the Russians and there were Serbs mixed in with them who had been up to all sorts. Apart from anything, we didn't want them nicking our kit.[3]

Behind the scenes, Commander of KFOR, Lieutenant General Mike Jackson, General Sir (retired) had been under pressure from the American Supreme Commander, Wesley Clark, to take the airport by force:
Tom Blakey recalled:

> We [the Pathfinders] were briefed that we were going to get pulled back in preparation to take part in a potential ambush on the Russian convoy heading for the airport. We dumped everything bar weapons, ammo, med kit and water. It was an incredibly dangerous mission alongside an SF contingent and some of the 1 Para anti-tank boys. The main firepower was to come from PF/SF Forward Air Controllers, who were ready to call in fast air support, as and when required. I don't think, if the truth be told, that any of us fancied our chances of surviving against the huge numbers of Russians involved. That said, we were all

to a man ready to go. Luckily, Mike Jackson stepped in and insisted on a different approach.[4]

Jackson averted hostilities by using diplomacy and tact. Risking his job, he told Clark that he would not be responsible for starting the Thirld World War and the situation was easily resolved. The Russians were not there to fight, they were there to be involved in the securing of Kosovo. The airport was finally handed over by the Russians and secured, and the paratroopers were soon on the move again.

The order came for the men to make their way to Pristina, and they set off once more, moving fast with just their day sacks and living off their belt kits. They made good progress, but they were running out of food and the situation was getting drastic. They had moved so quickly that they were miles ahead of their Bergens and support elements. There was no way of getting food to the blokes quickly and so, as paratroopers always do, they adapted and found their own way of coping by sharing aid packages that were being delivered to the refugees coming back into the city from the mountains. Finally, they saw Chinooks flying overhead bringing people from HQ and the rest of the battalion along with much-needed fresh food and water. When they got to a local park at the top of a hill in the outskirts of the city everything had been set up and the quartermaster was there dishing out supplies. The park then became the staging ground for moving into Pristina.

Putting on their famous maroon berets, the men calmly walked along the streets into the city centre to an emotional reception. The streets were lined with people cheering and waving; women and children hugged and kissed them and gave them flowers as they passed.

Battalion Headquarters were set up in an old government building and each company was designated an AOR to patrol and make the whole city safe. The Paras, with their vast experience of Northern Ireland, set about keeping the peace and providing protection to those that needed it with impartiality. They quickly went through the process of getting to know the area and understanding the situation to get things under control. They negotiated with the Kosovo Liberation Army (KLA) and gathered reports and evidence of war crimes. Patrols were generally accompanied by two Kosovan interpreters, one Serbian and the other Albanian, who helped them communicate with the different members of the population in the city. The Serbs had left a lot of booby traps but, now that most of the soldiers had gone, it was the Serb civilians left behind who were in danger. They quickly became victims of reprisals at the hands of the Albanians, including brutal attacks on vulnerable old people.

The men went into abandoned houses to check for traps that had been left by the retreating Serbs, and then set the properties up to act as operating bases. Many of these homes were still full of food, drink, and personal belongings. They had been left so quickly that they looked as if the owners had just popped out for a short while. Other houses had been burned to the ground. During the bombing campaign the Serbian forces had increased their regime of ethnic cleansing and instilled fear in the Albanian population through rape, torture, and extortion. A huge percentage of the Albanian population was displaced and soon hundreds of mass graves were discovered, revealing the horrific extent of the organised ethnic cleansing programme. The Paras patrolled the streets to try to prevent hostilities and to help the local people maintain a sense of order. When the Albanians returned to their homes, they were often caught out by booby traps left behind by the Serbs and inadvertently set their own homes on fire when they accidentally triggered these devices. Out on patrol, the blokes came across many fires. Joey recounted, 'As we were driving up the street, someone would come running out saying that a house was on fire and that there were people trapped inside. Us blokes just ran straight in, dragged the people out and then just cracked on with the patrol. We saved lots of lives and got a firm grip on the situation.'[5]

Both Serbs and Albanians greeted the soldiers warmly but over time things began to fray at the edges and the dynamics changed; tensions and the number of violent incidents rose. It was Northern Ireland or Palestine all over again, with the people starting to resent the paratroopers' presence in the city and inter-communal violence on the increase. Facing hidden snipers, mines and booby traps as well as open hostility, they were dealing with scared civilians as well as angry members of the KLA taking revenge. In the course of their patrols, they saved women from rape and men from torture or death while coming under fire, but, unfortunately, they couldn't prevent all the reprisals. Andy Rutherford said:

> We found bodies all over the place and it soon became clear that instead of fighting the Serbian military groups we needed to protect the Serbian civilians. I saw one guy tying down the tarpaulin on the side of a big truck when he suddenly came under fire. The rounds hit two of his tyres but somehow missed him and he just jumped in the truck and drove off at speed with two flat tyres. We patrolled around large blocks of flats trying to keep an eye on things. At one point we saw a car coming fast away from a dead end and stopped him. Bizarrely, he began chatting away to us in an English accent, but he was nervous and

gabbling on about football and all sorts of nonsense. We got him out and looking in the car I saw a tooth and a bit of blood on the floor. On further checking we found a grenade hidden in the door. Guys went up the road to have a look around and found a dead body in an orchard. We asked all the people living there what they had seen, but they all said that they hadn't seen anything. The body was of a man who had been dead a while; he had been brought to this place to be dumped. His hands were tied behind his back, and he had been executed with a single bullet through the forehead; the bullet was still lodged inside his head. Who knows what he had done to deserve that?[6]

There were a couple of other dramatic incidents as the men went about their professional duties, although both were dealt with very differently.

As 'A' Company were patrolling they made their way through a car park at the back of a pub and were confronted by an ex-Serbian soldier, who as a Kosovan had stayed behind. He came running out with a pistol and took a couple of pot shots at the lads thinking he could take them on, but the guys took cover. They called out for the man to drop his weapon, but he ignored all the clear warnings and then fired in the direction of the soldiers. One young paratrooper not long out of training got into a fire position and took the man out with four aimed shots to the chest. A full investigation showed that the soldier had acted correctly, and he was commended for his action. A separate incident later on was not viewed in the same light.

An announcement was made that all weapons should be handed in by the end of a ninety-day period. This was in a city where every house had an AK47 at the very least. The Para Regt policed the handing over of the arms and the people were giving in a variety of weapons, PKMs, AK47s, AKMs, numerous varieties of pistols and grenades, which were then handed over to the quartermaster. It was nearing the end of the tour and the NATO deadline for turning in weapons coincided with Kosovan Liberation Day, a day where the Albanian Kosovans celebrated becoming an autonomous province. They were not officially allowed to celebrate as normal with the firing of guns in the air but there was no stopping them. There was tracer everywhere, everyone was out with weapons that they hadn't given in, and the paratroopers prepared themselves to deal with any problems that might arise.

With his patrol, part of the CO's rover group, Joey Madden went to a building known as the Centre for Peace and Tolerance, which was being used as a shelter by a number of Serbian families frightened of being attacked. They went in to reassure the people and then outside they watched the road junction, which was swarming with people out celebrating. A massive cattle truck arrived with lots of people on it and it stopped at the edge of the road. It was dark inside the truck and the soldiers kept a close eye on it, wary of anything going bad; they weren't sure if they were going to come under some kind of attack.

Joey said:

> John Dolman, who was later tragically killed in Iraq, spotted a white car coming down the road on the other side with a bloke on top blasting rounds off into the air with an AK47. The car went out of sight, but John said to watch out for him coming back. Nothing was happening with the cattle truck, but the crowds of people were all getting stirred up and the atmosphere was very tense. The white Opel came back around with the guy still firing his weapon in the air. We ran out into the middle of the street and took cover behind a car calling out, 'Drop your weapon,' in English. 'Stop or I'll shoot!' in Serbian and using hand signals. Another guy joined us so there were three of us on the road. The car was crammed full of people with the man still on top with his weapon. The guy looked us in the eye and began firing on automatic. He then turned and started bringing down the gun towards us with his finger still on the trigger. Rounds were going up in the air and clearly arcing towards us. Knowing that within seconds we would be hit by these bullets, we made the decision to engage and blasted him.[7]

The car sped off and the Paras went running after it. The gunman took his last breath as they reached the car but beneath him sitting between his legs was another man, his cousin, who had also been hit. They got a drip into him and patched him up as best they could. Another guy in the back seat had caught a round while the driver, who had also been shot, ran off down the street. Luckily, there was a 3 Para call sign following up behind, so they helped him. They found the weapon that had been used against them hidden under the body of the cousin.

The Paras then got on with calming down the screaming, shouting crowd and got the situation under control as medics arrived to help the men in the vehicle. The guys were going through the procedure of Confirm, Clear, Cordon and Control when they were confronted by military policemen. The MPs were adamant that they must take their weapons, which did not go down well at all considering the situation and threat on the ground. A section of blokes then escorted them down the street to the battalion HQ, which was only 200m away. Unlike with the first contact, for whatever political reason, the guys were not commended for their actions or backed by their superiors, but on the contrary, they were treated like pariahs. Once back in the UK they lived with the fear that they would be court-martialled and sentenced to a long time in jail, but it soon became apparent that they had done nothing wrong, had acted fully within the rules of engagement and there was definitely not enough evidence against them. The case was thrown out and they were cleared of all wrongdoing. For the guys involved it left a bad taste in their mouths and was something that hung over them for the rest of their careers, but as genuine paratroopers they continued to serve with complete professionalism operating to the best of their abilities at all times.

The Paras finished their tour of duty and handed over the civil administration of the province at the end of July. They had once again proven their capability to be prepared for anything and went into Kosovo demonstrating their propensity to maintain order and cope with a community divided by hostilities. A DSO, a QCB and Mentioned in Dispatches were awarded to members of the battalion.

By the end of the twentieth century the Paras had found themselves involved in operations all over the world dealing with a wide range of deployments effectively and efficiently. Events in the twenty-first century provided them with even more extremely challenging situations that required all their expertise and led to some dramatic changes in their roles.

# Chapter 16

# Operation Certain Death

## Sierra Leone, 2000

The new millennium brought with it conflicts that shocked the world. In 2000, horrifying events in the African Republic of Sierra Leone led to the rapid deployment of the Parachute Regiment to take part in a large-scale operation to help organise the safe departure of personnel from the capital, Freetown. Demonstrating their ability to react quickly and take control of situations, paratroopers not only organised the safe passage of people under threat, but also pushed back vicious rebel forces intent on taking down the government. This was followed only a few months later by a dazzling display of courage, professionalism, and aggression when men from 1 Para, operating alongside Special Forces, took part in an incredible rescue mission in the heart of the jungle.

Civil war and unrest had been raging in the previously British colony since 1991 as the struggle went on for power and control of the country's great mineral wealth. Following continued coups and terrible acts of violence, UNAMASIL (the United Nations Mission in Sierra Leone) was established involving large numbers of military and peacekeeping personnel. In 2000, rebels known as the RUF (Revolutionary United Front), who had a reputation for committing horrific atrocities, were nearing the outskirts of the capital city and were on the verge of defeating the Sierra Leone Army and the UN peacekeeping force. Consisting of drug-crazed bandits and murderers, the RUF were known to go into villages and commit heinous crimes including rape, mutilation, and murder. Using sadistic practices, they cut open women and ripped their babies out of their wombs following a bet to see what sex they were. They made villagers pull pieces of paper out of a hat with instructions detailing their punishment, such as cutting off genitals, limbs, or lips. Girls from the village were forced to marry members of the groups and children were made to watch or even commit the murder of their parents before being forced to join the rebels. Using diamonds as their preferred currency and ransom money, they purchased weapons and were extremely well-armed and ferocious fighters.

In April 2000, the Sierra Leone National Army and the UN Peacekeeping Force were in retreat and the rebels were converging on the outskirts of Freetown, ready to move in and take control. The last time this had happened over 5,000 people had been tortured and murdered. At the beginning of May, the RUF attacked UN peacekeepers, including British soldiers, and took hostages; dozens were killed, and others were sexually assaulted and tortured. Commandeering UN vehicles and weapons, they put on the uniforms taken from UN hostages and, masquerading as peacekeepers, they closed in on the capital. With US backing, Operation Palliser, a non-combatant evacuation was launched.

A JRRF (Joint Rapid Reaction Force), predominately made up of 1 Para, bolstered by men from 2 Para plus the Pathfinder platoon, prepared to go into the beleaguered country with the main role of organising the evacuation of EPs (entitled persons): all British and allied nationals. The Paras were called back to camp from all over Europe to be ready to deploy within twenty-four hours, and on 5 May, rifle companies from 1 and 2 Para were stood ready for immediate overseas deployment.

The majority of the troops deployed by aircraft along with all vehicles and support weapons, but with the RUF rebels in striking distance no time could be wasted and an SLE (Spearhead Lead Element) consisting of paratroopers and SAS raced ahead in Chinooks and carried out a surprise TALO (Tactical Air Landing Operation) assault on Lungi airport just outside Freetown. They touched down and ninety men stormed off the aircraft to find the main airport in utter chaos without any air traffic control. However, they quickly took command of the situation. The men dug in around the perimeter while the systems were restored, and the rest of the paratroopers arrived on C-130 Hercules to reinforce the vanguard.

Around the outskirts of the city, the RUF gathered, waiting for the final push into Freetown from the south and north-east. After quickly securing the airport at Lungi, the Paras started organising the evacuation of those that were eligible, although with the arrival of the British troops many had renewed confidence and decided to stay. A cordon of mortars and heavy machine guns was set up around the airport in a ring of defensive fire. A Pathfinder patrol moved ahead of the main force and dug in around a key strategic road junction. In the local village, Nigerian peacekeepers lived in terror of the RUF. They had suffered terribly at the hands of these crazed rebels; among other heinous acts, some members of their group had been strung up by their feet and skinned alive.

The Nigerians received evidence of the RUF movements and passed the information on to the Pathfinders who dug in on forward positions. In the early hours of the morning, on full alert, movement was detected on the road ahead of the PF position. Using night vision aids they could see the RUF come into view wearing the UN uniforms and with the UN insignia on their vehicles. The Pathfinder force watched carefully as they came closer, they had to be sure that they weren't actually UN troops. Suddenly members of the oncoming group began peeling off and disappearing into the jungle surrounding the village. They were definitely rebels, and they were planning to take the village by surprise. They began shooting, but the PF were ready for them and the roar of GPMGs and other personal weapon systems split the air as the rebels were mown down or driven back into the jungle. A few hours later, the paratroopers from 'C' Company arrived to provide reinforcements and the men prepared for a counter-attack by creating an all-round defensive position. 'A' Platoon commander at the time, Captain (Retired) Danny Matthews MC was with 'C' Company:

> We set up ambushes around the area and kept watch for anybody coming down the road. At one point a blue-on-blue disaster was narrowly avoided. We were in control of the road and knew that anybody coming down it should be viewed as hostile. Reports came in of a vehicle heading towards us and we all stood ready. The men in the forward positions radioed in that they had eyes on the vehicles and asked for permission to engage. Suddenly the voice of the CO came over the radio telling the men to stand down; it was him coming down the road having been out to check on the ambush sites. Luckily, he had heard the radio calls and realised that he was the target.[1]

The RUF did not return, and the immediate threat had been neutralised. Commanding Officer of 2 Para at the time, Chip Chapman, summed up the ethos of the Paras succinctly:

> The incredible thing about Palliser (from a 2 PARA perspective) was that it was all done on old boy network when the Toms were on leave and Arms Plotting to Colchester. Everyone raced back, and once I heard, I had to apply the brakes for such is the nature of the beast that everyone wanted to pile out the door and get to South Cerney with a chance to be on the plane regardless of what 1 Para actually required! When they got back after the Op (as a duty of care sort of consideration) and because the company commander (as I recall) had taken his blokes down to a local hospital in Freetown to view the injuries of the kids who had been dismembered with machetes, I had a controlled study conducted by the RAMC (Royal Army Medical Corps) psychiatrists. It took guys who

had been there and some who had not. Perhaps unsurprisingly, it found a higher level of depression in those who had not deployed![2]

Due to the swift and decisive action of the Para battle group, a crisis was narrowly avoided, for the time being, and an IMATT (International Military Advisory and Training Team) was put in place with the mission to train the Sierra Leonean national army to the standard where they were ready to take on and defeat the rebel groups once and for all. The Royal Irish Regiment arrived in country ready to join this team and take on the IMATT role based in the military town of Benguema.

A few months later, Sierra Leone was enjoying a period of relative stability when, on 25 August 2000, a vehicle reconnaissance patrol, led by Major Alan Marshall, went out into the Okra Hills, 35 miles north of Benguema. The three-vehicle patrol included ten other members of the Royal Irish Regiment and a Sierra Leonean liaison officer, Lieutenant Musa Bangura from the Sierra Leone Army. A few weeks earlier, a massive operation had been carried out by UNAMSIL to secure all the roads in the Okra Hills region. Their aim was to clear the routes of rebel roadblocks and maintain the peace that had been established following Operation Palliser. Some members of a group known as the West Side Boys had initially surrendered but their self-proclaimed leader, Foday Kallay, had rallied the remainder of his rebels under threat of death, and they had continued to ambush travellers – attacking and looting aid vehicles, buses and cars that went along their route.

Major Marshall's patrol headed towards the village of Masiaka for a planned liaison visit with the Jordanian UN peacekeeping force based there and passed through territory controlled by the notorious West Side Boys. Masiaka was on the main transport link between the north and the east and the patrol had to pass through UN checkpoints and two West Side Boys' roadblocks. The rebels, numbering about 1,000, were generally high on drugs and alcohol and were known to be extremely erratic and violent. Trusting in voodoo magic, they believed that they were protected from bullets and were invincible. Like the RUF, they had a terrible reputation for cruel and sadistic acts, and they lacked any respect or care for human life.

The patrol was very well-armed, but Major Marshall was under the impression that the West Side Boys were deemed to be 'friendlies' and so the soldiers weren't overly concerned about any opposition to their presence. A few months earlier the West Side Boys had fought alongside the Sierra Leone Army and British government forces against the RUF. What Major Marshall had not realised was, that since then, after a series of hijacks and rapes, they had fallen out of grace with the government. The patrol's journey to Masiaka was uneventful but following the Jordanians' suggestion, Marshall decided to check out a village off the main track on the way back to base. As part of his remit, he was supposed to gather information and see if any villagers needed medical support or aid of any kind. It was a decision that was to have devastating consequences.

As the vehicles ventured down a dirt track with thick foliage crowding them on both sides, the patrol lost radio contact and couldn't report their position as they continued deeper into the jungle. Suddenly, they came into a clearing near the village of Magbeni on the banks of Rokel Creek and were surrounded by over one hundred heavily armed members of the West Side Boys. Men, women, and young boys, carrying numerous weapons including Russian-made PKMs and RPG (rocket-propelled grenade) launchers quickly gathered around, making it difficult to manoeuvre or make any sort of exit. An open-backed army truck full of rebels blocked their rear and the Royal Irish had no means of escape. The patrol members were quickly disarmed and ordered out of their Land Rovers. They were then taken across the river in dugout canoes to the rebel headquarters in the village of Gberi Bana, where they were held hostage. The village was surrounded by jungle with no roads in or out, making it virtually inaccessible except by the river or air.

With a stock of diamonds, the West Side Boys were buying arms and ammunition and a regular supply of liquor and powerful narcotics. The group, which had come into being in 1997, comprised of renegade soldiers, ex-RUF members and ex-prisoners who had been in jail for an array of charges including rape and murder. They were lawless, volatile, and unpredictable. The soldiers lived in terror as they were beaten, subjected to mock executions and forced to witness the unspeakable atrocities committed on other prisoners. After an attack on nearby Kamajor villagers, the rebels arrived back at camp with heads on sticks, including that of a baby girl. Liaison Officer Musa Bangura was horrifically beaten and tortured on a regular basis and was kept in a hole in the ground with stagnant, fetid water in the bottom of it. The other men slept together in a concrete room that was bare, apart from one small bed, and they were allowed outside under guard during the day. It was hot and humid, and the men were underfed, dehydrated, and lived in terror of being horrifically tortured or killed at any time. The village consisted of around twenty concrete bungalows with iron sheeting for the roofs and a few thatched mud huts in a clearing that had been cut out of the jungle.

The leader, Foday Kallay, aspired to become president and he was hell-bent on using the hostages to get what he wanted. He wanted the British out of Sierra Leone and had two plans; the first he called 'Operation Kill all British', and this was to be followed by 'Operation Kill all Your Families', meaning anyone who was related to any opposition to his rule. Drugs had turned him into an insane killer who worshipped blood and death and he was convinced that holding the hostages would protect him and his rebel followers from a British attack on the village.

Kallay announced to the authorities that he had the soldiers and negotiations began for their release. In return for medical supplies, food and a satellite telephone, five hostages were set free, while negotiations continued for the release of the other seven. As threats to the men's lives increased, British authorities began planning a daring, top-secret rescue mission, code-named Operation Barras.

The released Royal Irish soldiers were able to provide some valuable intelligence on the layout of the two camps and the erratic mindset of the rebels. A four-man surveillance team from the SAS rapidly deployed deep into the jungle to get eyes on the village of Gberi Bana and gather live-time intelligence on the whereabouts of the hostages and the real capabilities of the kidnappers. Their insertion by boat and then overland through the dense jungle made it quickly apparent that a large military rescue force would not be able to use this means of access. Fast currents on the River Rokel and the density of the jungle surrounding the village meant that the only feasible way in for a rescue team was by air. They knew they would lose the element of surprise with the noise of the helicopter rotor blades and needed to act swiftly and cohesively if they were to safely rescue the hostages and incapacitate the enemy force.[3]

The mission required careful timing and precision; if any part of the rescue went wrong, then the ramifications could be severe. One of the major problems was that while the hostages needed to be rescued from Gberi Bana, a large number of West Side Boys were based across the river in Magbeni. Heavily armed and holding the captured weapons and vehicles of the Royal Irish, the rebels there had to be prevented from supporting the rest of their gang across the creek in Gberi Bana when the SF rescue team dropped into action. With their natural skill set, in what was basically going to be a seek and destroy mission, the Paras were clearly the men for the task. The SAS would go in to get the hostages and the Paras would simultaneously land on the other side of the river with the aim of preventing hundreds more West Side Boys from providing reinforcements to their fellow lunatics on the other side of the creek.

In the UK, Major Lowe of 'A' Company, 1 Para was told that he needed to organise a force of 140 men, but that complete secrecy was essential. The call went out and many of the men were on leave. Danny Matthews was in Italy on a well-earned and much-needed holiday with his fiancée when he was told that he needed to get back to camp as soon as possible. 'I had no idea at the time why we were being called, but there was no question of not going. It was the end of the relationship, but the job came first. On Wednesday I was relaxing on a beach in Italy and late Thursday night I was back with the boys.' This was the price that many paratroopers had to pay. The need for rapid response and the indefinite, often long periods away from home put enormous pressure on relationships, and many suffered as a result.

The men were told that they were to prepare for exercises when they were sent to an operation-mounting centre in South Cerney, Gloucestershire. However, when their mobile phones were taken from them and they were put in isolation, it became clear that it wasn't just a normal exercise. Colour Sergeant (Retired) Keith 'Woolly' Woolgar was a corporal when he got the call:

> During Operation Palliser, 'A' Company had unluckily been on jungle exercises in Jamaica and consequently missed out, which is not something that any paratrooper likes to happen. So, when the hostage crisis in Sierra Leone arose a few months later, we were the obvious choice this time around. We were sent to South Cerney on Friday and had to stay inside a hangar. We were not allowed to leave for days, apart from going over the road for scoff due to the huge interest from the press. The rumour had gone around that the Paras would be supporting SF, so we had an idea what was going on, but we weren't told anything at first. There were three platoons, support weapons elements and a section of Patrols, which I was part of, bringing us up to one hundred and forty men in total.[4]

A lot of 'A' Company at that time was made up of 'crows', young guys just out of training with no experience of operations. However, they had passed all the Para Regt tests and were fit and ready to put their newfound skills into action. Warrant Officer 2 (Retired) Simon 'Si' Dawes, a mortarman and an experienced section commander at the time, recalled, 'My biggest concern was not wanting to lose a bloke. Four of my section were literally straight out of Depot and had only been in battalion for a few days. But they had finished their training and therefore, as qualified paratroopers, were ready to do the job, proving that the Depot system was still working well.'[5]

It was not so different to the Second World War volunteers who were deployed straight into the thick of the action. However, there was a huge amount of responsibility on the shoulders of the senior soldiers and non-commissioned officers during this operation to lead these new guys through what was going to be a complicated and dangerous mission. Orders were given and the men were transported to Sierra Leone in great secrecy.

Danny Matthews said, 'We eventually landed in Lungi and then we were transported in 4-tonne trucks, lying on the floor so that nobody could see us, which was absolutely horrendous. We crossed the peninsula on a ferry and went to what was code-named Waterloo, where elements of SF who had been there for a few days were hanging about in flip-flops in their usual airily relaxed manner. We joined up with 'D' Squadron as well as elements from the SBS at the FOB (Forward Operating Base) known as 'Hastings' and it was like a reunion as historically 'D' Squadron SAS is made up predominantly of paratroopers and, knowing nearly all the guys, an instant bond was established. 'D' Squadron had been on a live-firing training exercise in Kenya when the call came to deploy to Sierra Leone for Operation Barras, so they were the natural choice from the SAS.'

Intelligence was gathered and still not knowing if the mission would be given the green light, 1 Para began training on mock-ups of the village. Corporal (Retired) Dave Aitchison said, 'We had all these wooden pallets, and we created the layout of the village with the pallets used to mark the buildings we would encounter on either side of a central track. It was imperative that everybody knew what they were doing, and we went through our practice drills over and over again even though at that point we still did not know if we would get the chance to deploy on this op or not.'[6]

Despite all efforts to keep the mission secret, the BBC reported on the radio that the Paras were going in to rescue the soldiers and this raised fears that the West Side Boys would prepare themselves for attack or worse still, move or execute the hostages. Time was of the essence. Negotiators played down the news report by agreeing to all of Kallay's demands and sent in crates of beer and spirits along with other requests to give the impression that negotiations were still under way. In reality, they wanted to make sure that the West Side Boys were well and truly hungover when the insertion took place the following morning. Three Chinooks were available for the operation; two carried the SF troops to Gberi Bana and the third was used to drop the paratroopers in two lifts.

Danny Matthews said, 'We got the nod to go the night before. Negotiations were not going well; the West Side Boys' demands were getting more and more ridiculous, and the hostages were being subjected to mock executions. The possibility of the soldiers being split up and taken further up-river meant that we needed to act. Our objective was to hit them fast and hit them hard. Kill as many as possible and force the rest of them out of the village and away from Gberi Bana and then to get rid of all their kit and leave nothing that they could utilise in the future.'

In the dark pre-dawn with the sun just creeping up over the horizon, the green light had been given and the paratroopers quietly boarded the choppers fully geared up, weighed down by weapons and ammo, and having their last thoughts of family and friends before switching into game mode and ready to go. Three Chinooks roared into action and set off from FOB Hastings, and with the stunning mountains of Sierra Leone looming in the distance, the deep, throaty throb of the rotors broke the silence of the morning. A dozen paratroopers went in the first two aircraft carrying the SAS to provide covering fire as the 'D' Squadron boys fast-roped into Gberi Bana with the aim of getting onto the ground as quickly as possible and securing the hostages. Half of the men from the rest of 1 Para packed into the third helicopter and headed for Magbeni for the first drop with an aim of securing this location, whilst waiting for the second drop of paratroopers to arrive. A short distance from their target, still out of noise range, the Chinooks were ordered to hold their position waiting for the final go-ahead from GCHQ (Government Communications Headquarters).

Si Dawes recalled, 'My first thoughts had been to just get the job done but as we waited in the dark air with the rotors thrumming and the helicopter vibrating around us, the nerves began to creep in, and I worried about the new blokes. They had done their training, and some had been with us to Jamaica, but this was a very different jungle. Then the words came through on the radio, "It's a go. Go! Go! Go!"'[7]

The massive Chinooks came in low over the thick foliage, their powerful engines announcing their presence with a steady roar, and as they came down towards the village, the turbulence created by the giant rotors tore the roofs off some of the decrepit buildings. Supported by Lynx and Mi-24 gunships strafing and destroying anything that moved, the SAS men already on the ground bravely broke cover and rushed forward to clinically take out any West Side Boys guarding the hostages. 'D' Squadron fast-roped into Gberi Bana and quickly moved to achieve their objective as the rebels awoke to the terrible noise with their roofs falling in on top of them. The enemy may have been undisciplined and high on drugs and clearly no match for the SAS, but they were not afraid of anything, and with some of them wearing only their underpants, they grabbed their weapons and leapt into action. As they tried to get to the hostages, a massive gun battle ensued, with many of them being mowed down by the weight and accuracy of the British firepower. The SF team secured the hostages and held off the West Side Boys, who put up a strong resistance and were firing randomly and ferociously all over the place. Some of the SAS lads got hit by lumps of shrapnel and one SAS Trooper, Brad Tinnion, was seriously wounded.

At exactly the same time, on the other side of the creek, the first wave of paratroopers leapt off their Chinook near to their objective in Magbeni. Some dodgy surveillance on this side of the river had pinpointed an LZ that had appeared to be a clearing of solid ground. Dawes was the first man to leap off the tailgate of the chopper as it hovered above the ground and to his shock, he dropped into deep water that went over his head and rushed up his nose:

> When we took off from FOB Hastings, the ground had been wet, about four or five inches of water, and the whirr of the rotors had created a fine spray. It was the same kind of spray coming off the ground at the target location, so I just presumed it would also be the same shallow water. How wrong I was, I went straight under. I instantly pushed myself up off the bottom, desperately trying to gain a foothold somewhere. The radios were drenched, our weapons were full of dirty water, and it was fucking cold! We couldn't go straight onto target, so we went out at a different angle and had to cut our way through the jungle with our machetes to get eyes on our first objective.[8]

To the confusion and dismay of all the paratroopers, they leapt off the helicopter in darkness, carrying a huge amount of weight and wearing body armour, into deep swamp. With water sparking radio batteries and destroying equipment, they struggled to get over to firm ground.

Woolly Woolgar said:

> I was on the first lift. The sun wasn't even up as we approached the LZ, and the Chinook hovered over the ground below. The helicopter had been stripped of everything inside to get us all in, and we shuffled forward on our arses with all the weight we were carrying and jumped straight out. The swamp was deep and as I went in, I could see our gunships firing chain guns all around the target. We moved in a line, desperate to get to dry land. We had 51 mortar bombs and ammo to drag through that swamp and we couldn't do anything until we got out. 3 Platoon secured the start point and I was with 2 Platoon moving towards the tree line.[9]

Wading through the foul-smelling water, the men struggled with their heavy weapons and body armour to get to firmer ground. They were filled with a mixture of anticipation, dread, and adrenaline as they pulled themselves through the dragging, stinking bog. The noise of Lynx and Hind helicopters was deafening and the fire raining down on the village ahead of them lit up the sky. The landing zone was separated from the edge of Magbeni village by a thin strip of jungle and as the Chinook left them to go back and pick up the rest of the force, the Paras hoped that the rebels wouldn't spot them before they had got themselves organised and ready to fight. They were totally vulnerable at this point, unable to use any of the support weapons as they waded forward slipping and sliding in the slimy swamp. Dave Aitchison, company signaller at the time, described the scene:

> I was last off the first lift with the Officer Commanding, Major Lowe. I looked forward and realised that everybody was disappearing and thought, where the fuck is everyone? The swamp was deep and as I went in, I could see gunships firing chain guns all around the objective. That was the only light. The bottom of the swamp was uneven, and we were going up and down. Some of the shorter guys were up to their waists in water one moment and the next thing it was over their heads. Bob Crossman, not the tallest of blokes on a good day, completely disappeared. We were all taking in swamp water and laughing at our ridiculous predicament.[10]

The West Side Boys were kept busy as the gunships continued to pound the village from the air, causing mayhem and destruction, but they soon roused themselves and began firing back with ZPU-2 14.5mm anti-aircraft guns, which were mounted on flatbed trucks.

The lead sections moved forward, with Major Lowe and his command group close behind, and they waited for the Chinook to return with the rest of the lads. They soon arrived and once everyone was ready, Major Lowe gave the signal for the attack to begin. The men of 3 Platoon moved into the village as plumes of smoke billowed into the air from the blackened remains of the scant houses. They took up positions in the crumbling buildings as 2 Platoon moved forward to cover the riverbank in order to prevent any rebels from crossing over to Gberi Bana. The rebels emerged from their huts and opened fire as the men took what cover could be found and engaged the enemy. They took some out and dispersed the others. Major Lowe moved forward with his men and decided to cross the track that ran down the centre of the village. A shell of some sort exploded, lifting the men off the ground and shooting shrapnel into their bodies.

Corporal Aitchison, who was with Major Lowe, said:

I heard a loud 'boom!', which blew us all off our feet. I didn't know what had happened as the adrenalin kicked in and I looked at my hand and realised it was bleeding and my thumb was hanging off. I first thought we must have stumbled into a minefield, and then realised that my feet were okay and that others were also injured. Seven or eight of us had been hit, including the OC, and we all helped each other by administering morphine and patching ourselves up with first field dressings as best we could. I didn't even realise that I had also been hit in the arse, but it was an injury that got a lot worse as the day went on. Major Lowe handed command over to the company 2iC Captain Matthews and we stayed there as the operation went ahead, keenly listening to the radios to see how the other platoons were getting on.[11]

Danny Matthews described his experience:

Major Lowe, the OC moved ahead, and what seemed like a mortar came down and exploded close by. I thought they had dived for cover but then I heard the shouts for a medic and Major Lowe calling for me. I moved forward to where he was lying in open ground naked from the waist down. The explosion had literally blown his combat trousers right off him. I could see that his legs were badly fragged, and his arse and the back of his hamstrings were gone. He calmly said, 'I think I've been injured.' I agreed with him and then he asked me if I could carry on. I moved up to where the lead platoon commander was holding his badly injured triceps onto his arm, and suddenly realised that I was now in charge.[12]

Some of the radio equipment had been damaged in the blast and Captain Matthews was now unable to communicate clearly with the air support team. He realised that they had to get going so as not to lose the momentum of the battle and tackle whatever came their way on the ground in order to achieve their objective of preventing the rebels from reinforcing the rest of the West Side Boys over the creek in Gberi Bana. The men of 3 Platoon used white phosphorous grenades to create a cloud of cover and 2 and 3 Platoons made their way towards the mortars on the northern edge while 1 Platoon moved across to the southern side. The guys advanced to engage in some fierce and aggressive fighting as they forced the rebels towards their only point of escape in the east, away from Gberi Bana. Using the jungle fringe and the few buildings for cover, the guys proceeded down the central track employing fire and manoeuvre tactics and obliterated the walls of buildings using the old 66mm anti-tank weapons. Woolgar remembered seeing one of the young Toms who didn't know how to use this old weapon. 'It was used as more of a bunker buster and was ideal in the environment for taking out these flimsy huts. I remember using the 66 back in 1986 and it had already been superseded by a more effective anti-tank weapon, even then. I saw this young lad taking cover behind a mud hut and literally reading the instructions written on the side before then effectively putting it to good use and taking out a target in a swirl of dust and debris.'[13]

For nearly an hour the Paras fought their way through the village with the West Side Boys returning fire but eventually the sheer firepower and disciplined fighting skills of the men drove the crazy and unprepared rebels into the jungle, leaving trails of blood behind them. The Paras dug in on the edge of the village to ward off any counter-attacks from other rebels in the area and the mortar team managed to find a firm base and fired into the fringes of the dense undergrowth, killing or pushing any survivors further away. Their aim had been not only to kill the rebels, but to force them out of an egress away from Gberi Bana so that they could not interfere with the SAS rescue operation on the other side of the creek.

Si Dawes recalled:

> We dug in and prepared for a counter-attack. We had been told that reinforcements were forming up at a junction just outside the village and that was the scariest part of the whole op – just sitting and waiting for them to attack in greater numbers. Then the mortars got an accurate setting, thanks to some skilful MFC (Mortar Fire Controlling) by Evo. He relayed the enemy position to Glenn Colburn, who was in charge of the mortar line, and he, in turn, brought down some heavy fire from our 81mm on the junction and put paid to any plans the West Side Boys may have had about coming back at us.[14]

Major Lowe and the other injured men had been hauled back to the LZ. A Chinook picked them up and along with the badly injured Brad Tinnion and the hostages they were rushed to RFA *Sir Percivale* for medical treatment. Tragically, Tinnion, from 'D' Squadron, 22 SAS, did not make it.

The men in Magbeni secured the ammo dump and gathered up all the rebel weapons and vehicles. They found the Land Rovers that had been taken from the Royal Irish and, despite having been hit by bullets in the battle, they started up immediately and were driven to where they could be slung under the Chinooks that arrived to collect them. With all their objectives achieved, claymores and explosives were set around the perimeter of the village. The last paratroopers were lifted out, with Corporal Jim Collins being the last man off the ground from Magbeni. He had been injured earlier in the attack taking some shrapnel in his knee, but still carried on regardless and led his section through to the end. The explosives were then detonated, and the men watched from above as the village, including the ammunition dump, enemy vehicles and weapons, went up in a burst of flames, and smoke.

The fighting lasted no more than an hour and the hostages and other prisoners had been freed within the first twenty minutes by the SAS rescue team. The leader of the West Side Boys, Foday Kallay, was found cowering in his hut during the battle and had been taken prisoner. All objectives were achieved on both sides of the river and despite the tragedy of losing a man, it was a highly successful operation.

On board RFA *Argus* by late afternoon, the boys were allowed to relax and have a few beers. Woolly said, 'Along with the guys from "D" Squadron we had ourselves a few well-earned beers. It had been a good day at the office. Later that evening when a young petty officer was sent down like a sacrificial lamb to tell us that the bar was closing, we gave the poor guy absolute hell and told him to get lost. It was hard work getting into my high bunk that night.'

Many of the West Side Boys had been killed outright or died of their injuries with no medical aid and bodies floated down the River Rokel where they had been dumped. The British had one man dead and twelve injured. Following the rescue mission, forces, including airborne troops, went into the bush hunting for the remainder of the rebels. Many of the West Side Boys gave themselves up and Sierra Leone moved into a period of peace and stability with the help of the international forces, with around 45,000 rebel fighters surrendering their weapons.

The Paras had executed their part of the operation with their usual discipline, professionalism, and tremendous skill set. Not only did they assist in bringing an end to civil war in Sierra Leone and increasing confidence in British forces, but they also paved the way for a new permanent working relationship alongside the Special Forces. Numerous medals and gallantry awards were given to members of the Parachute Regiment for Operation Barras, including five Military Crosses and a Conspicuous Gallantry Cross. The men had truly proved their worth as professional and elite warriors.

According to the bestselling author Damien Lewis in his 2004 book, *Operation Certain Death*, 'No other army in the world could have done what the British Army did in Sierra Leone in 1999 – in terms of speed, decisiveness, ingenuity and above all, willingness to put the lives of its own men at risk in the face of overwhelming odds.'[15]

As the situation in Northern Ireland calmed, it looked as though the world might be a more peaceful place as the twenty-first century got under way. However, with only a brief pause to take a breath, the world was turned upside down and the Paras were about to be thrown into another two decades of mayhem in the Middle East.

Chapter 17

# Liberation of Kabul

## Afghanistan Part One, 2001

Everyone remembers where they were the day that the planes flew into the World Trade Center in New York on 11 September 2001. In Northern Ireland, Para Regt battalions were continuing tours of duty and going about their tasks as the peace talks made progress and over in Macedonia, 2 Para were on Operation Bessemer organising the collection and disposal of weapons owned by ethnic Albanians, as peace settled in the Balkans. However, any harmony in the world was shattered, and lives changed forever, when terrorists hijacked four commercial airliners and two flew into the Twin Towers in Manhattan. Responsible for this heinous strike on American soil was Osama bin Laden, leader of the Islamic terrorist group al-Qaeda, who was based in and operating out of Afghanistan at the time. The men of 2 Para watched in shocked awe as the news unfolded on the television at their base in Skopje and they were filled with hope that they might soon be deploying to the Middle East to meet this threat head on.

The Taliban offered bin Laden sanctuary in Afghanistan in return for his vast financial support and he had set up numerous training camps across the country, which trained thousands of radical Islamist terrorists. In response to the attacks, US President George W. Bush announced a war on terror across the world and an attack on both Afghanistan and Iraq was initially suggested as the necessary response. The US decided to focus on Afghanistan and come back to the Iraq question later. President Bush demanded that the Taliban government of Afghanistan deliver bin Laden and other al-Qaeda leaders to the US and when they refused, America began Operation Enduring Freedom. The aim of the operation was to destroy the Taliban and al-Qaeda, capture bin Laden and then help Afghanistan to rebuild under a new, more open-minded government.

On 7 October, less than a month after the terrorist attacks, the US carried out air strikes on Taliban military sites and al-Qaeda training camps. Air strikes on the capital Kabul and other major cities were followed by ground forces entering the country and joining with the Afghani anti-

Taliban Northern Alliance, whose leader, Ahmad Shah Massoud, had been assassinated on 9 September by al-Qaeda in clear anticipation of this response by Western powers. Kabul was taken and when the city of Kandahar fell on 6 December, Taliban rule in the country came to an end. The Taliban were driven out of power, but Osama bin Laden initially managed to flee into the mountainous area neighbouring Pakistan. Coalition forces were called upon to join US troops on the ground to work with the Northern Alliance to hunt down Taliban and al-Qaeda fighters and begin the process of rebuilding and stabilising Afghanistan with the interim leadership of Hamed Karzai.

An ISAF (International Security Assistance Force), overseen by NATO, was established and 2 Para were finally called into action. Brought back from Christmas leave, they quickly prepared for deployment to Kabul on what was known as Operation Fingal. They began their preparations with live firing exercises, fine tuning their personal weapons and patrolling skills, training in cultural awareness and receiving updates on the current situation on the ground, not totally sure what they might have to face on the streets of the Afghan capital once they arrived.

Corporal (Retired) Matt Shackleton remembered getting the call, 'I was in Macedonia when the Twin Towers went down, and it wasn't long before we were told that we would be going into Afghanistan. We were the spearhead battalion of 16 Air Assault Brigade at the time, and I remember some government guy flippantly saying, "You are going to Afghanistan, and you are going to be busy for the next thirty years."'[1] It was a prediction that proved to be not far off the mark.

The deployment was delayed, but 2 Para eventually arrived in Kabul at the beginning of 2002 with a mission statement very similar to that of Northern Ireland: to keep the peace, create good relations with the local people, control Taliban and terrorist activities, provide reassurance to the local population and to help train the new Afghan army. An initiative to improve the lives of the Afghani people was under way with improvements in schools and health facilities as the powers that be deemed Afghanistan had moved into a new era of peace and freedom from the oppression of the Taliban.

The first members of 2 Para arrived at Bagram airport on an Antonov transport plane flying in via Uzbekistan. British SF forces in the shape of the SBS, as well as a large number of American troops, had secured the old military airport and a couple of days later they were taken to set up the battalion HQ in an old telecommunications college that had been wrecked by the Taliban. Corporal Jim Kilbride was the first man of 2 Para to set foot on the ground in Kabul, but it was a number of weeks before the entire battalion were complete on the ground. Jim was later tasked with taking an artist into the centre of Kabul to do paintings of the parts of the city that had been previously destroyed by the Russians during the 1980s invasion and they narrowly missed being ambushed by an angry mob.

Jim recalled:

> During the day the city was thought to be reasonably safe to go around, and it was only at night that you had to be really careful but, on this day, we were taking the artist around with 'B' Company circling around us. It got to last light and I decided we needed to head back to base. We didn't have comms with 'B' Company, so we decided to make our own way back alone. As we were driving down a street, we saw a large group of protestors ahead of us and I told the driver to take a right turn and put his foot down, but there was no right turn, and we were getting closer to the mob. Suddenly, bricks and all sorts were thrown at us, and the windscreen shattered. I saw an Afghan coming towards me with an AK47 in his hand. I was in the jump seat of the DAF truck, and I instinctively cocked my weapon, making it ready with a round in the chamber. His AK was pointing at the ground, but I was prepared in case he decided to bring it up and aim it at us. He came towards us with a fag hanging out of his mouth and he waved at me and said that everything was alright. He was a policeman; he turned away and fired his weapon above the heads of the crowd, and they all bowed down low. He then casually pointed to his right and told us to go that way and we quickly moved off and got back to camp safely. The following day, I was at the 'B' Company location and the policeman appeared. I asked an interpreter to thank him for what he had done the day before and he smiled, and we shook hands. I asked what I could do to say thank you and the interpreter said that I should buy something from him. I agreed, and the guy went off and came back with a brand new AK47, still in its wrapper. I told him that I couldn't take that out of the country and so he went off again and came back this time with a bayonet, which I gave him twenty dollars for. The soldier's number on the bayonet was 3083 and coincidently my army number ended in 3803, so I thought that was a bit spooky![2]

Whoever had checked out the conditions in Kabul must have been there in the summer because the men were not issued with adequate cold weather gear and when they arrived in January it was freezing, particularly at night when it often snowed. A lot of the guys bought themselves coats and warm gear in the local market until that was put out of bounds for security reasons.

Terrance 'Moose' Millar, a sniper with the patrols platoon, remembered arriving in Kabul late at night, 'The C-130 came in at a very steep angle, due to the threat of ground-to-air missiles. It was quite a dramatic landing and we all raced off the tail gate and formed up on the tarmac before the plane turned around and flew out again, but then we had to wait for transport to take us to the main base near the American Embassy. The building had two towers so soon got nicknamed 'Twin Towers' or 'Telecom Towers' because of two red and white radio masts behind the building. We spent a couple of days there receiving intelligence briefings and then we were pushed out to various locations around the city.'[3]

The headquarters was a three-storey building in a compound and the men set about putting up sandbag defences and building sangars on the roof. The different rifle companies were then moved to bases around the city, taking over abandoned schools, colleges, and police stations. The accommodation was very basic, and the men tried to keep warm, living off army ration packs as they went about their duties and got to grips with the new operating environment. The buildings were sparse and unfurnished, so with typical airborne initiative, the men soon got themselves as comfortable as possible. They turned cardboard casings into shelves, put up pictures of their loved ones, and bought roll-up mattresses and simple gas cookers from the local market.

Moose said, 'Small teams of four men were given OPs to man and my team was initially sent up to "TV Hill", which was previously the location of a nice restaurant and was now a pile of debris. We had to keep an eye on local activities and report back to base on weather and traffic conditions and pass on the grid references for any incidents that we observed. We stayed on location for ten days before going back to the base for a couple of days off, and then would typically deploy out to another location.'[4]

The city was bustling with cars, open-backed trucks, carts pulled by donkeys, motorbikes, and bicycles, as people made their way around the decimated areas covered with bombed-out buildings, tanks and rubble. The patrols went out and about setting up checkpoints and trying to interact with the locals to gather information on terrorists who had remained in the country and had melted into the general population. Shackleton said, 'We spent time talking to people to see if we could get any useful intel and presented a friendly face to the locals. There was a curfew at night and there were a few tense situations where the Afghani militia confronted us. We were on the lookout for any Taliban or insurgent activity and aimed to dominate the area.'[5] The patrols were limited to one kilometre outside the city and any problems were mostly caused by the local militia. They had been controlling their areas and taking advantage of looting and robbing opportunities, which the Para presence inhibited, and there were a few contacts.

For many Afghans, the removal of the Taliban and its oppressive regime was welcome, but tensions were bubbling under the surface and incidents forewarned of an instability that would only get worse. Beyond the city limits, lights from continuing battles could be seen flashing in the mountains and the men knew it wasn't safe to venture into villages outside the city perimeter. A petrol bomb was thrown at the gates of the US embassy and when soldiers went in to investigate, they discovered IEDs and anti-personnel mines on the surrounding roads and paths; it had been a deliberate trap. The civil aviation and tourism minister, Dr Abdul Rahman, was beaten and stabbed to death at Kabul airport and initially the murder was blamed on Hajj pilgrims angry about delays to their flight, but President Karzai said that the killing had been a planned assassination by high-ranking members of the Afghan security services. However, nobody was ever arrested or punished for the killing.

In an effort to symbolise the good relations between the international peacekeeping force and the Afghan people, a 'Unity Football Match' was organised and held in February 2002 between ISAF and a team of the best Afghan players, aptly named Kabul United. Former Southampton Manager Lawrie McMenemy flew in to coach the Afghan side, while Spurs legend Gary Mabbutt arrived to take charge of the ISAF team. It was to be the first sporting event since the Taliban had left power and was played on a pitch previously used by the Taliban to carry out barbaric public executions. In the walled stadium with no covered areas, the pitch was on hard ground without a blade of grass. Thousands of people turned out to watch the match, and many did not have tickets so there were scuffles with security forces outside the stadium as people keen to see the game pushed and shoved to get in and tried to scale the walls. Jim Kilbride was on duty inside:

> I was there before the match, and I walked around the area looking for signs of blood as I tried to imagine the horrors that had taken place there. Men and women had been hanged, beheaded, stoned, shot, or beaten for the smallest things such as not wearing a head scarf or speaking out of turn. The match was a huge PR event to show the Afghan people that we were there as friendly forces who would protect and help them. The Barclay Premiership Trophy was flown in for

the winning team to hold and a dozen white doves were released as a symbol of peace. The match went well, the Afghan team lost, but they were extremely skilful and fast. Like all the people, they were weak and underfed and just not as strong as the ISAF team which had a couple of 2 Para guys playing for them. Two things stick out in my mind about the match. An American woman with blonde hair was watching and she kept taking off her headscarf. The Afghan men were going wild and every time the scarf came off, they surged towards her. The other thing was that when they released the doves, they didn't fly away and had to be picked up and thrown into the air. One poor bird didn't make it out of the stadium and went into the crowd, where I am sure its neck was stretched, and it went into a pocket for someone's family dinner that night.[6]

Despite the disturbances outside, the match was deemed an overall success and the situation in Kabul was described as under control. The men of 2 Para remained in Kabul for the next few months and, in comparison with what was to come, it was a successful and largely uneventful tour. With very little opposition to their presence and using their experience in Northern Ireland, they were able to handle most confrontations with diplomacy and the avoidance of force. The battalion established good relations with the local Afghan people and helped to train around 600 men for the new ANA (Afghan National Army). However, beneath the veneer of peace, insurgencies were growing outside the capital, and the Taliban were gathering their forces. The next deployments to Afghanistan were not so easy for the Paras but, for now, under a false sense of accomplishment, America turned its eyes towards Iraq.

## Chapter 18

# Freedom

### Iraq, 2003

At the end of 2002, the Parachute Regiment was called upon to prepare for an imminent invasion of Iraq. The men of 1 and 3 Para were called in after Christmas and given orders to prepare to deploy. They immediately began an intensive training package in the UK, honing their basic infantry fighting skills prior to being sent out to FOBs in Kuwait for Operation Telic.

Integrally connected to the invasion of Afghanistan following the attack on the World Trade Center in New York, the US war on terror now turned its focus to Iraq. Towards the end of 2002, tensions rose as Saddam Hussein continued to fail in disarming his country of alleged nuclear, chemical, and biological WMD (weapons of mass destruction) and an invasion of Iraq looked inevitable. Britain joined coalition forces led by the US and preparations for invasion began at the end of the year as the world waited to see if Saddam would agree to disarm and remove what was deemed to be a deadly threat to world peace.

In the first Gulf War in 1990 Saddam's forces were defeated and driven out of Kuwait but he remained in power under numerous crippling economic sanctions. With the main point of contention being the possession of WMD the US also intimated that Iraq had links with terrorist groups, including al-Qaeda. In early 2003, Bush and Blair claimed that Iraq was still not declaring its weapons and despite the lack of support from other countries, on 17 March, President Bush gave Saddam an ultimatum to leave the country within twenty-four hours. The deadline passed with Saddam still refusing to leave or to comply with weapons inspectors and consequently the war began.

The UK Prime Minister, Tony Blair, had waited for support from across the Houses of Parliament before agreeing to join the US and other coalition forces and so preparations for the invasion were behind the well-oiled US war machine, which had been preparing for months. In the UK, a force of 45,000 personnel from across the tri-services (Navy, Air Force and Army) was galvanised. Justin 'Sam' Salmon, Company Quartermaster Sergeant for

'C' Company 3 Para at the time, was one of the first to arrive in Kuwait, where he helped set up camp for the battalion, code-named Fort Longdon:

> Within a week we had built the whole camp, but compared to the extremely well-supplied Americans, our logistics chain was not good; we were desperately short of basic equipment such as NVG (night vision goggles) desert boots and body armour. We didn't have anywhere near enough proper goggles for the guys to protect their eyes from the dust that was blown all around when driving through the desert sandstorms and jumping on and off the helicopters. We had to make do with what were more like welders' goggles, typical British military equipment inadequacies. Our camp was miles from anyone else, all of the bases were dotted around because of the threat of attack and the night before the Americans went in there was a SCUD attack on one of their camps. We kept our respirators and NBC (Nuclear, Biological & Chemical) kit close to hand at all times.[1]

The men were there for a few weeks training hard with heavy kit and acclimatising to the heat and desert conditions. Sergeant (Retired) Paul Stoves said, 'The camaraderie between the guys was great, morale was high and as always, the guys were keen to get going. We had a good laugh, but all the time knowing that some serious business lay ahead.'[2]

In another part of the desert landscape of Kuwait, 1 Para set up in the aptly named Camp Pegasus. Colour Sergeant (Retired) Stuart Baillie, who was known to the blokes as Badger due to the streak of vivid grey that ran through his black hair, was one of the battalion's characters, well respected by his peers. He recalled:

> The camp was outstanding, the Regimental Quartermaster had done a great job and we began training hard for the high temperatures and dusty, sandy conditions that we were going to be expected to operate in. Even in March it was fuckin' hot, and we did 10-milers, always carrying our gas masks and full NBC suits, and even cross trained with the US Rangers. There was one very funny incident when we were doing a 10-mile advance to contact carrying 80lb Bergens with Land Rover WMIKs (Weapons Mount Installation Kit) vehicles coming up behind us, which were basically mobile fighting stations. The drivers had removed the windscreens ready for the operation and one of them had pressed the windscreen washer button by mistake, firing the liquid right up into the face of the vehicle commander. He screamed out, 'Gas! Gas! Gas!' thinking they were under attack as his eyes were stinging

and the whole battalion instantly went down on one knee in unison and put their gas masks on. It was an impressive reaction, although one guy discovered that he had no eyepiece in one of his respirator lenses, which had many of the lads in stitches of laughter. The NBC regiment guy checked the WMIK and quickly realised that the chemicals in the commander's eyes had come from the squirt of washer fluid. The guys took the task ahead very seriously but there was always humour to be found.[3]

The Parachute Regiment had become part of the 16th Air Assault Brigade in 1999 and Operation Telic was the first time that the Brigade had deployed as one complete battle group. The men of 3 Para, followed by 1 Para crossed the border, which was manned at the time by the RMP (Royal Military Police). They were attempting to maintain some semblance of control over the situation as the Para companies pushed through with the imperative mission to quickly secure the strategically important GOSP (Gas and Oil Separation Plants) in the Rumaila oil fields to prevent the Iraqis from setting them alight or sabotaging them as they had done during the first Gulf War. The Para battalions made their way across the desert ground using WMIKs and 4-tonne trucks; each company and then platoon had been given separate locations to reach and secure. Sam Salmon continued, '3 Para moved across the vast desert for a couple of days, digging in when we stopped for the night and heading for the main supply route. There were three or four trucks per company, but they were limited because there were only a few people fully qualified to drive them. I wasn't quite sure what difference that made in the desert. Our job was to secure the GOSPs in Rumailah and we met with little enemy resistance. I can remember being disappointed that we weren't going to be dropped in, as we had brought our para kit with us, but the plans were changing all the time.'[4]

Ahead of them, fierce battles took place as the lead coalition elements from the USMC (US Marine Corps) came up against initially strong resistance from the Iraqi Republican Guard and the Fedayeen as they made their way towards the capital, Baghdad.

The Pathfinder platoon, deployed in advance of 16 Air Assault Brigade, provided a surveillance blanket in front of the Para Regt battalions as they moved towards their specified targets. Tom Blakey said, 'At one point we were so far ahead of the Brigade that we came under the jurisdiction of the USMC Force Recon teams as they pushed hard, fast and aggressively across Iraq en route to Baghdad.'[5]

The Pathfinders operated in twelve-man teams, split between four WMIK vehicles, which were stripped down Land Rovers designed for fast reconnaissance and fire support, and could be mounted with various weapon systems, such as GPMG, .50-calibre machine guns and Milan anti-tank missile units, with three PF operators in each. Their mission was to establish ground truth ahead of the main force, carry out recces on specific enemy targets and direct-action raids where required.

Plans for 1 Para to form a blocking force to the side of the fast-moving US military push to Baghdad, in order to protect their exposed flank against any possible Iraqi counter-attacks, were discussed in the higher echelons of command. Allegedly the options for a TALO, a helicopter insertion, or even a parachute jump were all on the table for getting 1 Para onto the ground and into position. This was of course met with great excitement by the blokes, as well as understandable envy from their sister battalion, 3 Para.

On 24 March, a Pathfinder patrol consisting of three WMIKs with six PF operators and three Royal Engineers was dispatched to head up through the US front line with the aim of carrying out a recce on Qalat Sikar Air Base, where it was planned for 1 Para to be inserted onto the ground.

Intelligence had indicated that the area was relatively clear but as the Pathfinder patrol moved up to the outskirts of Al Nasiriyah, they witnessed the USMC and other American front-line fighting units engaged in heavy combat with elements of Saddam's forces and taking what seemed like numerous casualties. The patrol took this opportunity to link up with the US command post to get an idea of what was going on around them and to see if they could safely pass through en route to Qalat Sikar. The Americans told them that the area was extremely dangerous and that they had had a patrol attacked the night before and some personnel had been taken hostage. After taking this all into account and having a bit of rest and food, the Pathfinders made the decision to push on to the River Euphrates bridge, where they witnessed more heavy fighting. After setting up satellite communications with Brigade HQ, they were told that they had operational command on the ground and to continue if they felt it was achievable. The PF team decided to push on again, this time totally blacked out and moving in the dark using NVGs.

As the patrol pushed on through the darkness towards their target of the air base, they moved through heavy congregations of vehicles and men, which turned out to be Iraqi Fedayeen paramilitary. They did not initially realise who the British patrol were in the darkness. A little further down the road, their vehicles started to come under fire from small arms, Russian

DShK (referred to as Dushka) heavy machine guns and RPGs, which were flying in over their heads, and they ended up having to take evasive action. Breaking contact and getting off the main road, they set up a snap ambush and evaluated their situation. They watched silently as eight to ten enemy technical vehicles laden with troops sped by on the hunt for them. At this point, realising that their patrol had been compromised and unable to continue their task, the commander, Captain Blakeley, and second in command, Sergeant Nathan Bell, had a discussion about what to do next: whether to push on via another route to complete their mission, abandon the vehicles and move off on foot, call for a heli-extraction or otherwise to turn around and attempt to get back across the US front line. The senior members of the patrol were all consulted in the usual 'Chinese Parliament'[6] style and based on what had happened to guys in the first Gulf War, they did not want to risk being captured. It was decided that heading back down the road to the American front line was the best of the bad set of options available to them.

Warrant Officer 2 (Retired) Nathan Bell recalled:

> The guys agreed we had pushed our luck as far as we could, and the best option was to now drive back to Al Nasiriyah. I reversed all the routes on the GPS so we could go through a series of RVs and explained to the guys that if we came into any form of contact on the route back, we would return fire and engage any enemy targets we came across. We had our lights on this time just like any other vehicles on the road, which gave us a much better field of vision. I then physically led the vehicles back out of our lay-up point on foot at the front of the lead WIMK to make sure no one got bogged down before we reached the main road. I went through all the IAs (immediate action drills), so everyone knew exactly what they were doing and off we set.[7]

Reaching the edge of the next built-up area, the patrol started to come under enemy fire. The three PF WIMKs then opened up with all their vehicle-mounted GPMGs and .50-calibre machine guns. They took out the enemy targets as they passed by and threw white phosphorus grenades to cover their escape.

Continuing down the road, they came under fire on several more occasions. Taking out enemy positions that opened up on their three vehicles, they made their way to the main turning and into yet another enemy contact. Being careful to avoid a large bomb crater they had spotted on the way up, Sergeant Bell opened fire on the enemy gathered around this area and the patrol sped through. The main concern now was to make sure that they were easily identifiable to the US front-line soldiers, so they came back in with a green Cyalume light on the front of their vehicle showing themselves to be coalition forces.

Back behind the American lines, they assessed their situation and realised that as well as numerous bullet strikes over all three of the WIMKs, one round had passed through the corner of Captain Blakeley's trousers, and another had ricocheted off Royal Engineers Sergeant Healey's 9mm pistol, which was attached to his body armour. Nathan Bell said, 'We were lucky. There were strike marks all over our vehicles and one of the guys had a phosphorus grenade still in his hand, which he had pulled the pin out of earlier. The Americans wouldn't let us throw it, so luckily, I found a spare pin in my vehicle well, and inserted this back into the grenade to make it safe.'[8]

Sergeant Bell and Sergeant Healey were both subsequently awarded the Military Cross for their actions during this patrol, which Nathan Bell so aptly described as, 'An aggressive four-hour U-turn.' The plan to insert 1 Para into Qalat Sikar Air Base never came to fruition.

The two Para battalions continued to move up into the oil fields, carefully taking and clearing each drilling station, and fully expecting Saddam to defend these installations, or if not, attempt to destroy them to prevent them falling into the hands of the coalition. Recces were carried out on each target and, entering from the most vulnerable side, they set up fire-support bases with heavy weapons and snipers covering the approach into the locations and cleared them of potential enemy troops or booby traps. These GOSPs were then held by platoon strength for weeks on end, before the men were given orders to move on.

The Battle of Basra took place in early April, involving a massive tank battle that the coalition forces won, and 3 Para were sent into the Old Quarter of the city on foot because the tanks and armoured vehicles were too large for the narrow winding roads of the city. They were wary of getting caught up in street battles in a FIBUA situation, but it didn't come to that. Sergeant Stoves said, '3 Para tabbed in. We were expecting trouble and were very wary of being caught up in intense street battles, but they never materialised. A lot of the locals were looting banks and shops but the Iraqi soldiers, who were mostly conscripts, just dropped their weapons and ran at the sight of us. Any defence disappeared and the Iraqi soldiers melted away.'[9]

On 9 April Baghdad fell and Basra was secured by the British. The invasion phase lasted until the end of April and on 1 May, President Bush declared an end to major combat. President Saddam Hussein and other prominent Iraqi regime leaders went on the run and became the focus of intense searches as the country dissolved into widespread looting and saw the emergence of insurgencies fighting against each other as well as the foreign troops.

The initial shock and awe missile attacks and air strikes caused huge devastation, taking out key strategic installations and military targets. The ground invasion had followed soon afterwards, and coalition forces had moved over the Kuwait–Iraq border while more air strikes were carried out across the country on tier one locations. Despite the successful invasion and the collapse of the regime within a few weeks, Operation Telic was not over yet.

The war was declared officially over, and the Para Regt had been involved in little more than a few skirmishes during the initial phase of the invasion before their role changed. While 3 Para entered Basra along with the 1st Armoured Division, the rest of the Brigade moved north and crossed the Euphrates to occupy the historical site of the biblical Garden of Eden at Al Qurnah on the Tigris River. The men of 1 Para then moved north with other elements of the Brigade to begin the stabilisation phase in Maysan Province, while one of the rifle companies was quickly sent on to Baghdad to secure the vital British Embassy building. The Paras were now part of the stabilisation force and helmets were replaced by maroon berets as they patrolled in search of dissidents and tried to maintain peace. Stu Baillie said, 'The Iraqis surrendered, and it was officially peacetime but there were still a lot of dissidents, and our job was to hunt them down. "A" Company, 1 Para were based in the Al Amara sports stadium, patrolling the local neighbourhoods. We wore our berets in an attempt to soften our approach, but our helmets were on our webbing. Drawing on our experience of Northern Ireland, we moved around in multiples of twelve men, attempting to bring order to the situation and win the hearts and minds of the local people.'[10]

While the initial reaction to the fall of Saddam Hussein appeared to be joyous celebrations, the coalition forces had underestimated the backlash of local feeling. The number of troops on the ground was quickly reduced and wartime first-line ammunition quotas were cut back before any of the cities or smaller towns had been fully controlled. Support from the local population had been sorely misjudged and across the country sectarian violence was starting to break out. Corporal (Retired) Steve Thurtle of 1 Para remembered being based at the stadium in Al Amarah, 'We drove around in WMIKs which offered very little protection, but we patrolled freely in the soft-skinned vehicles doing welfare rounds between Abu Naji and Al Amarah. Initially we had good relations with the Iraqis but then there was a clear shift in feelings towards us.'[11]

Abu Naji camp near the city of Al Amarah became the main base for the British in the Maysan Province and from there patrols went out to numerous villages and towns in a large area of desert and marshland, much of which had been drained and ruined by Saddam Hussein's regime. The 1 Para rifle companies were based in and around Al Amarah and Basra, which were linked by the main route 6, but it was 3 Para who were initially in charge of controlling the town of Majar al-Kabir, which was 15 miles south of Al Amarah. The teams were using PRR (Personal Role Radios), but the region created great difficulties for communication and there were numerous blackspots in and around the towns. Ammunition and supplies were reduced as the men moved into what was now officially a non-combat phase of the operation and they neared the end of their tour. The area was deemed to be under control and no serious threats were expected. Sam Salmon said, 'There was very little resistance; we found a lot of abandoned kit, tanks, and empty troop barracks and ammo everywhere. We had to collect everything up and buried it all in a pit. There were a few minor skirmishes with local militia but nothing heavy and we did a lot of hearts and minds stuff, giving out medicine and food, but then that was stopped because it wasn't being co-ordinated properly. One of our biggest problems was trying to stop the locals from blowing themselves up as they tried to melt down ammo to get the brass.'[12]

Shortly after this 3 Para were pulled out and flew home after handing over to 1 Para in June 2003; for them Operation Telic was over. Now 1 Para took charge of patrolling the area, which was described as being peaceful. There was only a short amount of time left before they and the rest of the 16 Air Assault Brigade were due to leave Iraq. Everything was winding down and the guys were all looking forward to getting home and away from the intense heat.

Majar al-Kabir was a town with a population of around 60,000 living in mud huts or square, concrete houses with flat roofs. The locals felt that it was they who had got rid of the Saddam Ba'athist element whom they hated, and they now resented the foreign military occupation. Most importantly, they were extremely angry about any attempts to confiscate their weapons, which they viewed as their rightful means of protection. Feelings were also running high about the lack of help and improvements that had been promised. On 22 June 2003, 'C' Company, 8 Platoon, consisting of two multiples of twelve men, Two Zero Alpha led by Lieutenant Ross Kennedy and Two Zero Bravo under the command of Sergeant Gordon 'Jock Robbo' Robertson, had been tasked with patrolling the town from their base at the local police station for thirty-six hours. Kennedy's Alpha multiple were on first stag when angry protestors converged on the station. The shouting mob headed towards the station and began throwing stones. Windows were smashed and the vehicles were hit by the attacking crowd. The irate horde of around 500 Arabs surged towards the police station and a DAF 4-tonne truck and a Land Rover were destroyed. The Paras held off the angry Iraqis with rubber bullets until a QRF arrived with armoured Scimitars and the crowd was pushed back. Major Kemp subsequently met with local elders and an agreement was drawn up that there would be no more searches or confiscation of weapons. The agreement was written and signed but there was a massive miscommunication. The Iraqis believed that it meant that there would be no more military presence, but Major Kemp believed that it stated that there would be no house searches, but that patrols would continue. Both the multiples returned two days later on 24 June. Unbeknown to them, a patrol of RMPs was also making a routine visit to the town at the same time with the aim of understanding why the local Iraqi police force had not provided the expected level of support during the attacks on the 22nd.[13]

Lieutenant Kennedy asked for more supplies of rubber bullets for the next patrol, but this request was denied as they had been packed away in preparation for the departure of 1 Para in a week's time. On the morning of the 24th the two multiples, Alpha and Bravo, arrived in Majar al-Kabir and made their way to the outskirts of town, where the HQ of the FAWJ (local militia), who normally accompanied them on their patrols, was based. Alpha, led by Kennedy, set off on foot as normal, but they were intercepted by the leader of FAWJ, who told them that it wasn't safe to go into the centre of town. Kennedy informed Sergeant Robertson that he was returning to the militia HQ and that Robertson's Bravo multiple should patrol in vehicles instead of walking.

'Jock Robbo' Robertson, a highly respected and very capable paratrooper, who was held in great esteem by the blokes, set off with his multiple in two Pinzgauers and headed towards the souk with the militia following. As they drove down the narrow streets, they passed youths who glared at them with hatred etched on their faces. As the men continued down the claustrophobic roads with the sun already creating intense heat, the number of incensed Iraqis grew. They began crowding towards the vehicles as the Bravo multiple pressed forward. The Paras, wearing no body armour or helmets, gripped their weapons tightly as the crowd began to throw stones at them. They looked back and realised that the Iraqi militia unit was no longer with them. Rocks began to smash into the windscreens and clenched fists banged on the bonnets of the vehicles as the crowd was incited by loud voices from the mosque minarets urging them to attack the Para patrol.

Jock Robbo realised that they had no means of communication with the PRR radios in the tight alleyways and knew that they needed to get back to HQ to join up with Lieutenant Kennedy's multiple. With the aim of dispersing the angry mob, he fired the baton gun, but this only served to infuriate the massive throng. He then fired warning shots with his A2 SA80 personal weapon but again it had no real effect on the enraged people, who were being told that the soldiers were going to rape their women and that they should attack. More warning shots were fired from other members of Bravo multiple using the powerful GPMG and Minimi and the Iraqis backed off briefly, but only to return with more weapons. Private (Retired) Freddie Ellis was a young Tom at the time:

> As we pushed forward the crowd became more violent and Sergeant Robertson ordered us to get out of the vehicles in a show of force, but the crowd responded by throwing even more missiles at us. Jock Robbo fired a baton gun in the air again, and then again, this time directly at a target and then suddenly the Iraqis seemed to appear with AK47s and started firing at us. It was intense, there were hundreds of them. A gunman appeared at a window and opened up on us. A round ricocheted off some metal fencing and shrapnel split open Corporal John 'The Dolmanator' Dolman's lip. He was another highly experienced and steady hand and second in command of the Bravo multiple.'[14]

Dolman dived for cover and he and Jock Robbo fired up at the man in the window, while two other Toms got back to the Pinzgauers and provided covering fire. The Iraqi gunmen had gone down, and this enraged the crowd still further. Now they were truly out for revenge and were bloodthirsty. The men from Bravo multiple got back into their vehicles and took advantage of the lull created by their firing and drove away.

Alpha multiple heard the sound of British weapons and Kennedy ordered his men to board the 4-tonne truck and they set off into town with the aim of supporting Bravo. The Iraqis were now well-armed with RPGs and AK47s. Jock Robbo aimed to get back to the militia HQ to join up with the Alpha multiple, but Kennedy was already crossing the bridge to find Bravo and they soon faced the baying crowd. Kennedy told the men to debus, and they all ran for whatever cover they could find. It became clear that they needed to get out and, under the cover of fire, the driver ran back to the truck as the others carried out a tactical withdrawal, but the vehicle wouldn't start. With two men covering their back, the rest of the men pushed the truck along the road until it gained enough momentum for a jump start. Everyone jumped on board dripping with sweat, and they sped out of town, still coming under fire but reached the MSR (main supply route) without sustaining any casualties and quickly set up firing positions. From their location they could see the sugar refinery and a fish farm but there was no sign of any Iraqis following.

Bravo multiple heard that Alpha was in contact but had no idea where they were. They reached the river but there was nowhere to cross and, coming under fire from both sides, they set up in all-round defence. Sergeant Robertson was finally in a position to use the Iridium satellite phone he had been carrying as back-up comms and he attempted to get through to the operations centre. Back at base, the satellite phone lay on a shelf ringing for nearly two minutes before being answered by one of the duty signallers. Jock Robbo quickly reported the contact that Bravo were involved in and requested immediate support from the QRF. He told the signaller that they were in heavy contact and running low on ammunition. The Army Air Corps and a Chinook were warned off and the MSG (Manoeuvre Support Group) were mobilised. Lieutenant Kennedy was contacted and told that Alpha needed to go back in to support Jock Robbo's Bravo multiple.

Sergeant Robertson ordered a few of the guys to get back to the Pinzgauers, but as he spoke, a huge blast ripped through the air as an RPG landed a direct hit on a fuel tank. Not long afterwards, the second Pinzgauer was also hit, and the men were now stuck without transport. Jock Robbo knew that they had to get into a building where they could attempt to wait it out until the QRF arrived. Keeping close, the Bravo guys zig-zagged down the streets, covering each other as they went. Watching their backs as they fired, they manoeuvred along the hot, dusty roads followed closely by the Iraqis, who suddenly appeared with a Dushka, and the ground trembled as the weapon was fired. The men took out Iraqis, attacking them with RPGs and AK47s as they desperately looked for protection in the walled streets. Around them hundreds of Iraqis gathered, intent on killing.

Alpha multiple put on body armour and helmets and with their diminished levels of ammunition they headed back into town on their truck. The huge vehicle was peppered with rounds as they came under heavy attack, and wary of the threat of an RPG, the men debused once again. Both Alpha and Bravo were now coming under attack in different parts of the town as other swarms of enraged Iraqis now headed for the police station, where six RMPs were holed up. The Paras were only a few hundred metres away from the police station, but they still had no idea that the RMPs were there. Back at Abu Naji, the ARF (Air Reaction Force) and the QRF ground force MSG were mobilising. Sent to act as a re-broadcast unit between the two multiples and the ops room, the Army Air Corps' Gazelle was already en route as paratroopers and medics under the command of Corporal Buck Rogers boarded a Chinook and they set off on course for Majar al-Kabir to rescue the men. Like everyone else at this time, the paratroopers on the Chinook knew nothing about the RMPs being in the town.

Jock Robbo chose a house for cover and sent the interpreter, Joseph, in to persuade the family that they would be safe. The shocked Iraqi family shook in fear as the twelve grimy, dusty paratroopers piled into their house, trying to convey that they would not harm any of them. Robbo sent the father out into the street to look for the gunmen and he returned to report that they were close by. The men hunkered down; exhausted and with sweat pouring down their faces, they couldn't see how they were going to get out of the situation alive. Sergeant Robertson managed to contact the ops room and was told that support was on its way. They then managed to get in contact with the Gazelle pilot, who told the men that they were surrounded by gunmen but that the ARF Chinook was inbound. The men from both Alpha and Bravo multiples heaved a sigh of relief when they heard the familiar roar of the Chinook coming nearer. Robbo made the brave decision to give away their position and let off flares so that the ARF could identify Bravo multiple's location. He knew very well the risk he was taking because now the angry Iraqi mob also knew where they were.

The Chinook came in towards the town and the men on board crouched ready to jump off and leap into combat in support of their fellow paratroopers. The helicopter hovered 50ft above the ground, creating a tremendous blast of air on those below, but the Iraqis had been waiting for it and opened fire. Steve Thurtle, the ARF 2iC, was on board the Chinook:

> I was at the back of the chopper near to the tailgate and Tubs was in front of me. Through the porthole behind him I saw plumes of black smoke coming up from the town. I knew it meant trouble and that we were going into a hot contact. Before I could say anything, the rounds started coming in and I was the first to get shot. I was hit in the lower leg and then a couple more shots hit me in the back, and I called out for a medic. I looked across and saw Tubs, a 17-stone mountain of a

man with flaming red hair, stand up to come and help me and then suddenly he was shot in the stomach. For some strange reason this seemed hilarious at the time, and I was laughing hysterically until I looked over and saw Jingles. He looked as though someone had poured a tin of paint over his head and bright red blood was dripping down his face and off his chin. This sobered me up immediately as I realised that he had been hit in the head and I went into survivor mode as shots continued to penetrate the chopper and more of the blokes were hit, including Corporal Buck Rogers. An RPG just missed us and another one whizzed past the main cog of the Chinook by three inches. If that had been hit, it would have brought us down. The pilot took evasive action and banked away, just avoiding another RPG, and we had no choice but to return to base. I found out later that the Chinook had taken well over one hundred rounds and looked like a colander by the time it arrived back at base. Six paratroopers lay injured on the back of the Chinook. The Royal Army Medical Corps (RAMC) doctor was hit in the foot, but he continued to work on us and without doubt saved many of our lives on the trip back to base.[15]

The men of Alpha multiple were now trapped by a sniper and decided to hold their position in irrigation ditches and wait out the arrival of the MSG, but Bravo were still cornered in the villa compound, and they had now given away their position with the flares. The Iraqis turned their attention back to Jock Robbo's men and began climbing over the wall of the courtyard. Using controlled fire to conserve their limited ammunition supply, the men took out the encroaching Iraqis one after the other.

Freddie Ellis said:

Both Jock Robbo and John Dolman remained in complete control, super professional throughout. We young Toms were terrified, but as well-trained paratroopers we were fighting on and dealing with the situation at hand. The Iraqis were now coming in from all sides; one would get shot and go down, then another would appear as if from nowhere. The Chinook and the Gazelle going over distracted the gunmen and bought us some critical and much-needed time as the Iraqis began shooting at the helicopters. Two fast jets returning from another mission screamed overhead; they couldn't do anything because they didn't know exactly where we all were, but the threat of the plane did make the Iraqis go to ground for a short while. The devastating news then came through that the ARF Chinook had returned to base and that it was going to be another twenty minutes before the MSG arrived. I was sure we were going to die in that house.

Sergeant Robertson and Corporal Dolman made the decision to leave the confines of the villa they were taking cover in while the Iraqis were still distracted by the ARF. John Dolman stayed at the house with half the men providing covering fire while Robbo led the other men away. Pepper-potting their way down the streets, the first group of paratroopers made it to an irrigation ditch.

Freddie described what happened:

> I went first with Jock Robbo, and we moved with rounds coming from everywhere and landing in and around our feet as we desperately looked for some cover. We came to the corner of a building with a large, open, rock-filled farmer's field in front of us. I looked behind and saw that the others weren't following and then we made it to an irrigation ditch and the other guys joined us there. We heard the sound of machine guns being fired by the MSG and knew that the QRF had arrived. Jock Robbo told me that he needed me to run across the field to link up with them. It was a few hundred metres across open ground, and I took off my kit and just ran as fast as I could with the guys providing covering fire and picking off any Iraqis who were firing at me. I had nearly made it when I tripped over, and an enemy round landed within inches of my face. All I can remember thinking is that I'd better get up and keep moving or I would be dead. I reached the MSG and gave them a target indication as to where the enemy was and the location of the rest of my multiple. As I was standing there, one of the guys on a WMIK got shot in the stomach by an enemy round. The MSG moved up with the .50-calibre machine gun and suppressed the enemy fire so that the rest of the men could get over safely. The whole thing was a total adrenaline rush, we all thought we were going to die and I'm still not sure to this day how Bravo did not take any casualties.

All of the paratroopers from the Alfa and Bravo multiples eventually reached a point of safety, but for the RMPs at the police station it was tragically a very different story. Nobody knows the exact truth but the enraged Iraqis, out for blood, got to them and they were all savagely murdered. They had very little ammunition, just fifty rounds each, no smoke grenades, and no iridium satellite phone. The Paras knew nothing about their presence in the town until they were told the terrible news afterwards that six RMPs had been slaughtered at the police station. Freddie Ellis said, 'It was incredible that we all escaped unhurt and yet the six RMPs who were so close to us got massacred. We were very lucky. I saw them bring the bodies in and spotted their bloodstained boots but didn't know who they were. We all went as white as sheets when we were told. We were trying to work out where they were and if we could have helped them.'[16]

Sergeant Gordon 'Jock Robbo' Robertson received the Conspicuous Gallantry Cross for his actions that day in Majar al-Kabir, while Lieutenant Ross Kennedy and Corporal John Dolman received MiDs.

The reaction of the Iraqis in Majar al-Kabir was a sign of things to come all across the country as insurgencies grew and tribal warfare took over. Peace was very far away for the people of Iraq. For the Paras in 2003 it had not been the war that they were expecting. However, the two battalions had been kept busy and it had brought out the best in them, even though they didn't see the action that they had hoped for and for which they had trained so hard.

Operation Telic was one of the largest deployments of British forces since the Second World War. The 16th Air Assault Brigade lost eleven soldiers in Iraq, six of whom, the RMPs from 156 Provost Company, were killed by the hostile mob in the village of Majar al-Kabir that the Paras managed to evade without fatalities. In July 2003, the remainder of the Brigade returned to the UK. The Paras had demonstrated the ability to react under pressure and to work alongside armoured troops, with further tours of Iraq to come in the future, but their skills and resilience were soon to be put to extreme tests in the increasingly hostile environment of Afghanistan.

# Chapter 19

# Helmand

## Afghanistan Part Two, 2006–10

The troops of 2 and 3 Para were deployed into Helmand Province in the south of Afghanistan on three Op Herricks between 2006 and 2011. Between them they carried out five tours of duty and engaged in some of the fiercest and most intense fighting the British Army had encountered since the Second World War. They were tasked with patrolling and dominating the ground, as well as manning vulnerable FOBs in remote towns and villages, where they constantly came under ferocious attacks from a relentless and merciless Taliban fighting force. Often isolated, running low on ammunition, food, and water with little chance of resupply or support, it was reminiscent of numerous scenes from the past. The Parachute Regiment had gone full circle and continued to demonstrate the lasting ethos of the indomitable spirit of a warrior, as they fought on and triumphed, at least in the short term, against overwhelming odds to hold off the enemy and bring some semblance of normal life to the local people, who had suffered under the harsh Taliban dictatorship. With the mission of gaining the trust of the locals and offering them help and reassurance, the Paras came up against an enemy who ruled by fear, had no hesitation to use IEDs and suicide bombers, and had well-armed and militarily savvy fighters. Engaging in full-on battles, the Taliban used their overwhelming numbers in an attempt to dislodge the Paras from the key strategic locations. It was every operation the Paras had ever been engaged in rolled into one and it tested their skill set to the extreme. Operating in a harsh environment with temperatures reaching well over 50°C in the summer and freezing cold in the winter, the Paras demonstrated their courage, supreme soldiering skills and determination to never give up in what became known as 'Hell Land'.

Despite President Bush announcing the end of major combat and the move towards a stable and democratic society in Afghanistan in October 2001, the Taliban were never far away. When US and coalition forces turned their focus of attention to Iraq in 2003, the Taliban, with the support of Islamic terrorist groups such as al-Qaeda, began an insurgency. In the next few years, they reinforced their fighters during the winter months in preparation for 'the fighting season' when the snow disappeared and the passes were open. Kidnappings, assassinations, and bombings increased in Kabul, and as Iraq disintegrated into tribal warfare, the Taliban surreptitiously gathered support and grew in number. Britain joined the US and NATO forces in sending in more troops to Afghanistan to combat the situation in 2006. A large number of British soldiers, spearheaded by 3 Para, were sent into the southern province of Helmand. Their mission was to establish good relations with the local population in remote towns and villages and prevent Taliban forces from taking control.

With locals disillusioned by a new government that was doing little to help them, the soldiers didn't know who they could trust or when and where the next attack would come from. The main British air base, Camp Bastion, located near the provincial capital of Helmand, Lashkargah, began as a tiny base in a remote desert area with a dusty runway and tented accommodation. Engineers fortified the base, and over time it grew to the size of a large town with housing for 32,000 people, a fully equipped hospital, in-theatre training facilities and an airfield and heliport, which, by 2011, handled up to 600 aircraft movements a day. As the situation in Helmand escalated in 2006, the Paras prepared to be called into action.

*Herrick IV*
At the beginning of April 2006, the 3 Para battle group, under the command of Lieutenant Colonel Stuart Tootal (now Colonel Retired), were deployed into Helmand. They were quickly sent out to various FOBs in the region with the mission to keep a watchful eye on the Kajaki Dam and other key strategic locations and begin stabilisation duties in the farming communities of the region. Patrolling from fortified bases known as platoon houses, after a relatively quiet start to the tour, they soon found themselves engaged in ferocious fighting when coming up against huge numbers of well-armed and tactically astute Taliban fighters. Battles ensued in and around the towns of Gereshk, Nawzad, Sangin and Musa Qala. During this six-month tour, 3 Para engaged in over 500 contacts, often coming under sustained attack for hours on end, day after day. As the tour stretched over the summer months, the men operated in severe heat, confronting the enemy in heavy body armour and carrying weighty loads of equipment and ammunition. Despite the onslaught, and the high number of injuries and deaths, the men of 3 Para battled on with valour and resilience to hold off the enemy and continue with their mission to protect and reassure the innocent and often terrified civilian population.

The first democratic elections since the start of the war were held in Afghanistan in 2004 and Hamed Karzai was elected president of the newly named Islamic Republic of Afghanistan, but the Taliban grew in strength and gained support from villagers through fear and taking advantage of those who felt let down by promises of improvements to the critical infrastructure and standard of living as well as the lack of basic governance. NATO took control of the fight against insurgents in 2006 and Defence Secretary John Reid announced that Britain would send forces to relieve the American troops in the south of the country. Although he knew it would be tough, he said, 'Were in the south to help and protect the Afghan people to reconstruct their economy and democracy. We would be perfectly happy to leave in three years' time without firing a shot.'[1] The irony of that statement soon became clear. The Taliban promised to resist the incoming force; they increased their activities and began to surge through the land that they knew so well. As the US launched Operation Mountain Thrust against the insurgency in the south, troops had to hold back the determined enemy with insufficient numbers and lack of support and equipment in what quickly became a brutal war.

Helmand is a large area of predominantly desert with the River Helmand running through it to provide irrigation and produce fertile areas known as green zones. The Kajaki Dam is a major reservoir in the region and Helmand is one of the largest opium-producing regions in the world. The desert is hot and dry, while the farming regions around the towns are lush and humid. The men of 3 Para first heard about the upcoming tour of Afghanistan in late 2005; the first that some of the blokes knew about it was from article in the newspapers. Once mustered back in Colchester they soon went into a pre-deployment training phase that consisted of a series of lectures on the culture of the country and the basics of the Pashto language. They were, however, given very little information on the Taliban forces at this time. Sergeant (Retired) Stuart Pearson remembered, 'Helmand is about the size of England and so training consisted of moving from Salisbury Plain to Norfolk for a few days doing exercises and then up to Newcastle, covering a similar amount of ground as Helmand. Although, obviously, the conditions were very different.'[2] The second phase of training, which took place in Oman, was more useful, with some excellent live firing exercises. Eventually the men of 3 Para arrived in Camp Bastion, from where they were posted to basic and vulnerable FOBs in the green zones and simple bases around Kajaki Dam.

The arrival of all the troops took longer than expected and the first to arrive were 'A' Company in mid-April, who stayed in tents with no air conditioning at Camp Bastion before moving out to FOB Fort Price, just outside Gereshk. Initially, life was quiet; the soldiers patrolled out from their bases on what were fairly mundane and boring duties and chatted with the locals, but there was an underlying sense of unease, and the men were sure that they were being 'dicked', i.e. the locals were passing on information about their movements to the, so far invisible, Taliban. At the beginning of May 2006, a minor contact signified that all was not well. All of 3 Para were in country by the middle of May and the plan was to keep them mobile with the ability to react to the ever-changing environment and enable them to patrol areas without being fixed in one place for long periods of time.

The delay in the arrival of troops had given the Taliban time to move; many of their fighters in exile in Pakistan had come over and they took control of the northern district of Baghran. They remained low key while the poppy harvest went ahead, but then things began to heat up. In the middle of May there was an attack on the DC (District Centre) of Musa Qala, convoys were ambushed on the main routes, and reinforcements were sent to build up defences in the town of Nawzad after another Taliban attack there. As the paratroopers patrolled, they began to realise that the Taliban were organised and tactically cunning; their knowledge of the region enabled them to carry out effective ambushes on vehicles travelling along the almost deserted roads. Helicopters were needed for transport, resupply and casevacs, but with only five British Chinooks available at any time, it was clear that they didn't have enough. The fighting season began, and it was going to be a long, drawn-out tour for the men of 3 Para.

At the beginning of June, paratroopers were sent up to Nawzad to secure a compound believed to be a safe house for Taliban commanders and a weapons and ammunition dump. A cordon-and-search operation set up by Gurkhas came under attack and as 'A' Company, 3 Para, came off their Chinooks, they stepped straight into a firefight that lasted for four hours. It was an eye-opening experience as the men realised how difficult it was to operate effectively and fight in the small villages comprised of walled compounds with narrow streets and alleyways, which often led to dead ends. The compound walls were surrounded by irrigation ditches, high crops and orchards that all provided cover for the Taliban. The men clambered over fences and high walls and through tiny doorways trying not to injure any civilians as they came under heavy attack. Apache helicopters, being used for the first time, came in to provide welcome air support and eventually an A-10 provided cover for the men to get to an area of relative safety. There were more ambushes and an incident at Kajaki Dam led to a permanent base being set up by the Paras, which meant resources being even more stretched to keep them supplied.

'C' Company were based in FOB Fort Price just outside Gereshk and on 27 June a patrol went out to visit the village of Zumbelay, an oasis in the middle of desert surroundings. The plan was to meet with the elders for a 'shura' (a consultation between tribal leaders) to discuss the needs of the village and to see what help they could offer. A patrol made their way into the village, while an FSG (fire support group) lay up in the desert a couple of miles away to keep an eye on the surrounding area. The platoon, wearing berets to signify their peaceful role, walked into the strangely quiet village, and sat with a few men under a mulberry tree. One of the Afghan elders told them that it would be better to come back in a couple of days when there would be more people to talk to because they were all at prayer. It was not prayer time. He indicated for them to go another way out of the village where there was a bridge. Outside the town, the FSG moved to the outskirts of the village to RV with the platoon. Stuart Pearson said, 'We headed back to the village and suddenly came under enemy fire. My reaction was "Yes you dancer!" I was excited, this is what I had waited thirteen years for. We got into a base line and pummelled their position.'

Down in the village, 9 Platoon had walked into an ambush. Under contact from all sides, they quickly replaced their berets with helmets and dived into irrigation ditches to take cover. Scrambling out just in time before mortars crashed into the earth behind them, they manoeuvred across furrowed fields, returning fire and dodging rockets that slammed into the hard, sun-baked ground around them. The FSG got close to the village and put down some heavy covering fire. Using mortars, they created a distraction and provided smoke to enable the men of 9 Platoon, who had journalist Christina Lamb and photographer Justin Sutcliffe with them, to escape.

Stu continued:

> The firefight went on for about two hours and we were calling in air support, but apparently there had been another contact up at Sangin as well, and air support had been diverted up there, so we had to wait. The platoon managed to get out of the village, and we all headed out into the desert. The only way back to Gereshk was over the bridge, which they had tried to steer us across earlier, and the Taliban knew this, so they would have been waiting in ambush for us. The rest of the Company based at Gereshk crashed out to support us and secured the bridge so that we could come back in and get across before heading

back to camp. Finally, some air support turned up in the nick of time and covered our movement back to base.[3]

Sangin is a town further north, the centre of the opium trade and in a green zone with fields of poppies and maize irrigated by the River Helmand. 'A' Company took over from the Americans at the beginning of June and moved into the District Centre, a ramshackle compound about half a mile outside the main town with scant fortifications comprising of sandbags and trenches around the perimeter. Beyond the camp were derelict buildings, and compound walls with patches of tall crops and areas of higher ground providing the Taliban with vantage points from which to attack. The first few weeks were quiet and then the Taliban began their onslaught. Battles began and continued five or six times a day, every day for weeks on end. The troops, never more than 120-strong, were practically trapped inside the compound walls with only occasional patrols to try and clear the Taliban presence. It was often deemed too dangerous for helicopters to land with supplies and the men waited as long as five days while they repelled the Taliban, who were bombarding them with RPGs, rockets, mortars, and small arms fire. A direct hit from a Chinese 107 rocket smashed into the top of the District HQ and killed three men. The night sky filled with tracer fire, the clacking of machine guns and explosions resounded all around.

At the end of July, a patrol from 'B' Company, who had relieved 'A' Company, made its way through the narrow streets of Sangin and one section spotted Taliban gunmen on a roof, who engaged them. Two of the section were hit, and one of the blokes lay injured in open ground as bullets rained down all around him. Corporal Bryan Budd led a counter-attack on the building and forced the Taliban fighters to flee into an open field, where they were taken out. The move enabled medics to reach the injured man and get him out safely. A month later, Corporal Budd was out on patrol again. The Taliban were taking advantage of the high walls around compounds and the Paras planned to destroy them. Three sections headed out from the FOB with one group flanking left, the other going right and the middle section heading straight for the walls. Beyond the compound were fields of 6ft-high maize and the remains of old buildings. In the right-hand section, Bryan Budd saw a group of Taliban ahead of them and decided to move round and take them by surprise, but noise from another section alerted the enemy to the presence of the Paras and a firefight quickly ensued. As Corporal Budd led the way toward the Taliban, three of his eight-man section were hit, and the rest took cover. Despite being injured, Bryan realised that they were pinned down and could all die if they didn't do something to turn the momentum of the fight. He bravely moved forward alone to engage the enemy fighters, and ferociously went into the attack. His actions forced the Taliban to withdraw, and the rest of the paratroopers were able to get to safety. On the other flank, the first two sections joined up and made a safe route for reinforcements to come from the platoon house as an intense exchange of rounds began. As men from 3 section began appearing covered in blood, they realised that Corporal Budd was missing. The battle continued until an Apache came in to strafe the enemy locations and then the men went to look for Bryan. His body was found on the edge of the maize field, with three dead Taliban lying around him. For his courageous actions in both of these engagements, Corporal Bryan Budd was posthumously awarded the Victoria Cross. Over the course of the summer, one in seven of the original sixty-five men based at Sangin had been wounded or killed.

In Musa Qala, a town in an isolated green zone even further north, the Taliban had managed to get some of the locals onside and had gained control of much of the area by 2006. In May they attacked and killed a number of Afghan policemen, and the Pathfinder platoon was sent in to assist the police. Initially they weren't authorised to intervene, but eventually they helped force the Taliban out and fought numerous firefights to keep the Taliban from taking the key strategic location of the District Centre. Later on, in June, the Pathfinders were back there again to relieve the Americans at the base. They were given the remit that they would be there for forty-eight hours until 3 Para came in to take over control. Already stretched to the limit, 3 Para got caught up on ops in Sangin and with a strength of just over twenty men, the Pathfinders moved into the shabby, rat-infested platoon house, which was based in a compound on the edge of Musa Qala and was covered in holes from bullets and rockets. The Pathfinders took over a building in the centre of the compound that was surrounded by the low, flat-roofed cement and mud dwellings of the town and a market square. They put up sangars on the roof of their building, one facing the market and another on a structure just outside the high compound wall. Little did they know that it would be nearly two months before they were finally relieved. Tom Blakey arrived a couple of days behind the rest of the men on a Chinook bringing in supplies:

> I stepped off the heli in a wadi and realised that I was surrounded by Toyota Hilux trucks and a load of guys with long beards carrying AKs and wearing bandoliers, looking just like the Taliban. I thought I'd been dropped in the wrong place and wasn't sure until I saw a couple of WMIKs and a few of our guys walking towards me. We were only

supposed to be there for forty-eight hours but then all of the 3 Para companies got held up. Sangin kicked off and all anyone could do at the various FOBs was defend the location and carry out localised patrols. There weren't enough of us to dominate the ground; only twenty-one men were doing a job that required a full rifle company of around 120. We were prepared after the last mission and took in extra rations and ammo, but we didn't expect to be there so long, and it was tough keeping up the morale of the men as the stay was continually extended. We were not well-equipped, the FOB was pretty vulnerable, and conditions were harsh. We had a hose pipe for washing, a couple of cut-off oil drums for toilets and a limited supply of field rations, which often ran out because it was too dangerous for supplies to be sent in. We ate local food, and all of us suffered from diarrhoea and vomiting, plus we were faced by daily assaults from the Taliban. There was an attack on an American convoy in the desert, but we couldn't send anybody out to support, and I remember standing on the roof on lookout with another guy when a round passed right between our heads.[4]

The initial plan for the Helmand region was based on an ink-spot approach; each company had to clear their area and dominate the surrounding ground until all the territories merged like ink spreading on blotting paper. There just weren't enough resources or men to make this happen. The area was also a high-risk fly zone for Chinook helicopters, so resupply missions were few and far between. On occasion, supplies were parachuted into nearby wadis and the men had to go out to fetch them. They drove out in their non-armoured vehicles through Taliban-controlled areas to make the critical collections.

After nearly six weeks, a military Danish contingent was due to go in to relieve the PF team at Musa Qala and as a recce party of five Danes arrived in the compound the Taliban launched an attack and an RPG destroyed one of the sangars. Two Danish guys were trapped outside the compound; one of them had fallen two floors with the rubble from the explosion and he was injured and exposed to the enemy. Mark Wilson grabbed his weapon, ran over to the wall and looked over at the Dane, who lay with a broken leg and blood pouring from a head wound. The medic threw the guy a field dressing and Mark clambered down the wall using a makeshift ladder, got to the guy under incoming enemy fire and brought him back safely. He was later awarded the Military Cross for his actions. The full Danish Squadron followed, and Sergeant Major Andy Newell hitched a lift back to Camp Bastion on one of the resupply runs, to guide them in.

Corporal Blakely said:

We were really low on everything by now, including batteries for our NVGs. Under constant attack, it took three days for the Danes to fight their way in and eventually they moved into Musa Qala at night while air strikes distracted the Taliban. They reached the gates safely with Andy leading the convoy on foot, but a frightened ANP guard got spooked. He stupidly started shooting and hit Andy in the arm. It was a very severe wound; he lost a lot of blood and was very lucky not to lose his arm. The Doc attached to the PF, Tariq Ahmed, did a great job of stabilising Andy once he was brought into the DC and undoubtedly saved his arm. It was, however, great to see the Danish contingent; they had over one hundred men and were well-armed and equipped. After a short handover period, at last it was time for us to leave, but setting off into the desert in our WIMKs, we got ambushed in a wadi. Performing a contact drill, we returned fire, turned around and got back to the compound, luckily not sustaining any casualties. In all honesty, it could have been a lot worse. We had to wait a while for another opportunity to get out, whilst the daily contacts and intense scraps with the Taliban continued. A couple of days later a B-1 bomber dropped a huge incendiary which hit a mosque just outside the compound. It was a massive explosion with wriggly-tin and concrete blown into the air, but the compound wall protected us and even though there were guys on stag along the walls, thankfully, nobody was hurt.[5]

The local people moved out of Musa Qala, and it became a central point of focus for the Taliban attacks. Numerous attempts to relieve the Pathfinders failed due to lack of understanding of the ground conditions and it was finally realised that a full battle group operation was required. In Operation Snakebite, a landing zone was secured, and mortar lines set up to enable 'B' and 'C' Companies from 3 Para to air assault in. The battle group was supported by helicopters and bombers; a 500lb bomb was dropped before 300 men from 3 Para advanced to contact with bayonets fixed to clear the compound and check for IEDs. A Canadian unit of armoured vehicles linked up with the Danes and the Pathfinders drove out while 3 Para engaged the Taliban in battle, sadly with the loss of Pte Andrew Cutts, an RLC gunner on one of the WMIKs. Stu Pearson said, 'We had body armour, but it was very cumbersome and difficult to move in. We made a choice between ballistic protection and freedom of movement. We needed to get in and back out again fast. Carrying extra weight is very draining in that heat and you lose concentration, so we went without it.'

The Pathfinders finally extracted safely; the initial forty-eight hours had turned into fifty-two days. The Danish, along with Somme Platoon from the Royal Irish Rangers, continued to hold the DC and face the relentless daily attacks. With the Danish armoured 'Tiger' force, they were well-equipped to keep the Taliban at bay, however, after four weeks, the Danish squadron were ordered to leave by their politicians back home.

The plan was for the Danes to be replaced within the next forty-eight hours by a composite company of Para Regt and Royal Irish known as 'Easy Company' and led by paratrooper Major Andy Jowett. Andy met with the 3 Para CO, who explained the situation and laid out what he had at his disposal. The Royal Irish platoon already in situ were staying and were bolstered by a second platoon from their own unit. He also had a Para Regt sniper pair, a mortar section, some combat medics, and a LEWT (Light Electronic Warfare Team), which comprised a couple of signallers who listened in to the Taliban unsecured radio net, translated all key chit-chat, and used it to build intelligence and warn of impending attacks. Major Jowett asked for a couple of tip-top interpreters and a doctor, which he got, and was also informed that fifty new Afghan police were joining them as the previous local police had proved to be unreliable. Sergeant Major Scrivener, a well-respected and cool hand from 3 Para, joined Major Jowett in making up the ranks of the new company.

In the early hours of the morning, Easy Company set off from Camp Bastion in a Chinook. As the lights from the camp faded into the night, the men were excited to be getting into the action. Arriving on 23 August, the men scurried into the compound carrying as much food and ammunition as possible in the knowledge that resupply would be difficult. The men then watched in dismay as the Danes departed, taking all their heavy weapons, armoured vehicles, and medical team with them; eighty-eight men, including one doctor, were now left to defend the compound with greatly reduced defensive resources. With no civilians in town, the DC was even more vulnerable as the insurgents could move through the connected buildings and approach without being seen. In the desert, the Taliban did not know about the new arrivals and believed that they could walk in and take the town away from the remaining Afghan police force. The LEWT team, who monitored the Taliban radio net, heard them talking about drinking tea in the District Centre by the following evening, and this only served to galvanise Easy Company into proving them wrong.

The next morning, the Taliban attacked en masse in a determined attempt to take the DC compound. Huge numbers of insurgents moved forward in a well-co-ordinated and ferocious attack from all sides. The Paras and Royal Irish sprang into action, firing machine guns and aiming mortars almost vertically into the air to hit the targets, who were getting to within 50m of their position and were close enough to lob grenades into the camp. Finally, the Taliban retreated, and nobody had been hurt but they came again later that day and on multiple occasions every day after. Some attacks lasted twenty minutes, and others lasted for hours. Air support was called in on a regular basis to pummel the enemy and kill what seemed like a never-ending supply of Taliban fighters.

For five more days the attacks continued with the men constantly in the line of fire facing injury or death. The Taliban persisted with mortar and grenade attacks, but the men kept on defending and holding the DC compound. Getting supplies into the camp was extremely difficult. Warrant Officer 1 (Retired) Steve Tidmarsh, who was based in Camp Bastion said, 'One time we went in there on a logistics resupply mission with ammunition, food and water, protected by 3 Para Patrols Platoon. We drove to the wadi and immediately came under fire. The driver was incredibly nervous because he knew that if an RPG hit the drop, all the munitions in the back would take the entire patrol out. We dropped off the supplies and got out of there fast. The guys inside had it really tough.'[6]

Sometime later, after suffering what seemed like an unsustainable number of fatalities and injuries, the Taliban changed their tactics and began firing mortars and rockets from a distance into the DC on a far more frequent basis. It was very difficult to accurately locate the firing points at their bases 2 miles away, and the men constantly heard the whistle of the missile and waited for the explosion, not knowing where it would land. The compound was hit day in, day out.

Casualties became inevitable. A bullet zipped straight through a gap in one man's body armour, sliced into his flesh and killed him instantly. For the first time, the men heard the ominous shout of 'man down!' which they had been dreading from day one. As medics cared for his body, the soldiers continued fighting with everything they had to keep the Taliban at bay. The Para Regt sniper pair had to get to the roof at every opportunity to perilously try to spot the enemy and take them out. They made their way to their positions each day knowing that it could be their last. The emergency fallback position known to the guys as 'The Alamo' was manned by two soldiers when it took a direct hit by a mortar on 1 September. Men rushed to their aid but both soldiers died from their injuries. The following day the base sustained another direct hit and six more men were injured.

The attacks intensified and the guys were under relentless pressure going through a range of emotions including fear, anger and a sense of terrible loss. They got what sleep they could fully clothed and with a weapon close, often getting no more than two hours a night. Moving around in the oppressive, overwhelming heat wore them down and they struggled to keep hydrated. Supplies were running low; they had very little food left, but what they really wanted was more men and ammunition to be able to continue the fight and stop the enemy from taking Musa Qala DC.

A few days later the Taliban made another powerful attempt to storm the compound, but air support drove them back. A casevac was organised for two soldiers injured by flying shrapnel but the insurgents fired on the Chinook as it came in to collect the men. The helicopter had to return to base with damage from small arms fire and they were lucky to get back to Bastion with an almost severed rotor blade. A new plan was hatched, and a second attempt was made to get the injured men out that night, with air support and a huge barrage onto the Taliban position. This time the Chinook successfully got them out and also delivered some much-needed supplies and a small number of reinforcements. On 11 September, intelligence came through that the Taliban were being reinforced. The enemy numbers swelled, and they brought with them more weapons and ammunition. The men inside the compound prepared for an attack on the 12th and felt sure that the battle would come down to vicious hand-to-hand fighting. The thought of falling into the grip of the Taliban if they took the base was terrifying; they knew what these fighters would do to a British soldier if they captured one alive.

The attack never came, the Taliban disappeared. Major Jowett got word from the battalion HQ that the Taliban wanted a ceasefire, and he was to hold talks with them in the town the next day. The men of Easy Company made their views clear; they did not trust the Taliban, they believed that they were winning the battle and unanimously wanted to continue the fight. The bigger picture came into play and orders from above announced a ceasefire. Still not knowing if they could be trusted, Major Jowett went down to the market square to meet the Taliban leaders and local elders. The people of the village slowly returned, and a crowd gathered around the men discussing the way forward. Talks with the Taliban ensued and, although it was a tense time, eventually an agreement was reached. Easy Company remained at the base for another month while a plan for their extraction was agreed. On 13 October, the men were taken in local cattle trucks with an elder or member of the Taliban on board each vehicle to a location in the desert eight hours away. The men were on tenterhooks the whole way, sure that they would be ambushed, but then Apache helicopters came alongside and led them to where Chinooks were waiting to take them back to Camp Bastion, and eventually home.

To the east of Musa Qala lay the Kajaki Dam, an important installation that provided irrigation, controlled floods and produced electricity for the region. Members of 3 Para were deployed to small, rudimentary bases on the sandy and stony slopes where they endured the oppressive heat of the desert during the day followed by bitterly cold nights. They kept a close eye on Taliban movements to ensure the dam and village of Kajaki remained free of their control and came under sporadic attacks. On a fateful day in September, men from one team were subject to a horrific event that not only highlighted the lack of information and clear lines of communication, but also the added dangers faced by the Paras in their deployment to Helmand. While their fellow men from 3 Para battled against persistent Taliban attacks in the green zones, in comparison the men in FOB Camp Normandy led a mostly uneventful existence. On their elevated position living in very basic accommodation, the men attempted to stay hydrated in the sweltering heat and took occasional swims in the river below to cool off and take the opportunity to wash their clothes. On occasion the Taliban came up and took shots at the base and then disappeared into the dunes, but the limited number of men available to the Paras meant that they couldn't mount any operations against them. Half a mile away was a larger camp, FOB Athens.

On this particular day, 6 September, sniper Lance Corporal Stuart Hale spotted some Taliban down on the main road who had set up an illegal vehicle checkpoint and were stealing money from innocent civilian passers-by. The distance was too far for him to take an accurate shot, but he worked out that if he moved to a nearby ridge, the distance would bring the target in range, and he was keen to give it a go. Stu Pearson explained what happened:

> Stu Hale spoke to me, we got our wires crossed, and both thought the patrol had been cleared to go, then off he went on the route to the ridge. A short while after he departed, I heard a bang. It was an unusual sound, and I knew that it was something we hadn't come across before. We knew that the Russians had left millions of mines strewn across the country, but we hadn't been told where they were. I grabbed a couple of blokes, and we made our way down to where Lance Corporal Hale was lying at the edge of a wadi and could see that he had been injured. We got down to him and saw that part of his right leg and his finger had gone. Jay was putting a tourniquet on and giving him morphine. I called for a helicopter with a winch, but it was denied.

Shortly after this Corporal Mark Wright from Athens base came down with a team of nine men including Alex Craig and one other medic. My radio didn't have direct contact with Athens – calls had to be made through Normandy – but Mark could speak directly to Athens and so he too called for a helicopter with a winch, but he was denied as well. We identified two areas where a helicopter could come down and I got the blokes to check the sites. The path was cleared by the guys down on their belt buckles prodding with their bayonets as we had been taught in the pre-deployment training for mines, but as I went back to check on Stu Hale, I stepped on a fuckin' mine. I thought I was in a safe area that had been checked and the guys must have missed this one by millimetres. I heard the bang and immediately knew what I'd done and thought 'Fuck's sake', as I landed on my arse. Realising that we were in a minefield, I looked down at my left leg to see what damage had been done. It had been ripped apart, so I got out my tourniquet and Andy Barlow ran over to apply it for me. I couldn't feel any pain but knew it would be coming so I jabbed morphine into my right leg. Chris Harvey, or 'Jarhead' as we called him, was there helping Stu Hale, and Mark came over to see how I was doing. Despite clearly asking for a helicopter with a winch, after ninety long minutes a Chinook arrived and tried to land about fifty or so metres away, hovering just above the ground. The guys were indicating for us to go over to the helicopter, and we were waving to tell them to get away. We were in a fuckin' minefield and couldn't move, but as it lifted up into the air again, the incredible downdraft disturbed the ground and set off another mine causing even more injuries amongst our guys. Mark Wright was leaning over me, protecting me from the draft and took the main blast of the explosion, but my right leg was also hit this time, and Alex was hit in the chest. The Chinook lifted off and left us, Alex managed to get to the edge and Dave Prosser went to help him. Alex persuaded one of the guys to give him a needle decompression because his lungs were filling up with blood. Mark still had the radio and he kept in touch with Athens and passed on information to us even though he had severe injuries to his face, neck, arm, and chest. We heard that a helicopter was coming from Kandahar in about an hour and I didn't know if I could hold out for that long, but Mark would not let me sleep.[7]

There was a fourth explosion when a water bottle was thrown across to Andy Barlow and he stepped on another mine. His leg was blasted, Tug was thrown to the ground and Dave was hit. The men lay injured and in terrible pain spread out across the wadi with blood seeping into the earth around them, turning the yellow sand red. Tug threw his daysack onto the ground in front of him to check for mines before jumping onto it. By repeating this action, he got around to all the men to administer medical aid. Mark would not let anyone give up and go to sleep and the men bantered, taking the piss out of each other to keep up morale. It was Dave Prosser's birthday, and the guys sang 'Happy Birthday' to him as they lay on the hot sand with bloody flesh and gaping wounds, not knowing if they would ever have another birthday themselves, but all refusing to let their mates give up or think the worst.

The welcome sound of the Black Hawk helicopters finally reached their ears and after almost six hours since the first explosion and injury to Stu Hale, the men were finally winched up to safety. Medics fast-roped down into the gully to put the injured men in baskets and they were winched back up before the medic went down for the next man. They were then quickly cross decked to a nearby Chinook, but sadly Corporal Mark Wright succumbed to his terrible injuries and died en route to Camp Bastion. Stuart Pearson, Stuart Hale and Andy Barlow lost their legs. Mark Wright was posthumously awarded the George Cross for his leadership and bravery that day. It wasn't courage in battle or fierce and aggressive fighting, it was a tragedy that revealed the true inner strength of these paratroopers. They kept each other going, they laughed and took the mickey out of themselves and each other with their ever-present black humour and did what they could for the men around them to get through the horrendous ordeal.

Pearson said, 'Two of the guys went back to Kajaki and were shown a map that marked out all the old minefields. The information was available, but it had never been shared with any of us.'

Herrick IV came to an end six months after it had started, and the 3 Para battle group demobilised out of Afghanistan. They demonstrated their adaptability to a situation that demanded they show compassion and understanding to the local people and deal aggressively with an onslaught of attacks from the Taliban. Caught up in a number of intensive battles at FOBs and District Centres, they held out against an enemy that was determined and persistent. They never gave in, even when massively outnumbered and outgunned, and decisively won this phase of the battle. The men of 3 Para fought over 500 contacts, firing almost 580,000 rounds of ammunition. The award of over thirty decorations, including a posthumous Victoria Cross, showed the level of sustained combat the troops of 3 Para had been engaged in.

Operations continued in Helmand as coalition forces struggled to push through their commitment to providing the much-needed stabilisation programmes and improvements to everyday life that the Afghan people greatly desired, and in 2008 both 2 and 3 Para were sent back in on Herrick VIII.

## Herrick VIII

The Paras were keen to get back into Afghanistan in 2008, and both 2 and 3 Para Battalions were deployed as part of the 16 Air Assault Brigade. After Herrick IV, many men were lost through retirement, injury or death, but despite these losses many others stayed on ready to go again. Even some of those who had lost limbs carried on serving and a large number of young recruits, inspired by the actions of the guys during the 2006 tour, applied to join. Those that passed the demanding tests to join the Parachute Regiment were eager to deploy with their respective battalions. Despite the continuing mission to stabilise the country and complete development and improvement projects for the Afghan people, the enemy had gone nowhere. The Taliban had upped their game, swelled their ranks and were beginning to use more IEDs and suicide bombers. Herrick IV was tough, and for the paratroopers going in on Operation Herrick VIII it wasn't any easier in the hot, and testing environment.

Once again, the Paras were deployed in the summer months and had to endure the relentless sun beating down on them as they carried out their patrols and defended their bases. Experienced soldiers were joined by many fresh new faces. Steve Tidmarsh, Company Sergeant Major of 'A' Company, 3 Para at the time said, 'There was a massive recruitment drive after 2006. All the reports on television and in the media encouraged loads of new recruits. My future son-in-law joined up on the back of all the news. It had been a long time since the regiment had been in full-on battle and in 2006, we were tested and proved that we could deliver. We had an experienced core of guys who had been there and done it, and a lot of new, young lads joined who were inspired by the stories of battles and acts of courage and wanted to be part of the action.' The spirit and ethos of the regiment was as strong as it had ever been, and it needed to be as the situation in Helmand evolved.

The men of 2 Para were deployed to the Northern Districts of Helmand as part of Battle group 'North', manning FOBs spreading south from Kajaki along the course of the River Helmand to Inkerman, Sangin, Nolay, Gibraltar and Robertson. They were fixed in place while 3 Para formed part of Battle group 'South', who were more mobile and operating in and around the hot and humid green zones, the arid, scorching deserts of Helmand and Kandahar, the mountain borders with Pakistan, and the narrow alleyways of the towns and villages of Kandahar city in search of drug and ammunition stores and key Taliban players. As both battalions worked to gain the confidence of the local people, they also became involved in some heavy combat.

Major (Retired) Tony Hobbins, 2 Para Regimental Sergeant Major at the time, who took over in 2007 and had been on a recce of the region in February, said, 'The Bootnecks [slang for the Royal Marines] were there in winter, and I knew it was going to be a very different story in the summer when we took over. It was a completely different climate, and we were given the most difficult region to operate in. There was no doubt that we would be in contact in the green zones, in close-quarter fighting amongst the ditches, fields of poppies and maize where you couldn't see very far in front of you. On a precursor operation a month before our deployment we took a huge hit, and everybody was under contact. We smashed the Taliban back, but I knew that we would need more than a battle group this time around.'[8]

Hobbins was right. The men from 2 Para went in and took up their positions in the various FOBs, platoon houses and District Centres ready to face the incessant attacks and new dangers that the Taliban brought to bear when they patrolled out. 'B' Company were based at FOB Inkerman, which was soon known to the men as 'Incoming'. Out on patrol they had to wear full gear and carry heavy equipment as they went about with the task of mixing with the locals and intercepting the Taliban in temperatures well over 40°C. Imagine the hottest summer day and putting on enough layers for the coldest winter conditions, then moving around carrying heavy weapons and supplies weighing over 50lb along soft, marshy ground with crops reaching overhead, through mazes of streets and across stretches of hard-baked earth, crawling along ditches and clambering over walls. Each platoon rotated through 'point' (lead platoon) as they made their way around the village compound with its high walls and narrow paths, mixing with the people in a friendly and positive manner and keeping an eye out for Taliban, never knowing when they might be ambushed. Back at the basic camps fortified with Hesco and razor wire, most men slept outside with limited facilities. They built their own furniture and set up a dartboard to use when they had brief respites, always finding time to laugh, joke and mock each other.

On 8 June, after four hours patrolling in the draining heat, they headed back to base. Coming under attack from small arms fire and RPGs, the men diverted to the outskirts of the village and made their way along the outside of the walls with 4 Platoon on 'point', leading the way. They came to a T-junction and the section commander, Corporal David Baillie, wanted to secure the area for the platoon. Private Dave Murray was the front man and as he turned the corner, he saw an old man step out from a doorway into the path. Dave went forward to talk to the man and Dan Gamble, a Pashto speaker, went with him. As they reached the Afghan, he pressed the detonator button of his suicide vest and blew himself up. Shrapnel, screws, and nails fired out at high speed in all directions, ripping apart anything with which they came into direct contact. Dave, Dan, and the guys behind were caught by the blast and lay devastated on the path. Corporal Baillie was blown into a ditch, and with a bloody eye he quickly got back into action securing the area while medics and other guys from the patrol rushed over to attend to the injured men. Sadly, Privates Daniel Gamble, Nathan Cuthbertson and David Murray were killed by the terrible explosion. The new threat of suicide bombers was added to the list of dangers faced by the Paras whilst out on patrol. Hobbins said, 'The three men received catastrophic injuries. It was a lone action and marked the start of a new wave of attacks. We had to change our MO (modus operandi) and be even more aware of this new threat and treat the situations we came across accordingly. There had been some training for these types of scenarios, but most of the preparation had been for attacks on the bases. We now understood the lengths the Taliban would go to.'

The men started facing a multitude of contacts every day, and still tried to go out and meet the people with an upbeat attitude, not knowing who they might be coming up against.

Hobbins continued:

We could be hit by up to nineteen firing points at once, sometimes as close as 20m away. We were in a contact for three or four hours and then the enemy disappeared again. It was frustrating mayhem, but everything a Para could wish for. I was proud and privileged to see that the training we went through, everything done at the depot, the blokes were putting it into practice with grit and determination. 'B' Company were at Inkerman and 'C' Company were at Gibraltar FOBs fighting in the green zone day after day. We suffered casualties but saw the determination that guys showed for each other. Anything for your muckers to the left and right of you, you wouldn't let anyone down. The CO and I went out with a company-sized Fighting Patrol into the Green Zone. I attached myself with a few lads from the CO's Tactical

Group to the MSG whilst the CO went with his radio operator to a rifle platoon. During the task we came under attack from numerous enemy positions, and we quickly laid down effective fire whilst the MFC brought in mortar and artillery rounds onto the enemy positions that killed the group of insurgents, but then we started taking multiple contacts from all around us. I decided to move forward to where Sergeant Sykes and his platoon were under pretty heavy small arms and RPG fire. The forward platoons came into contact with multiple enemy targets. They cleared positions and moved forward to engage with the enemy. It was up to four hours of moving through ditches and crops, fighting through positions to clear objectives with the guys getting stuck in at close-quarters. I was on top of a roof when the guys below us got pinned down. The GPMG gunner next to me got hit and was concussed, unable to operate his weapon, so I took over the gun and started to suppress the enemy position. The blokes in the battalion demonstrated coolness under fire and were tenacious in battle, I was really impressed by the Toms and junior non-commissioned officers who were fighting these battles daily.[9]

As the coalition governments claimed that they were making good progress with their humanitarian projects, a hugely ambitious plan got under way to move an electric turbine to the Kajaki Dam. Operation Eagle Summit was an incredible logistical manoeuvre transporting the 200-tonne turbine and generator components in a convoy of 100 vehicles on a 160km journey from Kandahar. It took five days for the convoy to reach the hydro-electric dam on the Kajaki reservoir as it moved along at 3km per hour flanked by helicopters and heavy armour. Travelling through dry riverbeds and mountain passes, the route went through areas that were heavily armed and full of Taliban. US and British Special Forces went ahead to sweep through villages in the treacherous Helmand region, whilst other British troops led the convoy, with helicopters and jets in support, ready to fight off Taliban attacks. All kinds of operations were put in place to create diversions in preparation for the movement of the turbine up to Kajaki Dam. The Pathfinders set up at strategic points all the way towards the destination and engaged the Taliban at every opportunity so that the trucks bringing the massive turbine could get through. It was a joint US and British operation to provide more power to the region and show that they were there to improve the lives of the people. The turbine was successfully delivered but frustratingly couldn't be finally commissioned until 2016.

As part of the mission, the Paras were sent into the green zones to provide another distraction for the Taliban forces and keep them away from the convoy. 3 Para 'A' Company moved up to the Sangin area and set up a new base with the purpose of diverting the Taliban and taking the pressure off 2 Para 'B' Company at FOB Inkerman.

Tidmarsh said:

> We went to Sangin to support FOB Inkerman where they were getting absolutely smashed. We flew in and as soon as my guys went out of the gate they came into contact. In order to set up our new base we had to take a piece of high ground that would give us an unobstructed view into the valley. We were on the reverse slope and fought our way up to secure the compound and set it up as PB Emerald. It was pretty hardcore, but we did it. Then the Taliban attacked us from all four sides, the FSG commander was dropping grenades over the wall because they were getting that close to us. It was tough, really tough, but we achieved our objective of taking the attention away from the lads at Inkerman. It was good for the young guys to get this experience, they were straight into the breach, blooded for the first time in contact, and survived it. This boosted everyone's confidence; they now knew they could do it and that the enemy was real but could be beaten. 2 Para tended to be in more fixed positions while 3 Para were more mobile, but they all supported each other, and the main theme of the tour was working together to get these turbines up to Kajaki. 2 Para came under incredible attacks from the Taliban and Regimental Sergeant Major Tony Hobbins, an absolute legend in 2 Para and the most natural leader and commander I have ever come across, did an excellent job of holding the men together.[10]

On another occasion one of the 3 Para company locations was attacked, with some of the men sustaining injuries. In response, the guys from 2 Para fought through the buildings, compounds, and irrigation ditches, clearing positions to get the casualties out, taking the objective and moving forward. It was fluid and aggressive but always tempered. Hobbins said, 'We brought some artillery rounds down on a farm complex to where the Taliban were extracting to. We tore the place up, but when we followed in and were about to throw a grenade into a room, we saw a family was inside and stopped.'

The purpose of the FOBs outside Sangin town was to take the pressure away from the town itself to allow training of the ANA (Afghan National Army) and allow the PRTs (Provisional Reconstruction Teams) to reassure and improve the lives of the local population. Every day that the men patrolled out from Gibraltar and Inkerman they came into contact. In the first week of the tour there were five fatalities and from then on it was non-stop. The Taliban knew the ground, how to move on it and how to use it to their advantage. In an operation in the Musa Qala wadi, a man was killed, and the men couldn't reach his body immediately as they came under sustained fire. The Paras cleared the whole wadi whilst under constant attack, but when they were coming back down, they were bombarded again. The Taliban were clever; they knew how to move around and use the terrain to their advantage. The contacts and the ongoing battles were incessant and intense.

FOB Gibraltar was called 'The mouth of Hell' by the Taliban and for the men of 'C' Company based there, it was Hell. More men were hit during the six-month tour at Gibraltar than anywhere else; almost one in three were killed or wounded as they took on the Taliban in cornfields, open swathes of dry land and irrigation channels. They got caught up in close-quarter fighting and dragged their injured or dead back under fire from RPGs. Despite the constant battles, the remit of the men was still to garner good relations with the locals, and they endeavoured to fulfil this task never knowing who they could trust. Smiling children ushered them into a deadly ambush, IEDs were placed in their paths and suicide bombers mounted attacks. The base itself was very exposed and as soon as the men stepped outside, they came under sniper fire. Added to the constant dangers were the tough conditions. At one point over the summer a ground temperature of 78°C was recorded; it was so hot that their desert boots melted.

The Paras did an impressive job under unbelievable stress and as Tony Hobbins said, 'The men should be very proud of what they achieved. The loss of life and the number of casualties was devastating. I made a point of visiting all the families of those killed and went to see the injured in hospital with the CO. The men spent most of the tour in contact with the enemy or under huge pressure, and they came back different people.'

Once again, the Paras had held off the Taliban forces intent on preventing ISAF from delivering much-needed improvements to the local Afghan population. Some had made the ultimate sacrifice, but they had all shown themselves to be courageous and indefatigable in their duties and ability to fight. The men of 2 and 3 Para returned home having demonstrated their superior ability, even under extreme duress, to switch from aggressive fighters in a combat situation to politely dealing with the local people. However, their work in Afghanistan was not done and they were back again in 2010.

*Operation Herrick XIII*

In 2010, 2 and 3 Para were again deployed together to Helmand Province on Herrick XIII. They moved out into many fixed locations across the region but often cross-pollinated and supported each other in different sectors. The operation was deemed to be much more focused on building relations with the Afghan people and handing over security to the new and ever-growing Afghan forces. To mark the progress made in the establishment of good relations, British and Afghan dignitaries attended a 'Friendship Feast' at the headquarters of the Helmand PRT in Lashkargah. The Paras arrived in Camp Bastion and prepared for the latest deployment in the new FOBs across the Province. They were excited to be back doing what they do best, tinged with a slight wariness about what to expect this time around.

The men of 2 Para, with support from 3 Para, moved through the night to reach their destination of Tor Ghai. Wading across irrigation channels and climbing over 10ft-high compound walls with heavy equipment, they moved into position before sunrise and began their advance into the town. Within minutes the teams heading in from different directions were under contact and engaged in a heavy firefight for the next thirty minutes. The ANA arrived in large numbers with further British support and the enemy disappeared, leaving the paratroopers to secure the village and hold a shura with the village elders. The Paras took up their places in selected bases and began to patrol, but it soon became clear that this was a different scenario to previous tours.

The Taliban realised that full-on battles could not work against the British soldiers. In response, they began utilising IEDs as their main form of attack. The deadliest year was 2009 as the Taliban began laying down hidden devices and the army had to change their methods in combating this deadly tactic. The insurgents laced roads, ditches and pathways with explosive devices, making it extremely difficult for the men to move around freely. The local people were also affected and endangered by the sheer number of improvised bombs, and many towns and villages were deserted. Vallon metal detectors were brought in so that the paratroopers could continue with their patrols and dominate the ground. Searching for the well-hidden explosives, often disguised inside children's toys and other common everyday items, was stressful and slow and the men still had to contend with a number of contacts and ambushes. Although the battles were nothing like the intensity of Herrick IV and VIII, the casualty rate was even higher.

Steve Tidmarsh said:

> We had a lot of young lads who were a little nervous about going back into Afghan. One of my former guys, Sean Sexton, who had recently

left 3 Para was working for a private security company in Afghanistan when he got killed. 3 Para made sure that he got a full military send-off – even though it wasn't the norm, it was the right thing to do. He had served in Afghanistan, and it gave the guys confidence that they would be looked after if anything happened to them. 2 and 3 Para were locked into several fixed locations in Helmand, and it was a very different tour. The earlier tours had been all about close-quarter contact but in 2008 the Taliban started using IEDs and by 2010 they had laced the area with them; you couldn't move. They knew they couldn't continue with normal contacts because we just smashed them.[11]

Due to this change in tactics by the Taliban, the number of deaths and casualties more than doubled in 2009 and 2010. In the village of Char Coucha insurgents out to get British soldiers had forced villagers to flee by laying down IEDs on paths leading into compounds and on roads used by the local people. When 2 Para arrived there in October, they discovered an eerily empty town, deserted because of the high possibility of injury from these hidden bombs. The soldiers immediately went about clearing the streets of explosives and a team of counter-IED specialists moved in to begin the excruciating task of completing a fingertip search of the whole village. The task was completed, and the villagers were persuaded to start returning to their homes as redevelopment projects got under way.

The remit was still the same: the men went out on patrols and came into contact as they worked to dominate each area. However, they now had to check the ground for lethal devices with metal detectors as they made their way around. In February 2011, 'C' Company, 3 Para were out on patrol in the Nad e Ali district to interdict a Taliban movement around the village of Shaheed when they came under fire. The men moved into cover, some went into a nearby mosque and others jumped into an irrigation ditch. Company Sergeant Major Colin Beckett, known as 'Tom', began to move out of the trench he was in to provide cover fire when he triggered a device and was killed by the explosion. As the men went forward to help him, another man was injured by a second device. The Taliban knew that the men used the ditches for cover and had begun to pepper them with IEDs.

Every day the guys went out on the increasingly perilous patrols and although the incidence of contacts had decreased as the Taliban protected their numbers; they were still very active. Tony Hobbins said, 'We were making improvements for the locals and putting things in place to move forward. Girls were going to school, there were medical facilities and security was in place to allow the infrastructure to be improved and people were going about normal business, but the Taliban had changed, there were more IEDs and stand-off attacks, but it was still very kinetic.'

'D' Company were in a remote outpost in Nahr-e Saraj when the Taliban tried to take over the compound. Corporal Martin Windmill was wounded by shrapnel when an enemy grenade detonated, but he lobbed one back at the insurgents and despite being injured he pulled two other men away to safety as a firefight ensued. Armed with only his pistol, he killed oncoming fighters and ran into a field to fire a rocket launcher. He maintained control over his men and refused to call in a rescue helicopter to avoid risking any more lives as he continued to fight in a contact that lasted for four hours. Hobbins said, 'Corporal Windmill had already proved himself in an earlier tour and should have got the Military Cross for that; he thoroughly deserved the MC that he was awarded for this action. All of the guys were fantastic.'

The men of 2 Para, 'C' Company, were at Patrol Base 2 in the Nahr-e Saraj district. A patrol went out to intercept Taliban fighters in a small village, where one of the guys was injured by an IED. Disregarding the dangers, Private Martin Bell rushed over to the fallen man and proceeded to administer first aid. As he helped to move him to safety, he triggered a second device and was killed by the explosion. The Taliban had deliberately laid numerous devices in the same area to inflict as much carnage as possible on soldiers moving to help the injured. Bell received a posthumous George Medal for his actions on that day, demonstrating the bravery of the men and their natural reaction to help their airborne brothers.

While things were being put in place to reach the objective of handing over security to Afghan forces in 2011, the Paras worked hard under extreme stress to combat the threat of the Taliban and provide reassurance to the locals. The presence of explosive devices made their work extremely dangerous and impeded their movement, but, as always, they got on with the tasks presented to them. They were involved in a myriad of tasks as they continued to fight the enemy, clear IEDs and also open schools, radio stations and distribute food. During this last period, they had still been engaged in some heavy contacts, but not on the scale of the 2006 and 2008 tours and they were able to engage more with the local people and helped to persuade them to work with the government and ISAF. When they left in April 2011 there was an air of optimism, but the Taliban had not given up in their determination to bring their country back under their dictatorship. The Paras were taken off the arms plot following Herrick XIII, and many had the difficult task of adjusting to more mundane duties. The men who served in Afghanistan had been pushed to the extreme and had come out on top. For some the intense battles were over, but others moved over to 1 Para, who had been hard at it as part of the SFSG (Special Forces Support Group).

# Chapter 20

# Special Forces Support Group

The Parachute Regiment was originally formed as a specialist service unit taking only volunteers into their ranks due to the extremely dangerous missions they were asked to embark upon. The natural bond and synergy with the Special Air Service has always been strong, not only because of the number of paratroopers who join the SAS, but also due to their MO: the way they train and think on operations.

August 2000 was a key moment in the evolvement of the Paras. The daring jungle rescue of the hostages taken by the West Side Boys in Sierra Leone by 22 SAS supported by 1 Para firmly cemented the foundations of a future, much closer working relationship between the two forces. It was only a matter of time before this relationship was formally acknowledged with the formation of the SFSG.

The Paras have always been kept very busy, and this has tended to keep the spotlight off them when it comes to potential MoD (Ministry of Defence) cuts, but they have had to fight hard to maintain their structure. When some desk-bound Rupert (colloquial derogatory term for an Army officer) in Whitehall floated the subject of cost savings, fortunately the head of the army at the time was General Sir Mike Jackson, a staunch supporter and former officer in the Paras. Jackson was able to make a bold call and move one of the battalions into a role as the backbone of the newly formed SFSG. Working hand in glove with the SF, the future of the three Para battalions was secured once again.

For many years the Paras cross-trained in the US and back in Aldershot with the 82nd Airborne and the US Army Rangers. The Rangers had evolved into a role providing direct support to the US special forces teams, as well as executing their own direct-action raids in hostile or sensitive environments. Many direct comparisons had been made between the Paras and the Rangers, but nothing had officially changed. Now was the time to move the Paras into a similar role, and 1 Para was quickly confirmed as the first part of the Support Group, based in St Athan, Wales, a tactical bound away from the SAS in Hereford.

Both 2 and 3 Para remained in Colchester as part of 16 Air Assault Brigade, the heart of the country's global RRF (Rapid Reaction Force). Even though 1 Para was officially now separated from the other two sister battalions, they remained in close touch. As part of the airborne brotherhood, they continued to support each other with the ability to cross-deck personnel and skills wherever necessary. Soldiers from 2 and 3 Para could apply to join SFSG, and if successful they moved across and joined 1 Para after the appropriate training and selection process.

Formed officially on 3 April 2006, SFSG provide specialist infantry and support weapons capabilities to the UK Special Forces on operations worldwide. The Paras had already proven their value in previous conflicts, providing ad hoc manpower and skills that just did not exist, for varied reasons, within the SAS at that time.

Like all new ideas and concepts within the UK Armed Forces, there were compromises and deals to be made first, and both the Royal Navy and the Royal Air Force commanders wanted a role in this new unit. It was eventually agreed that a company of 100 Royal Marine Commandos and a platoon of twenty-five from the RAF Regiment would be added to the 600 Paratroopers of 1 Para to make up the SFSG manning levels, thus making it a truly inclusive unit with a multitude of skills and experience.

First of all, the new SFSG needed to prove to the SAS, and the other parts of the Special Forces community, that they were ready and up to the task in hand. They needed to show that they were worthy of joining this specialist group of men and capable of deploying at their side, into places such as Afghanistan and Iraq. Six weeks of live firing, living under field conditions in Brecon, lay ahead of them as part of an exacting test of soldiering skills, fitness, and the ability to operate under pressure.

The Paras were the hosts and moved into the area early to prepare. They set themselves up in and around a few of the old skill houses that were old shells of buildings with nothing but concrete walls and leaky roofs. There was no running water or electricity and they started to make ready for what they knew would be an arduous and extremely important six weeks under the watchful eyes of the SAS Directing Staff.

The RAF contingent turned up, not a regiment that the Paras had tended to have too much time for in the past. However, and all credit to them, they had taken this seriously and clearly sent down their best twenty-five guys who were prepared, fit, switched on and reasonably experienced. They fitted in well with the Para Regt blokes, and got on with it, making a good impression on those observing.

On the other side of the coin, the Royal Marines rocked up and from the moment they arrived it was clear that they had not quite grasped the overall concept. Para Regt had already decided, as the Marines were still their guests at this stage and to promote good feelings between the two rival units, to give them use of the small number of buildings that had some running water and electricity. Despite this, they still came out with some unbelievable questions such as, 'Where can we charge our mobile phones?' and 'When do the liberty wagons go to town?' Queries that the Paras had never even considered, and what the hell was a 'Liberty Wagon'? The reply given to the Royal Marines was simple, 'We are here for the next six weeks working day and night on our skills, fitness, and live firing to prove ourselves worthy of being part of SFSG. There is nothing else to think about!'

For the record, the Royal Marines are great soldiers and without doubt the closest thing I have come across in the forces to Para Regt. They tend to have the same mentality, determination and will to win, a dark sense of humour with a sprinkling of arrogance, just like us. However, for whatever reason, they were not properly prepared for this and had not sent down their best guys. A few of them were clearly cast-offs from units who had taken the opportunity to get rid of a few weak links. More worryingly though was that they had not worked together in the past and were mostly out of touch with the basic bread and butter skills of soldiering. This was clearly highlighted when they were put through their paces across the wet, cold, and rugged live-firing ranges of Brecon over the next few weeks.

The lieutenant colonel in charge of the six-week range package was an ex-Marine and SBS officer, who was based in Hereford with the SAS. He was less than impressed and failed them hands down. After giving them a long weekend to recuperate, he had them do it again, but they failed for a second time. They finally passed on the third attempt, which took them eighteen weeks in all.

Stu Baillie said:

After the marines finally passed the range package, with a few tweaks here and there to their personnel and overall attitude to the task in hand, the marine Company Sergeant Major, who to be fair was a stand-up character, put his hands up during a meeting in the Sergeant's Mess and admitted that they had been caught woefully unprepared, and with their trousers down on this one. He accepted that his guys' personal soldiering skills were not up to the Para Regt standards, and they would now go away and get their house in order and quickly get up to par, which to be fair they did. After this meeting, the 1 Para Regimental

Sergeant Major held his senior non-commissioned officers behind and made it clear to them what was going to happen. He said, 'We have more than proven our point gentlemen, and now is the time to pull together as a team, and not a time for us to gloat. Leave the piss-taking to the Toms. We, as the senior non-commissioned officers, now need to put aside inter-regimental rivalry and work together. I want you to get around the marines, get stuck in on the next stage of the training and get them up to standard to prove to the SF instructors, who we know are watching this whole process unfold carefully, that we are worthy as the SFSG, and can operate alongside them as one finely tuned unit.[1]

Initial teething problems were overcome and the lads in SFSG started to get issued some decent kit, which had always been a point of contention within the battalions. All of a sudden, they had new weapon systems, lightweight body armour and helmets, expensive navigational devices, and all the bells and whistles you would expect in an SF unit.

Iraq became a major commitment, especially for the SAS and SBS Sabre squadrons working full out on counter-terrorist operations. At a time when the public beheadings of kidnapped Western workers and local Iraqi community leaders were rife and being gratuitously displayed across the internet, they were working hard to counteract these activities and the SFSG worked in support of these efforts as part of a multinational task force.

A rotational British SAS Sabre squadron, Task Force Black was now joined by a platoon of paratroopers from SFSG, who soon became known as Task Force Maroon, a nice link to our heritage and famous beret. SFSG's primary role was to secure and cordon the areas where the SAS teams were operating and provide close support and a QRF where required. Due to the heavy number of operations, once SFSG were brought up to speed, they soon ended up taking on many of these raids by themselves. They went on to carry out numerous successful operations during this time. Between 2006 and 2009 they supported the SAS in raids against Ba'athist and al-Qaeda targets, killed or captured terrorists and gathered valuable intelligence.

As part of the famous Basra Prison break, SFSG supported the SAS to get back two of their own operators. Two undercover British SAS soldiers were on a covert surveillance operation mounted against a known corrupt and brutal high-ranking Iraqi police officer. Disguised as Arab civilians, they opened fire on policemen when they were stopped at a roadblock. Tensions were already high between the Iraqi police and the British Army and as the police tried to pull the operators from their vehicle, they opened fire and killed two of the policemen. The SAS guys made a quick getaway with Iraqi police in pursuit. However, feeling that they had no chance of getting away as the net closed in, they decided to stop and attempt to talk their way out of it. The two SAS men were arrested, beaten, and then subsequently taken to the Al Jameat police station.

In response, twenty members of 'A' Squadron, 22 SAS, and a platoon of paratroopers from SFSG flew down from Baghdad to Basra. Racing against time with credible intelligence that the prisoners may get handed over to a hard-line group, or be murdered at any time, they set up a daring rescue operation. The mission was successful and helped in cementing the close working relationship between the two units.

Each of the SFSG platoons was made up of forty-five men, very different to the normal manning levels back in 2 and 3 Para, with a selection of skills at their disposal, which they called the Golf Bag. Each club in the bag, just like in golf, had a specific job which was represented within the platoon. This included assault teams, sniper pair, mortar crews, MFC (Mortar Fire Controller), FAC (Forward Air Controller), heavy weapons, anti-tank, demolitions, medics, signallers, and a command element. This enabled them to adapt to and deal with any situation without having to wait for outside support.

Members of the SFSG often wore American army combat uniforms to blend in when operating alongside American special forces teams in Iraq and Afghanistan. This always seemed to cause confusion when US army officers approached them and found out they were British soldiers and gave the guys a good laugh each time. Similarly, when British officers heard the accent, they were left completely perplexed as to who they were. However, in the great scheme of things it worked very effectively on operations and, most importantly, confused the enemy on the ground.

SFSG supported SF operations across Iraq and were part of an SAS operation to stop a group of would-be suicide bombers. Surveillance and human intelligence had identified the building being used as their base so listening devices were set up close by that allowed the teams to eavesdrop on their conversations and learn their plans. This revealed that three of the bombers had explosives strapped to their bodies and were planning to hit specific targets throughout Baghdad that day. It was decided that raiding the building might lead to a detonation of one or all of these devices, so instead, snipers were set up in positions where they could take them out as they left the house. The SFSG team were positioned close by in order to take immediate action if things escalated. As the bombers left the building, all three were simultaneously shot, successfully preventing the murder of many unsuspecting and innocent civilians.

The following year, SFSG were involved in an operation to free the British peace activist Norman Kemble, who had been kidnapped along with two Canadians and an American. The task force had built up an intelligence network on terrorist and kidnapping organisations throughout Iraq, and when the American hostage was suddenly and unexpectedly murdered by the kidnappers, they sprang into action, using all their human and intel resources in a bid to discover the whereabouts of the remaining captives. They received reliable information regarding the location of the peace workers in a downtown suburb of Baghdad and immediately put a rescue plan into operation. The SF rescue team arrived at the location in low-profile taxis and pick-up trucks, while helicopter gunships flew overhead. SFSG set up a security perimeter and the SAS entered the building and successfully found and rescued the three men unharmed.

SFSG also deployed to Afghanistan in support of the SBS and SRR (Special Reconnaissance Regiment) and became part of what was known as Task Force 42. The task force was heavily involved in pinpointing key players within the Taliban network and focused on specific capture or kill missions. In September that year they were involved in Operation Medusa, joining other NATO forces in attacking and cutting off the Taliban in the Panjwayi district.

In 2009, they were tasked with creating diversionary attacks in support of an SBS raid on an old fort that was being used by the Taliban as a storage and bomb-making facility. In one of the most successful operations of its time, British and Afghani troops were inserted by helicopter into the local area. The SBS assaulted the fort as SFSG troops carried out a secondary attack that succeeded in destroying hundreds of IEDs and killing several members of the Taliban. Again, in September that year, the SBS, supported by SFSG, conducted a rescue mission to free the journalist Stephen Farrell and his interpreter, who had been captured and held at a compound in Char Dara District, Kunduz Province, by Taliban insurgents. The SBS rescue team assaulted the buildings where the hostages were being held, whilst SFSG set up a secure cordon around the nearby area. The Taliban tried to flee, and a fierce firefight ensued during which Farrell was safely rescued but a Paratrooper from SFSG and Farrell's Afghan interpreter were tragically killed.

SFSG worked hand-in-hand throughout Helmand Province with an elite unit of Afghan commandos in 2013. Known as Task Force 444, they mounted numerous assaults against the Taliban, including a series of raids on suspected Taliban bomb-makers after three British soldiers were killed in a roadside bomb. The unit also targeted insurgent supply lines in the desert near the border with Pakistan and Taliban command bases in the centre of the province.

During this period in Helmand Province, 1 Para Lance Corporal Joshua Mark Leakey was on a routine patrol to search a local village, thought to be a Taliban stronghold, for illegal weapons. British paratroopers, US Marines and Afghan soldiers were airlifted into the area on Chinook helicopters, which landed on a hill near to their destination. Leakey was with three other paratroopers and an Afghan soldier providing fire support and protection for the forces going in to clear the village. Moments after they got onto the ground, the forward patrol was attacked by machine gunfire and RPGs. Over the radio, Leakey heard that someone had been injured and although he was only a lance corporal, he took control and decided that they needed to act. He led his men down the hill towards the contact.

Under heavy attack, he got to the injured Marine Corps captain and got him away from the incoming fire. He then ran across the hill to where a machine gun team were surrounded by the enemy. He provided medical aid and arranged the evacuation of casualties. Still coming under heavy fire, he quickly moved a machine gun into a position from where he could attack the Taliban force. He came under constant fire with bullets ricocheting off the machine gun he was carrying, and his actions galvanised the rest of the men around him into fierce action. They were inspired to support him as he put the gun into use. Firing at the enemy, he continued to call into the radio with situation updates and soon realised that more than one machine gun was needed. One of the other soldiers took over his weapon, and he ran carrying 60lb of equipment on his back to retrieve a second gun. He then ran back up the steep hill with the insurgents bombarding the hillside around him to set up the second machine gun in a suitable position to return fire.

The assault lasted just under an hour, during which time eleven insurgents were killed and four wounded. Finally, air support arrived, and the fighting stopped. Leakey handed his gun to another man and went back to the injured captain to check on his condition and make sure he was evacuated safely.[2]

Leakey was awarded the Victoria Cross, the highest military decoration for valour in the British and Commonwealth armed forces, for his brave actions, which, without doubt, prevented the loss of lives. He was the only living soldier to receive the award during the Afghanistan war and demonstrated the very essence of the professionalism and courage associated with the Parachute Regiment. In an interview with the BBC he said, 'We're paratroopers. We are well-drilled in what we do, and we train for moments like this. You're taught as a member of the Parachute Regiment to think on your feet and to think outside the box and to step up to the plate when you have to.'[3]

Due to the ever-increasing and almost unsustainable workload on the Sabre Squadrons in both Iraq and Afghan, SFSG were tasked with taking over the CTT (Counter-Terrorist Team) role in the UK for a while. Since the time of its inception, and height of its fame when the guys stormed the Iranian Embassy, 22 SAS, and more recently the SBS, were the only units who possessed the required training and consequently had the responsibility for counter-terrorism operations within the UK. The guys from SFSG embraced the new challenge, and quickly mastered the required skills to take on this key role in the bid to prohibit terrorist activity in the UK.

SFSG also act as the hunter force during the escape and evasion phase of the UK Special Forces Selection, bringing some real intensity and impetus to this part of the process. The formation of the SFSG understandably caused some initial concern amongst the Para battalions, as Major Curt Vines, who served with 1 Para during the inception of the new role explained:

> It took a few years for the regiment to fully embrace the new SFSG role, develop and exploit the concept. Certainly, during the inception and early period, 2 & 3 Para felt perhaps a little threatened and were hesitant to send their best and most experienced soldiers to their sister battalion 1 Para in their new SF supporting role. However, the regimental command elements worked hard on developing a system which sustained both the conventional infantry airborne/air assault role within 16 Air Assault Brigade Field Army and the SFSG. The system now works well, having established a cross-regimental pollination rotation, which affords a broad understanding right down to the lowest level. It ensures SFSG officers and soldiers of all ranks have had experience in operating in their core function as airborne soldiers in the first instance and at a more enhanced and niche skill level in a specialist role. It is no coincidence that the regiment was selected to provide and lead the SF support element, providing 80 per cent of the group, and their success to date speaks for itself.[4]

As I have stated previously in this book, I will not be divulging any information on current deployments and operations but, needless to say, the guys from SFSG are active in all current war zones and areas where British interests and Special Forces are involved. As their role has become more defined, they have become recognised as an integral part of UK special forces' capabilities and have become an extremely capable force in their own right. The Ministry of Defence does not comment on SF matters, therefore little verifiable information exists in the public domain, and it will remain that way until it is declassified in years to come. I have no intention of deviating from that line, but wherever they are, the men from 1 Para will be doing us proud. Rest assured that the Special Forces Support Group is still as active and busy today as when they were first formed, operating alongside the British and US special forces worldwide.

# Chapter 21

# Return to Kabul

## Afghanistan Part Three, 2019–21

*Operation Toral*

In 2014, British combat troops withdrew from Afghanistan, and in January 2015, ISAF was replaced by NATO's RSM (Resolute Support Mission) to help Afghan security forces and institutions develop the capability to defend the country themselves and protect its citizens without international support. Working closely with the government, the police, the army, and the air force, the focus was on training and offering advice and assistance without engaging in military operations themselves. After 2011 the Parachute Regiment was involved in numerous training exercises around the world but with America holding ongoing peace talks with the Taliban, 2 Para deployed to Afghanistan once again as part of the RSM for a six-month tour in November 2019.

After their involvement in Operation Herrick, the Paras went through a difficult transition. For the decade after the invasion of Afghanistan the battalions had been fully involved in the fight against the Taliban. The training of both new recruits and the longer-serving men had been centred on contact drills in areas of intense fighting. The men were psychologically geared up to put these skills to use and, despite the horror of the reality of war, they were keen to get into action and play their part. As Steve Tidmarsh explained, 'I went back to 3 Para as Regimental Sergeant Major, and we soon realised that we had to manage the expectations of the men. 1 Para were part of the SFSG and were kept busy throughout the twenty-year war in Afghanistan, so a lot of cross-pollination went on. Men from both 2 and 3 Para spent time with 1 Para on special forces support operations, in part so that the skills were brought back to all the battalions and also to give the guys from 1 Para some respite. As the MO changed the combat diminished, and it was important to manage the expectations of the soldiers and keep them interested. In 2012 we had the Olympics in London and paratroopers were part of the security team. It was a big change to go from being front-line combat soldiers, to taking on guard duties and stagging on.'

As always, training was adapted to suit the conditions and the focus turned to psyching the men up for the importance of their task, however mundane. The men were geared up as an aggressive fighting force and now they needed to be able to deal with security and guard duties but still be prepared to respond with aggressive combat action if the need arose. Managing the two elements of behaviour was extremely good experience for the men.

The task in Kabul was to enable NATO advisors to meet with the Afghan Ministry of Defence and other government departments in a secure environment. The Paras planned the missions and set up the security to enable the meetings to take place. It was in complete contrast to their usual role. Normally, logistics were about enabling them to get where they needed to be and to have the resources that they required in place to perform their tasks and fight the battles. Now they were the ones enabling, and the pre-deployment training developed to provide the men with the motivation to stay alert at all times and remain flexible and positive in their attitude.

Many of the blokes in 2 Para at this time were just 18 years old; they hadn't even been born when terrorists flew into the World Trade Center in New York in 2001. They were often involved in over 100 missions a week to the same secure building in the Green Zone in Kabul, but they maintained their high standards throughout and never dropped their guard. Junior non-commissioned officers were put in charge of the missions, and this meant a huge amount of responsibility for them to shoulder; despite the monotony of the tasks, they weren't going to let anything go wrong on their watch.

Beyond the secure area of the Green Zone, life in Kabul was anything but peaceful as the Taliban claimed responsibility for continual suicide bombers and VBIEDs (Vehicle-Borne Improvised Explosive Devices). Men of 2 Para, who were part of the QRF, were stationed at the New Kabul Compound. On 13 November, a VBIED detonated on a busy street during rush hour and injured four Canadian security contractors. The QRF rushed to the site to locate the casualties, who had been taken to a nearby hospital, and brought them to the army medical facilities for further treatment. Going into scenes such as this was a very disturbing experience; the explosions caused multiple injuries, mainly involving the loss of limbs, and were harrowing to witness. The people of Kabul were often innocent victims of these attacks. Even if not injured, the blasts broke windows and threw people off their feet, and they were traumatised by the experience. In their reaction to these events, the Paras dealt with the carnage and offered support to the local people.

Up in the mountains the men were stationed at Camp Qharga, where Afghan Officer Cadets were trained. Known as 'Sandhurst in the Sun', the role of the RSM force at the Afghan National Army Officer School was to offer advice and assistance but not actually run the courses. The syllabus was taught by Afghans and after just under one year the officers were sent to study specific skills at Branch Schools before deploying to the provinces to fight against the Taliban and the new threat from ISIS (Islamic State of Iraq and Syria). For the Afghans the war was as real and intense as ever and with air support from the US they were still fighting running battles with the insurgents. The number of casualties was extremely high and there were problems with many Afghan soldiers going AWOL because they didn't want to fight or because they were not being paid.

Despite all the effort by NATO forces to train up the Afghan army and allow them to take over security of their own land, in the summer of 2021 the plan went horribly wrong, and paratroopers were deployed to the country for a very different and unexpected task.

## Operation Pitting

Between April and August 2021, Taliban forces swept through Afghanistan in a lightning offensive that took the world by surprise. Suddenly, it became a race against time to get people out of the country by the 31 August deadline. In the UK, Operation Pitting was launched and the lead battle group, 2 Para were deployed to facilitate the extraction of eligible personnel. With the Taliban about to move into Kabul, thousands of people descended on the airport in the hope of getting out before the Taliban took over. What had been viewed as a fairly relaxed and protracted evacuation plan turned into heart-breaking pandemonium and the Paras went in to deal with an unforeseen humanitarian crisis that put their adaptable skills to the test again.

The US and the Taliban signed the Doha Agreement in February 2020 to bring an end to the war in Afghanistan by removing all international forces by May 2021. In April 2021, the US began withdrawing their troops, confident in the belief that they had provided the Afghan forces and the government with all the skills, equipment and training necessary to hold power and fight the Taliban. It was thought highly unlikely that the Taliban could overrun the country. As the military forces moved out, the Taliban charged through the land at unanticipated speed. Taking over equipment provided by the Americans and coalition forces, they quickly captured more than two thirds of the country. The Afghan National Army clearly did not share the same confidence as the Americans and, despite all the years of training and support, in many areas they just gave up without a fight. Even as Taliban forces took the major cities of Mazar-i-Sharif and Kandahar, politicians still believed it would be months before they could get into Kabul.

One member of 2 Para said:

> Once we knew that the US forces were withdrawing, we kept a close eye on events and at the beginning of May plans were put in place expecting the extraction to be quite protracted. In July, the attitude was still fairly relaxed and by the beginning of August, I was stood down ready to go on summer leave with my family. Suddenly everything changed, and it was full speed ahead as the Taliban spread across Afghanistan. They reached the outskirts of the capital and denied all requests to extend the deadline of 31 August. As the lead Air Manoeuvre Battle Group, 2 Para were always ready to go at short notice. The battalion got back within ten hours of the call; we were aware of what was going on in Kabul and were ready to immediately deploy thinking that with our various attachments we had sufficient numbers to get the job done. A small advance party quickly moved into theatre. Groupings based on the traditional rifle companies then deployed led by 'A' Company flying in and staging via the UAE.[1]

At this point, civilian flights were still operating, and everything was fairly normal. The first phase of Operation Pitting was to secure Kabul International airport and then to expand out from there. Turkish and US forces had secured the perimeter, and the Turks had assumed control of Covid checks and passport control. Paras supported the task of securing the perimeter of the military side of the airport and, unable to use the British Embassy, the heavily fortified and well-protected Baron hotel near the airport was selected as the Battalion HQ and processing centre for all those eligible for flights out of the country. It was predicted that around 5,000 British passport holders, dual-nationals, and those with permission to extract as part of the Afghan Resettlement and Assistance programme would be evacuated. Although they were UK-centric, their position on the ground meant that they also helped with the recovery of eligible people from other countries. The Baron hotel became the staging point for checking papers before transporting eligible persons to the airport, where they went through the normal processing and security measures before they boarded flights out.[2]

On 15 August, there was panic and pandemonium in Kabul as the Taliban arrived at the outskirts of the city and President Ashraf Ghani fled the country. Hoisting their triumphant white flags, the Taliban quickly took control of the roads, moved into the city and took over the Presidential Palace. The following day thousands upon thousands of Afghans rushed to the airport. A crowd found a gap in the perimeter of the civilian airfield and raced towards a plane lined up on the runway. They clambered up the sides and clung on even as the plane started to take off, and witnesses watched as they fell to the ground.

A basic barrier was put up outside the Baron hotel using a chevron of concrete blocks and abandoned cars as they tried to manage the overwhelming quantity of people. The limited number of men in 2 Para was not going to be enough and they held on under tremendous pressure for four days as reinforcements arrived.

The men of 3 Para, who were normally on a twenty-day notice to move, were ready within twenty-four hours and along with medical support, engineers, and search dogs, they were transported to Kabul. Troops from Alma Company, the Yorkshire Regiment based in Cyprus, flew in later to take over driving duties.

The situation around the airport was carnage. People crammed into the roads leading up to the airport, they pushed and shoved in a sea of bodies as mothers clung onto their babies and families got separated. In the dense, milling crowd, crying, shouting Afghans waved their papers in the air and desperately tried to get out of the country.

The Paras moved swiftly into action. They needed a clear route from the hotel to the airport so that they could process those eligible and then move them quickly to the airport and get them loaded onto planes. The 400m stretch between the Baron hotel and Abbey Gate into the airport, code-named Route Leeds, was cleared and people moved into the deep sewage channel running alongside the road. To control the crowd surging towards the hotel, the soldiers increased the barriers around the complex, with engineers moving shipping containers into place forming a perimeter and makeshift funnel. They were eventually able to manage the flow of people coming in for processing and going out to the airport for flights in a very organised and efficient manner, with volunteers from UK Border Force coming in to administer the clearing process. The hotel and grounds were crammed full of families waiting to be processed, sleeping wherever they could, but outside the situation was dire.[3]

As the numbers grew, some at the front were crushed to death in the hysteria. The people had no food or water apart from what they had managed to bring with them, and in the soaring summer temperatures, many were collapsing from heat exhaustion and dehydration. In the street, the soldiers helped as many as they could. They pulled people out of crushes and while the medics worked non-stop administering first aid, they tended to the wounded or sick and tried, wherever possible, to save lives. On top of the containers, paratroopers looked out for those with the right papers and pulled men, women, and children up from the mass of shouting, distressed people.

To the surprise of many, the Paras were joined by members of the Taliban, and all memories of past combat had to be put aside as they worked together to control the vast crowds. A member of 2 Para commented, 'We were standing on one container and opposite us on the other platform were the Taliban. They helped facilitate the process and co-ordinate the crowds with us. The past was put to the back of our minds; we had a job to do.'

News teams filmed the unfolding scenes and captured poignant images of paratroopers holding babies, helping women and children out of danger, using hoses to spray the crowd with cooling water, performing CPR, and covering dead bodies in white sheets. The waiting people slept rough, waded through stinking sewage water, and overheated in the scorching daytime temperatures.[4] The human misery and anguish could be seen everywhere and for the Paras it was a deeply emotional operation, stretching them both physically and mentally.

The member of 2 Para continued:

> For the whole time we were there it was non-stop. The medics bore the brunt of the emotional stress; people were getting trampled to death, babies died, there were heat and crush injuries. The people were queuing there for days without access to food or water. Everyone had their own story of people they tried to help, contact with a particular family, kids left alone, helping a family with a five-week-old baby; trying to help as many as possible to get out and into a better life. The emotional strain of the task was immense, it was an intense hearts and minds operation and completely unlike anything we had done before. We helped anybody that we saw in distress, but we didn't have an endless supply of things that we could dish out.[5]

Over the evacuation period the paratroopers distributed 300,000 litres of water, 20,000 ration packs, baby milk, nappies, sanitary packs, blankets, sunshades and over 1,500 colouring books and pencils amongst other things to try to alleviate the hardship.[6]

The Paras slept on the floor, just metres away from their posts, grabbing what rest they could, before carrying on as the evacuation continued around the clock. At the hotel, they oversaw the processing procedure and arranged for British passport holders and Afghans with the right paperwork to move to the airport. Many arrived with falsified documents and had to be shepherded back into the streets. Initially planners had expected to process 300 people per day, but this ended up being nearly 2,000, and they ensured that all the planes were full to capacity before they left.[7] There had been no time to plan for the situation that arose and vehicles for taking people from the Baron to the airport had to be sourced locally. The member of 2 Para explained, 'Nobody had expected the situation we faced, and so no military vehicles had been sent over. We utilised whatever facilities we could get our hands on, using both the military and private security networks to locate vehicles in the area and in some cases hot-wiring to gain use.'[8]

Due to the overwhelming number of people, it was proving difficult for the legitimate ones to get to the hotel. So many people who did not have the right paperwork were making it difficult for those that did to get through. The men were receiving messages via various sources about people they knew in Kabul who were struggling to get through the enormous crowds to the Baron hotel. They needed to find a way in which these people could be easily spotted by the paratroopers on duty. One ingenious paratrooper came up with the idea of holding up signs for the Paras on the containers to see. What was written on the sign had to be something that would attract their attention and not be wording that anyone else might understand and copy. The message chosen was, 'I hate Crap Hats.' Based on the long-held tradition in the Parachute Regiment that all other regiments in the army are not as good as they are, paratroopers refer to all other soldiers as crap hats. The signs were very noticeable, and the plan worked well.

In the midst of all the chaos, intel continually warned that there was the possibility of a terrorist threat. Despite the heightened awareness, there was little to be done with the masses of people packed into the tight area. On 26 August, two ISIS suicide bombers made their way to Abbey Gate undetected and detonated themselves in the midst of hundreds of people in the sewage canal, decimating those closest to them. The response from the military personnel on the ground was swift and efficient as they rushed to take care of the injured and the dead, but the two blasts killed at least seventy-three people including thirteen American servicemen and wounded well over 100. It was a heinous act of violence that only added to the already tragic situation; misery was piling onto misery. The Paras had been operating in the same patch of ground and were incredibly lucky not to have been affected by the explosions.

The UK government decided to get everyone out before the situation escalated, and on 28 August the final plane carrying civilians departed and was followed later on that day by all the military personnel. The member of 2 Para said, 'The government made the call as to when we should stop processing to enable us to extract before the Taliban deadline. We closed down the operation at the hotel but when we left there were people still queuing outside. The operation was tough and heart-breaking, but it was what we had signed up to do.' They succeeded in evacuating 15,000 people and in very difficult circumstances had exceeded expectations.

The men of 2 and 3 Para flew to the UAE, where they were fed and given clean clothes before flying back to RAF Brize Norton. They spent a week in Covid isolation and received operational stress management involving speakers and group therapy before going on leave. It was a far cry from the fervent battles of the Herrick tours but tested the men in their ability to react to a completely unexpected, highly emotive situation requiring empathy and consideration. Faced with an organisational nightmare while witnessing the horrendous suffering and despair of thousands of people fearing for their lives under Taliban rule, the Paras created calm, controlled order. They demonstrated compassion and care as they helped as many people as possible in an ever-changing, dynamic environment. Their actions were a testament to the resilience, mental strength, and broad skill set of the men. The Parachute Regiment used the experience to improve their training and operating methods, ever evolving, and incorporating lessons learned to remain an elite and supreme force in times of both war and peace.

# Chapter 22

# The Circuit

This story would not be complete without tackling a subject very close to my own heart, and if I didn't include it, I would be doing a great injustice to the many former paratroopers who have paid the ultimate sacrifice in the line of duty operating within the private security industry, known to those who work in this world, as the 'Circuit'. I feel I now need to take the time to explain what this sector is all about, how it links into the modern-day history of the regiment, and what these ex-Paras have brought to this secretive, often misunderstood, and sometimes fatally dangerous industry.

Members of the Parachute Regiment are often asked, 'What will you do when you leave?' It is a very difficult question. How do they start to fill the void that is left after being part of such a close-knit airborne brotherhood? In what way can they replace the daily adrenaline buzz that comes with being an elite paratrooper?

When the time comes, some guys just genuinely want a change of pace after risking their lives so many times in the service of their country. Some married men want to spend more time at home with their families, from whom they have been separated for such long periods of time. There may be numerous other personal reasons why the lads decide to leave the army and there are different ways in which each of them deals with it and makes a new life outside of the regiment.

Many, just like myself, search for something new, something to replace our old lives in Para Regt. Depending on who you talk to, it could be a new and different way of finding that adrenaline rush we talk about, or a way to continue to serve whilst still working in the war-torn parts of the world to which we have all become strangely accustomed. Continuing to work with like-minded individuals around you might play a big part in decisions, or it could be the financial incentives, which, on the Circuit, are far more than the guys ever earned whilst serving in the armed forces. One way or another, many former paratroopers find their way into the world of the Circuit, and many quite honestly see it as a natural extension of their military service.

Back in the 1980s and '90s the private security industry was far smaller and very little was known about it; there was a lot of cloak and dagger stuff. It was really a case of who you knew, rather than what you knew, and therefore very difficult to break into and make a decent living. Most of the work was carried out by retired special forces operators, and it involved close protection for private families, high-net-worth individuals or celebrities, training team tasks, and a relatively small amount of work in Africa working as security managers for oil companies. I know this because I was one of the few paratroopers operating in this small and tight-knit circle in the late '90s. However, events in the early twenty-first century led to an unprecedented increase in security work.

After the 9/11 terrorist attacks the world changed dramatically and the Afghan and Iraq wars followed soon after. The industry literally exploded into action overnight and quickly grew out of control. Numerous new security firms were formed providing support in Afghanistan, but mainly in Iraq for government agencies and commercial entities. The natural mentality and ultra-professionalism of the former paratroopers helped them to easily transition from the traditional forces' environment into the new and ever-growing world of the security circuit and made them a highly sought-after commodity.

The guys leaving the Para Regt to join the Circuit were able to take full advantage of the military resettlement system, which allowed them several thousand pounds to spend on Close Protection Training Courses. If they did not qualify for these grants, some paid out of their own pockets. The courses were generally designed and run primarily by former soldiers, many of whom came from an SF background. They knew exactly what skills the security companies required the guys to have in order to be able to fit right into their operations on arrival in theatre. It became big business and many guys from the Para Regt had their heads turned by what they saw as a new and exciting career with some great financial rewards.

Many of the large commercial contracts in Iraq had several similarities to how life was whilst serving in the Parachute Regiment and on the whole, the transition from soldier to contractor was a relatively smooth path for all concerned. The contracts were run with military precision, with an internal rank structure and nightly prayers where the guys analysed what they had just done and what was on the itinerary for the following day. SOP (standard operating procedures), the law when it comes to how you conduct yourselves when on the ground during operations, were followed, and if you were lucky enough, you were provided with some decent kit and weapons, along with some training and range time. Just as important was who you found yourselves working alongside and often these were fellow former paratroopers.

Richard Stacey, who left the Paras in the late 1990s, worked worldwide, and spent his last eleven years on the BBC security team operating in just about every front-line conflict you can imagine. He commented, 'Due to the amount of Para Regt guys who worked over in Iraq and Afghanistan in the 2000s with the likes of Kroll and Olive, they became unofficially known as the 5th Battalion, which was epitomised by the photo of them under the famous Baghdad Crossed Swords on Airborne Forces Day in 2005.'

However, there were also many differences. There was less bullshit, which is always a plus, but also there was no high-end logistical and political support. This time there was no reliable back-up, no glory or medals to be won, or flag-draped coffins, just a group of former soldiers risking their lives in remote and hostile environments on behalf of government or commercial clients.

In the post-conflict recovery stage of a country, the tasks they were contracted to perform always had one purpose in common: to protect and save the lives of those clients who were entrusted into their care. Working with a huge sense of honour, duty, patriotism and a large portion of military black humour, they spent months away from their homes and loved ones. The Paras moving onto the Circuit put their lives on the line once again.

Of course, the powers that be knew that by contracting out to the private security sector for some of the government contracts and diplomatic security team tasks it saved tying up an already stretched and over-deployed army who could be better used elsewhere. This also put the onus on the privately owned companies running these new contracts to provide the blokes with the required kit and manpower to get the job done. It also shifted the burden of responsibility for any injuries or deaths that undoubtedly occurred. When a serviceman is killed, it becomes big international news, and the government is rightly scrutinised and held to account. You will never hear it on the news when a private security contractor is killed abroad; these deaths go unreported.

The year 2003 saw the US-led invasion of Iraq. In less than four weeks Baghdad had fallen, and Saddam Hussein had gone into hiding. Large, mostly American and European, companies won huge contracts to move into Iraq to begin the reconstruction programme in what was now a very unstable and turbulent country with insurgency on the rise. Looting, bomb attacks, shootings, organised crime, and the emergence of local militias were becoming the norm across the major cities. Iraq was the new Wild West, and at the time, regardless of the politics involved, what this meant for the Circuit was new opportunities with a boom in security contracts to protect clients, government embassies, and news teams covering the unfolding events.

They were crazy times; the militants were running riot around Baghdad between 2003 and 2008, as well as outside the capital. There was no getting away from the harsh facts. Attacks were commonplace, and the guys got hit by IEDs (Improvised Explosive Devices) and got involved in some fierce firefights, especially on the convoys that were run between remote locations outside the main cities. Some of the blokes were injured or tragically lost their lives in these attacks. The job at that time was just about as real and kinetic as anything they had experienced while serving in the Paras. However, this was now the commercial world and things worked differently; it was something to which some guys had difficulty adjusting. The lads were really earning their money with plenty of accolades from clients, employers, and peers alike, but they had none of the support and back-up that they were used to in the army.

The road between Baghdad International Airport and the city, code-named Route Irish by the American military, became known as the most dangerous road in the world. It was a magnet for insurgents because they knew that coalition forces as well as private security companies protecting international business and embassy staff were using it on a regular basis to get to and from the airport and there were no other viable options. The insurgents used the slip roads, which had very little security controlling them, to get onto the main highway in cars containing VBIEDs. They drove alongside obvious-looking Western transport in these mobile bombs and detonated themselves as suicide bombers, causing many casualties and fatalities.

If any story is able to bring home the harsh reality and extreme danger of working in the private security industry, then it is the tale of Private (Retired) Steve Johnson. His story highlights the indomitable Para Regt 'never give up' attitude, pure selfless bravery, and incomparable, dark army humour.

Hailing from Bedlington, he joined Junior Para in 1986, served eleven years in 1 Para and ended up on the Circuit via a second career in the prison service. A straight-talking typical paratrooper, admired by his peers and held in high regard by the clients he worked with, Johnson's life changed dramatically and permanently on 19 June 2011 in Basra, Iraq. Whilst operating as a bodyguard on a commercial security contract, his armoured

Toyota Landcruiser was struck by an EFP (explosively formed penetrator), which severely wounded him. He lost an arm, an eye and consequently sustained a brain injury. Steve relayed the incident in his typical no-nonsense manner:

> The missile entered the vehicle through the driver's side window, then went straight through Luay's, my driver's, head. The missile missed my face by approximately three inches before exiting the vehicle through my door window. I was showered with shrapnel and my body was ripped apart as the shrapnel tore through my clothing, body armour and flesh. I felt Luay slump across onto my chest and looked down to see a huge hole that had been made in his head with arterial blood pumping from his brain. I leaned forward to my medical kit and pulled out a Haemostatic bandage. I pushed the dressing inside his head, feeling for the end of the ruptured artery. I knew there was very little chance of anything I did saving his life, but you cannot just sit idly by and let someone bleed to death. Leaving the bandage inside Luay's head, I used my right hand to move him back on to his own side of the vehicle in order to survey my own injuries. It was at this moment I became aware of how serious my own plight was. I was covered in blood from head to toe, most of it my own. My left hand was hanging on by a small piece of skin and tendon. I could see most of the bones in my hand, wrist and lower arm as the flesh had been ripped away by the blast. Blood was pumping out of my arm in time with my heartbeat and I knew an arterial bleed like this would surely spell my own death within minutes if I could not do something to stop it. At this point my medical training kicked in and I remembered what I had been taught. I put the fingers of my uninjured right hand inside the gaping wound and found the end of my artery. I applied as much pressure as possible, and the flow of blood slowed a little. As I contemplated my own death, my door opened and my friend and colleague, Colin appeared, 'Can you walk?' he asked. I somehow found the strength to climb out of the wrecked Toyota and followed Colin to his vehicle.
>
> At the same time, two pick-up trucks pulled up full of Iraqi militia armed with AK47s. They were clearly there to finish the job the missile had started. Colin told his driver to tell the militia to leave, in no uncertain terms, or they would be shot. They got back in their vehicles and departed. Running on pure adrenalin, I somehow got into the back of Colin's vehicle, and he applied a pressure bandage to my badly injured arm. He then covered it in tape to apply more pressure

and this action stopped me from bleeding to death. The rest of my team got me back to the American Army base at Basra Airport at top speed. Luckily, our company had informed the Americans of our imminent arrival, so thankfully they were prepared with further medical care, and quickly arranged for a helicopter. As they were lifting me onto the chopper, I momentarily woke up and asked Colin if my genitals were intact. He replied that he had checked during the journey, and they were indeed still attached to my body. I remember placing my phone between my legs when I initially sat in the vehicle. My iPhone had taken the majority of the blast as it swept across my body, unfortunately disintegrating my phone, but in the process, protecting and saving my plumbs![1]

Steve was lucky and he survived, mainly by the sheer willpower that comes from being a paratrooper. After twelve and a half hours in surgery to save his life, he was then moved to Dubai, where he spent another eleven weeks going through forty-eight operations, mostly in a coma. It was during this time that he suffered a brain haemorrhage and lost the use of the right frontal lobe of his brain. Despite all of this he never lost his sense of humour. Steve relayed a conversation he had with another former Para, Martin Adams, 'Martin had warned me prior to going to Iraq that it was far more dangerous than people would have you know, and had said, "Don't risk it pal. It's not worth it. You have a good job and decent money; you don't need it." When I saw Martin on Airborne Forces' Day, I said, "Well mate I've got to admit you were right, it was fuckin' dangerous!" Martin stared at me for a second with a look of disbelief, then we both burst out laughing and shared a few drinks together.'

There were some big, high-profile security companies along with the military, but there were also plenty of smaller, but high-quality firms who had non-government contracts in Iraq on the commercial side of life. Working in a more low-profile manner, they knocked around the city in old armoured B6 Mercedes or soft-skin saloons. Surviving by using their wits and thinking outside the box, procuring weapons and kit on the ground in Baghdad, the companies who employed them tended to look for guys who had a little more experience in the industry, mostly from the SF side of life, as well as Paras and marines who were well used to working in this specialist way.

Many paratroopers choose to move onto the Circuit and the work can take them all over the world for varying contracts. Everyone's story is different, but all have a similar theme, and it is important to point out the clear difference between those who work on the Circuit, whose primary aim is to protect the lives of the clients who are entrusted to them, compared to mercenaries who fight on behalf of the highest bidder and are purely driven by financial gain. The definition of a mercenary, sometimes known as a soldier of fortune, is an individual, usually a former soldier, who takes part in military conflict for personal profit and is otherwise an outsider to the war that they are involved in and is not a member of any official military unit. Mercenaries fight purely for money or other forms of payment, rather than for political interests, and certainly do not adhere to any rules of engagement or the Geneva Convention. The ex-Paras who work on the Circuit have never taken on any contracts that run against Britain's national interests or any other recognised governmental organisation. All have served their country at one point or another with pride and honour and a paratrooper would take great offence if ever described as a mercenary. If anything, the opposite is true, and the facts bear this out. Many of the lads find themselves on government-funded contracts, protecting diplomats and other high net worth assets. In essence they work as private armies on behalf of the governments they used to serve in uniform, who do not have the physical assets or ability to fill these roles with serving troops.

What really matters to the ex-paratrooper is making sure that those clients, who are just in the country to do a job, go safely back home to their families once their contracts are up. We should honour those who have paid the ultimate price in the line of duty, names who will live forever within the Parachute Regiment brotherhood and will never be forgotten, whether they died on active duty in the army or working on the Circuit.

The former paratroopers who work in this industry carry out important work on behalf of their country. These guys are not after any sort of recognition, or a slap on the back, they fully understand the rules of the game and how things work. However, it is important, as the final part of this book and to accurately chronicle the history of the Parachute Regiment and its magnificent troops, to recognise the role they have played in these modern-day conflicts. Albeit out of uniform this time, there is a clear pathway between the time spent serving in the Parachute Regiment and British Army as a whole, and then the private security industry, on the Circuit. The two are intrinsically linked to the history of the Parachute Regiment.

Once a Para, always a Para.

# Afterword

Reaching the end of this phenomenal challenge, I sat back and reflected on the journey I have been on, the valuable lessons learned and the inspiring stories I have heard along the way. It was a humbling, and at times emotional, process to speak to so many members of the regiment who have fought in some unbelievably challenging conditions whilst keeping their well-known Para Regt humour and wits about them.

After a long hard journey, it took every ounce of energy I possess to get this book over the line and ready in time for the anniversary. It was extremely tricky to write about my own regiment and all their achievements, with the self-imposed pressure to ensure that I was doing them the justice they so richly deserve. What a challenge to write eighty years of history in only 100,000 words whilst still giving the reader a clear summary of all of the noteworthy actions the regiment have been involved in over that time. I certainly never realised when I started this how difficult it would be, but I am proud to have completed it. Above all, the process of writing this has further cemented in my mind that the Parachute Regiment is without a doubt the finest fighting machine in modern history.

At the time of going to print, people around the world are at home watching Russia invade Ukraine, and we can only wait and see if this heinous act by Vladimir Putin opens a new chapter involving the Paras.

I couldn't think of a better way to end this book than with a quote from former colleague and friend from my 1 Para mortar days, Major Curt Vines. A Late Entry Officer, he joined up at junior level at the age of 16, climbed through the ranks and has served with the Parachute Regiment for the last thirty-six years.

> The regiment's brand is its key asset, the Paras have never been diluted or amalgamated since its establishment in 1942. We are a proven entity, during war, battle, conflict and peacekeeping missions. We are purposely a broad church, and everyone wants to be a part of it, with many officers and soldiers from all ranks applying to transfer in from their own regiments. The selection process demands a high standard

by which we judge ourselves and each other. It sets the conditions for our inclusive respect, trust, reliability, physical ability, resilient mindset, and, arguably arrogant, self-belief of being superior. We are an exquisite band of brothers. When a Paratrooper adorns the famous maroon beret, he looks at himself in the mirror and checks where that legendary cap badge is. He always takes a second look and gives himself an invisible wink. He knows his history, the fundamental regimental roots, the ethos he is part of, and hence what he is capable of, which in turn motivates and drives him to excel in all aspects. He goes about his business with a spring in his step and utter pride in what he represents. Every Man an Emperor.[1]

# Acknowledgements

There are so many people to thank and acknowledge that I apologise in advance if I miss anyone out. Every bit of encouragement, feedback, and constructive criticism that I have received throughout the journey of writing this book has been very much appreciated – thank you all.

Firstly, this book would never have happened if it were not for my co-writer Sian M. Williams, whose professional guidance in developing the manuscript was key to the success of this project. Thanks also goes to Damien Lewis for taking the time to read my manuscript, write the foreword, as well as his friendship and the endorsement of the book.

The team at Pen & Sword for turning my manuscript into the book it has become, and my gratitude to Phil Patterson, Literary Agent, for his support and sound advice.

The Airborne Assault Museum Curator Jon Baker and Para Data Manager Ben Hill for the many hours of their time and constant support throughout the last eighteen months and for the tireless task of fact checking my work and allowing me to use photographs from their archives.

Craig Allen for very kindly providing photos taken during operational tours and all the individuals who have sent me their own personal images taken in theatre.

Major General (Retired) Chip Chapman for the time he spent proof-reading and the invaluable advice and straight-talking feedback provided. Stuart Hepton Lieutenant Colonel (Retired) for his enthralling stories and contagious enthusiasm. Jolene Turner for her overall support and advice, and of course Caroline Frost for her wonderful accounts of her father.

Richard Stacey MiD for not only his contributions to the book, but also his constant support of the ABF community, the Memorial Fund, Airborne Soldier Statue, and careful conservation of the final bastion of the Parachute Regiment and Airborne Forces community in Aldershot, the Trafalgar Inn, whilst fighting his own very personal battle with the humility and bravery we have all come to know him for.

Major Curt Vines for his input as well as his constant support of the Para Regt community and ongoing service to the airborne community.

A special mention for Sergeant (Retired) Fred Weaver, who at the age of 89 provided me with some vivid accounts of his time in Malaya with the Independent Parachute Squadron; Private Freddy Crompton, who at 19 years old jumped into Suez in the last airborne assault to date and was able to share his stories; and lastly, an old friend, Warrant Officer 2 Steve Parker, who always provided me with great support. These great men sadly died before the completion of this book. A true inspiration and airborne warriors. RIP paratroopers.

To all the amazing men who took the time to give me their personal accounts and experiences, which enabled me to have the privilege of penning the first book to cover the eighty years of the Paras. I really enjoyed talking to you and reconnecting with my former peers who went on well past my own time to have magnificent careers and have been awarded the medals to prove it. I feel honoured and very grateful to have been given the opportunity to present so many true and previously untold personal tales of the tenacity and bravery of the men involved.

I take the knee to all my airborne brothers who have ever served within this legendary regiment over the past eighty years. I am proud to have been a small part of this regiment's illustrious history and would not have become the man I am today without the training, experiences, and lifelong friendships I built whilst being part of this unique band of brothers.

Thank you to all the members of the airborne forces and TA units such as 4 Para, 7 RHA, 9 Squadron, 216 Signals amongst many others, who support the three regular Para battalions so well and without whom we could not deploy and operate on the ground as we do. Also, the wider British armed forces serving across the world, who fight the good fight, risk their lives on a daily basis and sometimes pay the ultimate sacrifice to keep us all safe in our beds at night, and who never seem to receive the recognition or after-support they so deserve.

# Select Bibliography

My thanks go to the numerous former and serving members of the Parachute Regiment and independent experts who willingly gave their time to me during this process, far too many to mention, you know who you are, including but certainly not limited to:

Jon Baker, Curator of the Airborne Assault Museum
Ben Hill, Para Data Manager, at the Airborne Assault Museum
Caroline Frost, daughter of Major General (Retired) Jonny Frost
Major General (Retired) Chip Chapman CB BA
Lieutenant Colonel (Retired) Stuart Hepton, PRA & Former Airborne Assault Museum Curator
Major (Retired) David Collins
Major (Retired) Tony Hobbins MBE
Captain (Retired) Danny Matthews MC
Captain (Retired) John Meredith DCM
Warrant Officer First Class (Retired) Gil Boyd
Warrant Officer First Class (Retired) Jamie Clarke
Warrant Officer First Class (Retired) Richard Turner
Warrant Officer First Class (Retired) Steve Tidmarsh
Warrant Officer Second Class (Retired) Joseph Madden
Warrant Officer Second Class (Retired) Nathan Bell MC
Warrant Officer Second Class (Retired) Simon Dawes
Warrant Officer Second Class (Retired) Steve Morris
Warrant Officer Second Class (Retired) Steve Parker
Colour Sergeant (Retired) Colin Edwards
Colour Sergeant (Retired) Justin Salmon
Colour Sergeant (Retired) Keith Woolgar
Colour Sergeant (Retired) Paul Bishop
Colour Sergeant (Retired) Stuart Baillie
Sergeant (Retired) Andrew Rutherford
Sergeant (Retired) Fred Weaver
Sergeant (Retired) Martin Margerison
Sergeant (Retired) Paul Stoves
Sergeant (Retired) Stuart Pearson
Sergeant (Retired) Terrance Millar

Sergeant (Retired) Tom Blakey
Corporal (Retired) Dave Aitchison
Corporal (Retired) Matt Shackleton
Corporal (Retired) Richard Stacey
Corporal (Retired) Steve Thurtle
Lance Corporal (Retired) John Campbell
Lance Corporal (Retired) Michael Murtagh MiD
Private (Retired) Bernard Cribbins
Private (Retired) Brian Fleetwood
Private (Retired) Freddy Crompton
Private (Retired) Freddie Ellis
Private (Retired) Paul Stoddart-Crompton
Private (Retired) Steve Johnson
Private (Retired) Steve Taylor
Private (Retired) Tony Costello
Royal Air Force Parachute Jump Instructor (Retired) Rick Wadmore

## Books

*3 Days in June: 3 Para's Battle for Mt. Longdon*, James O' Connell, Octopus Publishing Group, 2013.
*3 Para*, Patrick Bishop, Harper Press, 2007.
*A Drop Too Many: A Paratrooper at Arnhem*, John Frost, Cassell, 1980 (reissued Pen and Sword, 1994).
*Danger Close – Commanding 3 Para in Afghanistan*, Colonel Stuart Total, John Murray, 2013.*Last Round: The Red Caps, the Paras and the Battle of Majar*, Mark Nicol, Weidenfeld & Nicolson, 2005.
*Men of the Red Beret: Airborne Forces 1940–1990*, Max Arthur, Random House, 1990.
*No Way Out: The Searing True Story of Men Under Siege*, Adam Jowett, Pan MacMillan, 2018.
*One Jump Ahead*, Nigel Riley, John Clare Books, 1984.
*Operation Certain Death*, Damien Lewis, Cornerstone, 2018.
*Operation Colossus: The first British Airborne Raid of the Second World War*, Lawrence Paterson, Greenhill books, 2020.
*Our Boys*, Helen Parr Penguin, Random House 2018.
*Para! Fifty Years of the Parachute Regiment*, Peter Harclerode, new edition Brockhampton Press, 2000 (originally published Cassell, 1992).
*Ready for Anything: Parachute Regiment at War 1940–1982*, Julian Thompson, Weidenfeld & Nicolson, 1989.
*Soldier, The Autobiography*, General Sir Mike Jackson, Bantam Press, 2007.
*The Day the Devils Dropped in*, Neil Barber, Pen & Sword, 2002.
*The History of the SAS*, Chris Ryan, Coronet, 2019.
*The Making of a Para*, Rory Bridson, Sidgwick and Jackson, 1989.
*The Paras: The Inside Story of Britain's Toughest Regiment*, John Parker, Metro Publishing, 2000.

## Websites

Hundreds of websites were accessed for articles, scholarly papers, memoirs, diaries, personal accounts, reports, essays, documentaries and films, below are the most frequently used.

Archived articles from *The Guardian*, *The Telegraph*, *The Times*, *New York Times*, *Financial Times*, *The National*, *Business Insider* and the Al Jazeera website.
Api.parliament.uk/historic-hansard
Britannica.com
British Journal for Military History
Eliteukforces.info
Forces war records.co.uk
Gov.uk/uk-forces operations
Historycollection.com
historynet.com
Iwm.org.uk
Jstor.org
Nam.ac.uk
News.sky.com
Parachuteregimenthsf.org
Paradata.org.uk
Reuters.com
Warfarehistorynetwork.com
Weaponsandwarfare.com
Worldhistory.org
Youtube.com

# Glossary

| | |
|---|---|
| 1 Para | 1st Battalion, the Parachute Regiment |
| 2 Para | 2nd Battalion, the Parachute Regiment |
| 3 Para | 3rd Battalion, the Parachute Regiment |
| 4 Para | 4th Battalion, the Parachute Regiment |
| 2iC | Second in Command |
| ANA | Afghan National Army |
| ARF | Air Reaction Force |
| ASU | Active Service Unit |
| ABI | Airborne Initiative |
| Bangalore Torpedo | Explosive charge used to clear obstacles |
| Basha | Malayan word for a hut with a thatched roof |
| Bergen | Rucksack for carrying medium-size loads |
| BIAP | Baghdad International Airport |
| Bootnecks | Slang for the Royal Marines |
| Brick | Four-to-six-man patrol, commonly used in Northern Ireland |
| Casevac | Evacuation of a battlefield casualty |
| CCTV | Closed-circuit television |
| CO | Commanding officer |
| COP | Close Observation Platoon |
| CIVPOP | Civilian population |
| CQB | Close-quarter battle |
| CPO | Close Protection Officer |
| CT | Communist terrorist |
| CTT | Counter-Terrorist Team |
| Crows | Combat Recruit of War (First World War term for the new boys) |
| CSM | Company sergeant major |
| CQMS | Colour quarter master sergeant |
| DC | District Centre |
| DCM | Distinguished Conduct Medal |
| Dead letter box | Covert place to pass on messages or items |

| | |
|---|---|
| DF | Directional fire |
| DS | Directing Staff, usually SAS |
| DZ | Drop zone |
| EFP | Explosively formed penetrator |
| EP | Entitled person |
| FAC | Forward air controller |
| FIBUA | Fighting in Built-Up Areas |
| FLOSY | Front for the Liberation of Occupied South Yemen |
| FOB | Forward operating base |
| FSG | Fire Support Group |
| GCHQ | Government Communications Headquarters |
| GOSP | Gas and oil separation plants |
| GPMG | General-purpose machine gun |
| ICP | Incident Control Point |
| IED | Improvised explosive device |
| IMATT | International Military Advisory and Training Team |
| ISAF | International Security and Assistance Force |
| IRA | Irish Republican Army |
| ISIS | Islamic State of Iraq and Syria (also known as Daesh, IS or ISISL) |
| JOE | Joined on Enlistment |
| KLA | Kosovan Liberation Army |
| LE | Late Entry (Officer) |
| LEWT | Light Electronic Warfare Team |
| LLP | Low-level parachute |
| LO | Liaison officer |
| LOE | Limit of Exploitation |
| LUP | Lying Up Point |
| LZ | Landing zone |
| Kampongs | Small Indonesian jungle villages |
| MFC | Mortar Fire Controller |
| MPAJA | Malay People Anti-Japanese Army |
| MiD | Mention in Dispatches |
| MO | Modus operandi (the way in which something is done) |
| MOD | Ministry of Defence |
| MSG | Manoeuvre Support Group |
| MSR | Main Supply Route |
| NBC | Nuclear, biological and chemical (weapons or suit) |
| NCO | Non-commissioned officer |

| | |
|---|---|
| NITAT | Northern Ireland Training Advisory Team |
| NLF | National Liberation Front |
| NVG | Night vision goggles |
| OC | Officer commanding |
| OP | Observation post |
| Para Regt | Parachute Regiment |
| P Company | Pegasus Company (Test prior to jumps course) |
| PF | Pathfinders |
| PJI | Parachute Jump Instructor |
| PKM | Machine gun |
| PMC | Private military contractor |
| PSC | Private security contractor |
| PRT | Provisional Reconstruction Team |
| PRR | Personal role radios |
| QRF | Quick Reaction Force |
| RAMC | Royal Army Medical Corps |
| RMP | Royal Military Police |
| RSM | Regimental sergeant major |
| RSM | Resolute Support Mission |
| RQ | Regimental quartermaster |
| RTU | Returned to Unit |
| RPG | Rocket-propelled grenade |
| RUC | Royal Ulster Constabulary |
| RUF | Revolutionary United Front |
| Rupert | Colloquial derogatory term for an army officer) |
| RV | Rendezvous |
| SAS | Special Air Service |
| Sangar | Temporary fortified position |
| SBS | Special Boat Service |
| SF | Special Forces |
| SF | Sustained fire |
| SFSG | Special Forces Support Group |
| SLA | Sierra Leone Army |
| SLE | Spearhead Lead Element |
| SNCO | Senior non-commissioned officer |
| SOP | Standard Operating Procedures |
| STICK | Ten to twenty men in parachute grouping |
| SRR | Special Reconnaissance Regiment |
| SPOOSY | Send Paras Out of South Yemen |

| | |
|---|---|
| TA | Territorial Army |
| TAB | Tactical Advance to Battle |
| TALO | Tactical Air Landing Operation |
| TAOR | Tactical Area Of Responsibility |
| Thunder box | Army portable toilet |
| Tom | Nickname for an ordinary British soldier, from Tommy Atkins |
| Trainasium | P Company test of nerve, 40ft in the air |
| Tri-services | Navy, Air Force, and Army |
| UDR | Ulster Defence Regiment |
| UNSCOP | United Nations Special Committee on Palestine |
| UNAMASIL | United Nations Mission in Sierra Leone |
| USMC | United States Marine Corps |
| VCP | Vehicle checkpoint |
| VBIED | Vehicle-borne improvised explosive device |
| Wadis | Dry riverbeds |
| WAAF | Women's Auxiliary Air Force |
| WMD | Weapons of Mass Destruction |
| WMIK | Weapons Mount Installation Kit |
| WO1 | Warrant officer first class |
| WO2 | Warrant officer second class |

# Notes

**Introduction**
1. Speech made by Field Marshall Bernard Montgomery *circa* 1945.

**Chapter 1**
1. Letter from Prime Minister Winston Churchill to General Ismay, 22 June 1940, copy on Paradata.org.uk
2. Interview between the author and former RAF Parachute Jump Instructor, Rick Wadmore (2021).
3. Major (Retired) Tony Hibbert's memoirs on Paradata.org.uk
4. 'The Tragino Aqueduct Mission' article posted by Mitch Williamson Weapons and Warfare.com (15 February 2019).
5. Ibid.
6. Interview between the author and Regimental Sergeant Major (Retired) Pete Edgar Lane (2021).
7. Interview between the author and Caroline Frost (2021).
8. Interview between the author and Warrant Officer First Class (Retired) Gil Boyd (2021).
9. Interview between the author and Major (Retired) Tony Hobbins (2022).

**Chapter 2**
1. Interview between the author and Warrant Officer First Class (Retired) Jamie Clarke (2020).
2. *The Day the Devil's Dropped In* by Neil Barber, article in 1940.co.uk and book published by Pen and Sword, (2002).
3. Interview between the author and Warrant Officer First Class (Retired) Jamie Clarke, (2021).
4. Interview between the author and Jon Baker, Curator of the Airborne Assault Museum (2021).
5. Interview between the author and Major (Retired) David Collins (2021).
6. WW2 Heroes – The Story of Major Digby Tatham-Warter, history.co.uk
7. Interview between the author and Caroline Frost (2021).
8. Interview between the author and Caroline Frost (2021).
9. Major (Retired) Dan Jarvis MP. Quoted from hansard.parliament.uk Battle of Arnhem 75th Anniversary (14 October 2019).
10. 'Flexible Enough to Adapt' British Airborne Forces' Experience during Post Conflict Operations 1944 to 1946 by John Greenacre, *British Journal for*

*Military History* (2017) quoting Terence Otway, 'Airborne Forces' (London Imperial War Museum, 1990).
11. Article by Lieutenant (Retired) R. W. Butcher, 'Salisbury to Semarang: The Odyssey of a Parachute Brigade' provided by paradata.org.uk
12. Interview between the author and Jon Baker, Curator of the Airborne Assault Museum, (2021).

## Chapter 3
1. Article by Lieutenant (Retired) R. W. Butcher, 'Salisbury to Semarang: The Odyssey of a Parachute Brigade' provided by paradata.org.uk
2. Ibid.
3. 'After Arnhem' by Alan Whitworth Gauntlet on Paradata.org.uk
4. Interview between the author and Private (Retired) Tony Costello (2021).
5. Interview with Dennis Edwards on the YouTube documentary AIRBORNE! British Paras 1945 to 1968.
6. Vincent Leonard memoirs on Paradata.org.uk
7. Interview between the author and Private (Retired) Tony Costello (2021).
8. Captain John de Grey on Paradata.org.uk
9. Interview between the author and Private (Retired) Tony Costello (2021).
10. Interview between the author and Private (Retired) Tony Costello (2021).

## Chapter 4
1. Interview between the author and Sergeant (Retired) Fred Weaver (2021).
2. Interview between the author and Sergeant (Retired) Fred Weaver (2021).
3. *History of the SAS: As told by the men on the ground*, Chis Ryan (Hodder & Stoughton, 2019).
4. *History of the SAS: As told by the men on the ground*, Chis Ryan (Hodder & Stoughton, 2019).
5. Interview between the author and Sergeant (Retired) Fred Weaver (2021).

## Chapter 5
1. 'Describe 3 Para's Operations Against EOKA in Cyprus 1956', report by Lt M. A. Swann provided by Paradata.org.uk
2. Interview between the author and Private (Retired) Frederick Crompton (2021).
3. Ibid.
4. 'The Suez and Cyprus Crisis II' by Mitch Williamson, Weapons and Warfare.com (17 January 2019).
5. Interview between the author and Sergeant (Retired) Fred Weaver (2021).

## Chapter 6
1. Interview between the author and Private (Retired) Frederick Crompton (2021).
2. Memoirs of Corporal Tony Lowe on Paradata.org.uk

3. Interview between the author and Private (Retired) Frederick Crompton (2021).
4. Ibid.
5. Interview between the author and Private (Retired) Frederick Crompton (2021).
6. Interview between the author and Private (Retired) Frederick Crompton (2021).
7. Ibid.
8. Ibid.
9. Interview between the author and Private (Retired) Frederick Crompton (2021).

## Chapter 7
1. Interview between the author and Private (Retired) Brian Fleetwood (2021).
2. Interview between the author and Private (Retired) Brian Fleetwood (2021).
3. Interview between the author and Private (Retired) Brian Fleetwood (2021).
4. Interview between the author and Lieutenant Colonel (Retired) Stuart Hepton (2021).

## Chapter 8
1. 'We Were There: Return to the Jungle', Forces TV (2015).
2. Interview between the author and Lance Corporal (Retired) Mick Murtagh (2021).
3. Interview between the author and Warrant Officer First Class (Retired) Gil Boyd (2021).
4. Interview between the author and Lance Corporal (Retired) Mick Murtagh (2021).

## Chapter 9
1. Interview between the author and Private (Retired) Tony Costello (2021).
2. Interview between the author and Warrant Officer Second Class (Retired) Steve Parker (2021).
3. Ibid.
4. Interview between the author and Private (Retired) Frederick Crompton (2021).

## Chapter 10
1. Interview between the author and Private (Retired) Paul Stoddart-Crompton (2021).
2. Interview between the author and Warrant Officer First Class (Retired) Richard Turner (2021).

3. Interview between the author and Warrant Officer Second Class (Retired) Steve Morris (2022).
4. Interview between the author and Warrant Officer Second Class (Retired) Steve Morris (2022).

## Chapter 11
1. Interview between author and RAF Jump Instructor Rick Wadmore (2021).

## Chapter 12
1. Interview between the author and Warrant Officer Second Class (Retired) Steve Parker (2021).
2. Reprinted from an article on parachuteregimenthsf.org with kind permission from Steve Taylor.

## Chapter 13
1. Major General (Retired) Chip Chapman confirmed the landing time for 2 Para on 21 May was 0630z.
2. Interview between the author and Sergeant (Retired) Martin Margerison (2021).
3. Interview between the author and Sergeant (Retired) Martin Margerison (2021).
4. Interview between the author and Colour Sergeant (Retired) Colin Edwards (2021).
5. Ibid.
6. Interview between the author and Colour Sergeant (Retired) Paul Bishop (2021).
7. Interview between the author and Captain (Retired) John Meredith (2021).
8. Interview between the author and Colour Sergeant (Retired) Paul Bishop (2021).
9. Interview between the author and Captain (Retired) John Meredith (2021).

## Chapter 14
1. Interview between the author and Corporal (Retired) Richard Stacey (2021).
2. Interview between the author and Colour Sergeant (Retired) Justin Salmon (2021).
3. Interview between the author and Corporal (Retired) Richard Stacey (2021).
4. Interview between the author and Lance Corporal (Retired) John Campbell (2021).

## Chapter 15
1. Interview between the author and Sergeant (Retired) Andy Rutherford (2021).

2. Interview between the author and Sergeant (Retired) Tom Blakey (2022).
3. Interview between the author and Warrant Officer Second Class (Retired) Joey Madden (2021).
4. Interview between the author and Sergeant (Retired) Tom Blakey (2022).
5. Interview between the author and Warrant Officer Second Class (Retired) Joey Madden (2021).
6. Interview between the author and Sergeant (Retired) Andy Rutherford (2021).
7. Interview between the author and Warrant Officer Second Class (Retired) Joey Madden (2021).

## Chapter 16
1. Interview between the author and Captain (Retired) Danny Matthews (2021).
2. Interview between the author and Major General (Retired) Chip Chapman (2022).
3. *Operation Certain Death*, Damien Lewis (Cornerstone, 2018).
4. Interview between the author and Colour Sergeant (Retired) Keith Woolgar (2021).
5. Interview between the author and Warrant Officer Second Class (Retired) Simon Dawes (2021).
6. Interview between the author and Corporal (Retired) Dave Aitchison (2021).
7. Interview between the author and Warrant Officer Second Class (Retired) Simon Dawes (2021).
8. Interview between the author and Warrant Officer Second Class (Retired) Simon Dawes (2021).
9. Interview between the author and Colour Sergeant (Retired) Keith Woolgar (2021).
10. Interview between the author and Corporal (Retired) Dave Aitchison (2021).
11. Ibid.
12. Interview between the author and Captain (Retired) Danny Matthews (2021).
13. Interview between the author and Colour Sergeant (Retired) Keith Woolgar (2021).
14. Interview between the author and Warrant Officer Second Class Simon Dawes (2021).
15. *Operation Certain Death*, Damien Lewis (Cornerstone, March 2004).

## Chapter 17
1. Interview between the author and Corporal (Retired) Matt Shackleton (2021).
2. Interview between the author and Corporal (Retired) Jim Kilbride (2022).

3. Interview between the author and Sergeant (Retired) Terrance Millar (2021).
4. Ibid.
5. Interview between the author and Corporal (Retired) Matt Shackleton (2021).
6. Interview between the author and Sergeant (Retired) Jim Kilbride (2022).

## Chapter 18
1. Interview between the author and Colour Sergeant (Retired) Justin Salmon (2021).
2. Interview between the author and Sergeant (Retired) Paul Stoves (2022).
3. Interview between the author and Colour Sergeant (Retired) Stuart Baillie (2021
4. Interview between the author and Colour Sergeant (Retired) Justin Salmon (2021).
5. Interview between the author and Sergeant (Retired) Tom Blakey (2022).
6. Term used in the forces to mean that everyone has their say.
7. Interview between the author and Warrant Officer Second Class (Retired) Nathan Bell (2021).
8. Interview between the author and Warrant Officer Second Class (Retired) Nathan Bell (2021).
9. Interview between the author and Sergeant (Retired) Paul Stoves (2022).
10. Interview between the author and Colour Sergeant (Retired) Stuart Baillie (2021).
11. Interview between the author and Corporal (Retired) Steve Thurtle (2021).
12. Interview between the author and Colour Sergeant (Retired) Justin Salmon (2021).
13. Last Round' Mark Nicol, Weidenfeld and Nicolson (2005).
14. Interview between the author and Private (Retired) Freddie Ellis (2021).
15. Interview between the author and Corporal (Retired) Steve Thurtle (2021).
16. Interview between the author and Private (Retired) Freddie Ellis (2021).

## Chapter 19
1. Spoken by Defence Secretary John Reid in April 2006, Ministry of Defence article published on gov.uk (3 June 2011).
2. Interview between the author and Sergeant (Retired) Stuart Pearson (2021).
3. Interview between the author and Sergeant (Retired) Stuart Pearson (2021).
4. Interview between the author and Sergeant (Retired) Tom Blakey (2022).
5. Interview between the author and Sergeant (Retired) Tom Blakey (2022).
6. Interview between the author and Warrant Officer First Class (Retired) Steve Tidmarsh (2022).
7. Interview between the author and Sergeant (Retired) Stuart Pearson (2021).
8. Interview between the author and Major (Retired) Tony Hobbins (2021).
9. Interview between the author and Major (Retired) Tony Hobbins (2021).

10. Interview between the author and Warrant Officer First Class (Retired) Steve Tidmarsh (2022).
   11. Interview between the author and Warrant Officer First Class (Retired) Steve Tidmarsh (2022).

## Chapter 20
   1. Interview between the author and Coloured Sergeant (retired) Stuart Baillie (2021).
   2. Citation for the award of Victoria Cross to Joshua Mark Leakey British Army video on YouTube (26 February 2015).
   3. Interview with Siân Lloyd bbc.com (26 February 2015).
   4. Interview between the author and Major Curt Vines (2022).

## Chapter 21
   1. Interview between the author and a member of 2 Para (2022).
   2. Royal United Services Institute Operation Pitting: The British Army's Experience in the evacuation of Kabul (12 October 2021).
   3. Royal United Services Institute Operation Pitting: The British Army's Experience in the evacuation of Kabul (12 October 2021).
   4. Reports by Stuart Ramsey news.sky.com (21 August 2021).
   5. Interview between the author and a member of 2 Para who wishes to remain anonymous (2022).
   6. Royal United Services Institute Operation Pitting: The British Army's Experience in the evacuation of Kabul (12 October 2021).
   7. Ibid.
   8. Interview between the author and a member of 2 Para (2022).

## Chapter 22
   1. Interview between the author and Private (Retired) Steve Johnson (2022).

## Afterword
   1. Interview between the author and Major Curt Vines (2022).